The Politics and Strategy of the Second World War

A series edited by
Noble Frankland and Christopher Dowling

The North African Landings
1942

Keith Sainsbury was born in 1924 and educated at Christ's Hospital and Oriel College, Oxford. After service with the Royal Artillery and the Intelligence Corps in the Second World War, he was appointed lecturer in History and Political Science at the University of Adelaide, South Australia, from 1951-54. He became a Lecturer at New College, Oxford in 1955, and he has been Lecturer and Senior Lecturer in Politics at the University of Reading since 1955. He is a member of the Political Studies Association and of the Royal Institute of International Affairs. From 1971-1974 he was Senior Tutor in Charge of Faculty Admissions at Reading University, and he has been, on various occasions, a Member of the Court, Senate, and Letters Faculty Board. He has contributed to two previous books, and has published numerous articles on politics and international affairs.

KEITH SAINSBURY

The
North African Landings
1942

A Strategic Decision

NEWARK
University of Delaware Press

Copyright© 1976 by Keith Sainsbury
Introduction copyright© 1976
by Noble Frankland and Christopher Dowling

FIRST AMERICAN EDITION PUBLISHED 1979

Associated University Presses, Inc.
Cranbury, New Jersey 08512

Library of Congress Catalogue Card Number: 79-52242
ISBN 0-87413-158-8

PRINTED IN THE UNITED STATES OF AMERICA

CONTENTS

MAPS

EDITORS' INTRODUCTION

Numerous books and articles have been written about the weapons, battles and campaigns of the Second World War, and the problems of command, supply and intelligence have been extensively surveyed. Yet, though the fighting has been so fully described from these and other points of view, the reasons why the various military operations took place have attracted less study and remain comparatively obscure. It is to fill this gap in the understanding of the Second World War that this series has been conceived.

The perceptive have always understood the extent to which war is a continuation of policy by other means, and the clash of armies or fleets has, in intention, seldom been haphazard. Battles and campaigns often contain the keys to the understanding of the grand strategies of supreme commands and the political aims and purpose of nations and alliances.

In each of the volumes in this series an important battle or campaign is assessed from the point of view of discovering its relationship to the war as a whole, for in asking the questions Why was this battle fought? and What effect did it produce? one is raising the issue of the real meaning and character of the war.

As the series progresses, its readers, advancing case by case, will be able to make general judgements about the central character of the Second World War. Some will find this worthwhile in its own right; others will see it as a means of increasing their grasp of the contemporary scene. Thirty years have now passed since the death of Hitler and the capitulation of Japan. These momentous events were the culmination of a war which transformed the political and social, the economic and technological and, indeed, the general conditions of society and politics in virtually every corner of the world.

NOBLE FRANKLAND: CHRISTOPHER DOWLING

PREFACE

A number of strategic decisions made during the Second World War have been singled out by historians as of crucial importance. One of these is clearly the Anglo-American decision to invade North Africa in November, 1942. This book is an account of how that decision came to be made, and what followed from it. It was a decision which had a decisive influence on the course of the war, since it largely determined the course of Anglo-American strategy not only for 1942 but for 1943 as well. The commitment of troops on a large-scale to North Africa and the difficulty and cost of bringing them back to the United Kingdom led inevitably to the conclusion that it was better to deploy them in further operations in the Mediterranean in 1943 than to seek to use them in a cross-Channel attack. From the North African decision therefore flowed the invasion of Sicily and the Italian campaign. Because of this the cross-Channel attack – the invasion of Western Europe – eventually took place in 1944 instead of 1943.

The course of events which led to this decision throw a revealing light on Anglo-American relations in the early years of the alliance; and also on the relationship between the political leaders of both states and their military advisers – Churchill and Roosevelt on the one hand and the British and US Chiefs of Staff on the other, especially the Army Chiefs, Brooke and Marshall. On the first count, this story illustrates the point that the year 1942 was the last period in which a fully mobilized Britain was able to make its ideas prevail over those of a largely unmobilized United States. It was clear from the beginning that the vast resources of the United States made it inevitable that the British would become junior partners in the alliance. The fact of the United States' unpreparedness, however, together with the particular character of the North African decision, ensured that a largely British stamp would be put on allied strategy in Europe for the first two years of that alliance. On the second count, the point does not need to be laboured that Churchill played a very active role in the direction of the war and concerned himself with the details of operations, in a way that Roosevelt in general did not seek to do. What is not always so fully appreciated is that Churchill, hard as he fought for his strategic conceptions, seldom overruled his military advisers on a major question of strategy. Roosevelt, who developed a profound respect for Marshall's judgement, was equally loth to do so. But the North African decision was one occasion when he *did*. There was only one other instance during the war when Roosevelt overruled Marshall's advice on a major issue of strategy; and none on which the two men so profoundly disagreed. On the British side, there is no doubt that Brooke shared Churchill's belief that a 'Mediterranean strategy' in 1942-3 made more sense than a 'cross-Channel' strategy. But Brooke was always more cautious than Churchill as to the implementation of that strategy, and it was the latter's unremitting pressure for the North African operation which was the decisive influence on the British side. In short, in a way that was true perhaps of no other strategic decision of the war, this was Roosevelt and Churchill's decision. Whatever credit, and of course whatever blame, attaches to it, is primarily theirs.

It will be clear also from this account that during this controversy there were occasions when the leaders on both sides were not absolutely frank with each other. This was natural. There was a certain degree of suspicion of British motives on the American side, particularly at levels just below the top; while the British view was that a certain amount of tact was required in educating the American newcomers in the realities of global warfare. What is surprising is not that, in these early days of the alliance, Churchill, Roosevelt and Marshall did not always feel that they could say all that was in their minds: it is more remarkable that they felt able to be as frank as they were. As time went by and the political and military leaders got to know each other better, that frankness and unreserve

developed to a marked extent and contrasted very strongly
with the state of affairs in the Axis camp.

All of these men were aware of the gravity of the decisions they were taking and how many lives depended on
them. One aspect of this which is touched on in these
pages was the unavoidable fact that a decision not to invade Western Europe in 1942 meant that the Soviet
Union had to bear the brunt of the German war effort
and the fearful losses involved for the whole of that year,
and as it turned out for 1943 as well. It is the essence of
the argument in this book that, harsh though it was, no
other decision could wisely have been taken; and no other
decision that *might* have been taken could have measurably relieved the pressure on the Russian front.

It is also of course the essence of the argument that
there was a fundamental error in the American approach
to this controversy, epitomised in the position of the US
Army Chief of Staff, General George Marshall. No one
who has studied the history of the Second World War is
likely to question Marshall's stature, certainly not the
present writer. But there was perhaps a twofold error
here on his part; firstly an error of oversimplification, of
believing that textbook military principles could be applied without dilution to the complex problems of a war
fought in many different theatres and with many different
allies; and secondly an error of political psychology, in
thinking that it would be possible for the United States
to enter the war and immediately impose its strategic conceptions on an ally which had been fighting for two years,
was already fully mobilized, and would have to continue
to provide the bulk of forces for any Allied operation that
could be launched in the immediate future. Much of the
controversy which is described in this book derived from
this twofold error.

I have drawn mainly on British official sources for this
book, and have not, to my regret, been able to consult
American, French or German documents. The deficiency
is I hope partially compensated for by the use I have
made of the official American histories of the war and

other sources which draw freely on official documents other than British. My debt to such historians as Matloff and Snell, Pogue, Ambrose, Warner, Howard, Kammerer and others will be obvious enough and I am glad to acknowledge it. Many people have contributed in one way or another to the writing of this account, but I should like to acknowledge particularly my debt to Admiral of the Fleet the Earl Mountbatten of Burma, who has not only allowed me to draw on his unique recollections of the wartime Chiefs of Staff Committee, but also directed me to other sources of information; to Mr Averell Harriman who, from the other side of the Atlantic, kindly answered some questions I put to him; to Lord Duncan-Sandys, Lord Sherfield and Mr Alan Campbell-Johnson; and especially to Professor Geoffrey Warner, of the University of Hull, who suggested I should write this book and has been a source of encouragement and help during its composition. My thanks are due also to Mr A. Harrington, Miss V. Graham-Green and the Staff of the Public Record Office, London for their helpfulness; and Mrs M. McNamara, Mrs D. Duckmanton, Mrs S. Simpson and especially to my wife, all of whom typed portions of the manuscript. I should perhaps add the customary warning that none of the above are in any way responsible for any errors or shortcomings in this account. I dedicate this book to my wife and family, who bore with me during its composition.

KEITH SAINSBURY
Reading, 1975

PRINCIPAL CODE-NAMES USED IN
THIS BOOK

(1) North African Operations

GYMNAST   British or Combined Anglo-American invasion of French North Africa: the latter sometimes referred to as 'Super-Gymnast'.

TORCH   New code-name given to 'Gymnast', when, in July 1942, the decision was finally made to launch the operation.

(2) Cross-Channel Operations

SLEDGEHAMMER   Small-scale Cross-Channel attack in 1942; either in the form of a raid or designed to achieve a permanent bridgehead, as a prelude to full-scale operations the following year.

ROUND-UP   Large-scale Cross-Channel invasion of Western Europe in 1943.

BOLERO   Transport of US troops to Britain for Operations in the European theatre. In its early stages referred to as 'Magnet'.

(3) Middle East Operations

CRUSADER   British offensive against Rommel's forces in the Western Desert in November 1941.

ACROBAT   Proposed British invasion of Tripolitania, following a successful 'Crusader'.

WHIPCORD   Proposed British invasion of Sicily, following a successful 'Acrobat'.

The War in 1941

(i) GREAT BRITAIN

In June 1940 it was evident to most people outside the British Isles – and to some in Britain itself – that Germany had won the war. At that moment the British position seemed well-nigh hopeless. It was questionable whether a resolute German invasion could be successfully resisted with the limited forces rescued from France and the scanty equipment available; and even if defeat in 1940 *were* avoided, it was difficult to see how the war could ever be won by Britain alone. An alliance with the Soviet Union or the United States – certainly with both – would make the prospect very different. But at that moment neither seemed at all likely. The Soviet Union, having partitioned Poland in collaboration with Nazi-Germany, had stood idly by while France was overrun. However little love was lost between Russia and Germany, the USSR preferred to avoid involvement in war with the Axis unless actually attacked. As for the United States, President Roosevelt was still waging an uphill battle against a predominantly isolationist Congress and a public opinion which wished above all to avoid the sacrifice of American lives. It was not until the autumn that Roosevelt felt the danger to American security had become sufficiently obvious for him to risk asking Congress to accept conscription, and to recommend an agreement with Britain to exchange fifty destroyers for facilities in British bases in the Western Hemisphere. Although both measures could be represented as primarily designed to strengthen American defences, in neither case was it easy to secure Congressional approval.[1]

In June 1940, therefore, there seemed little likelihood of either a Russian or an American alliance. Yet Churchill chose to fight on, and in this was supported by public opinion and political leaders of all parties, however doubtful some of them may have felt about the outcome.

The question then was 'what should British strategy be and how should the goal of ultimate victory be pursued?' Churchill pinned his hopes on gradual US involvement in hostilities and an ultimate American alliance. In addition he hoped for revolts by the subjugated peoples of Europe, once it became apparent that Germany had not finally won the war. In the meantime there was nothing for it but the endurance of one of those long slow delaying actions which Britain had fought before, with blockade, air-bombardment and occasional raids on enemy occupied coasts as the main weapons. Against Napoleon such a struggle had lasted nearly twenty years. Only the prospect of an American alliance made it seem at all hopeful that this time it would take a little less.

The first essential was to hold on to what we had. That meant firstly strengthening home defences, naval, military and air, to a point where a German invasion could be resisted; secondly ensuring the security of British sea communications, especially with the United States, so that this island could still be fed and provisioned; and thirdly putting the remainder of the sprawling territories of the British Empire into some condition of defence. The Middle East was more immediately threatened than the Far East, so long as Japan remained neutral, and that theatre was also regarded as more strategically vital; it was therefore to that area that any forces which could be spared from Home Defence were sent. These forces, with assistance from India and East Africa, were put to good use by General Archibald Wavell, the Commander-in-Chief, Middle East. During the course of the year after the Fall of France a decisive defeat was inflicted on the Italian army in Libya; Cyrenaica and the vast Italian Empire in East Africa were conquered; a pro-Axis revolt was suppressed in Iraq; Syria and Lebanon, held by the Vichy French after the Fall of France, were occupied and brought back into the Allied camp;[2] and Iran was soon afterwards occupied by British and Soviet forces. Meanwhile at home the Battle of Britain had been won and the threat of invasion averted.

There were also set-backs. Forced to detach troops to assist the Greek resistance to the Axis – a gesture that was politically necessary but militarily questionable – Wavell suffered a reverse in Cyrenaica at the hands of the reinforced Italian army, now led by General Rommel with the support of the Africa Corps. In the spring of 1941 Hitler's armies, diverted from the invasion of Britain, raced through the Balkans, mopping up Yugoslav, Greek and British resistance and sweeping Hungary, Rumania and Bulgaria into the Axis camp. In May they moved on to Crete, taking it from the Greek and British forces after a fortnight's heavy fighting. The Germans had suffered substantial losses, including vital airborne troops: but Britain had also in these campaigns lost heavily in men, ships and equipment which she could ill afford to spare.

A different complexion was put upon affairs by the German attack on Russia in June 1941, a decision which seemed then, as it has often seemed since, one of unexampled recklessness. Yet the strategic gamble very nearly came off. In the summer and autumn of 1941 the Soviet forces suffered heavy defeats, and by October had been driven back to the outskirts of Leningrad, Moscow and Sebastopol, losing the whole of Russian-occupied Poland, the Baltic states and much of White Russia and the Ukraine to the Germans. The main fear in the minds of the Western leaders at this time was that the Russian armies might collapse completely, or alternatively that, fearing such an eventuality, the Soviet leaders might sue for peace.[3]

Neither of these two things happened. The Russian armies re-grouped, stabilized their position and launched counter-attacks. In December 1941 the Germans were held on the line Leningrad, Moscow, Kharkov, Rostov, Sebastopol. In that same month Hitler, recognizing that

another spring and summer campaign in Russia would be
necessary, withdrew an Air Corps from the Russian front
and transferred it to Sicily with a view to finishing off
Malta. With Malta out of the way, the costly interference
with Rommel's supplies in Libya could be brought to an
end and the way made clear for a victorious and decisive
Axis campaign against Egypt in 1942.

After June 1941, therefore, Britain had a powerful ally,
but an ally short of tanks, aircraft and guns, and clamour-
ing for British and US supplies which could ill be spared
and which could only be conveyed to Russia by incurring
heavy shipping losses via the Arctic route, or by a long
and tortuous passage round the Cape and across Iran. In
either case the drain on Anglo-American resources was
considerable. Nevertheless it was also an ally with the
manpower capability, the determination, and ultimately
the military skill to match the German armies. From this
time, therefore, it might have been expected that British
views on future strategy against the Axis, and particularly
the views of Churchill and the British Chiefs of Staff,
would be radically re-shaped in the light of this new
factor.

This was not to be the case, however, for two reasons.
One was that so long as there remained any doubt about
Soviet ability and will to continue resistance at all costs,
the British leaders were unwilling to gamble too heavily
on their new ally: and these doubts persisted well into
1942, even to some extent until the conclusive German
defeat by the Russian armies at Stalingrad in February
1943.[4] The second reason was that, with or without
Russia, the problems of successfully assaulting German-
occupied Europe, in a major amphibious operation, remained formidable. In spite of the drain of the Eastern
Front, the Germans were still able to keep about twenty-
five divisions in France and the Low Countries, which
could be quickly reinforced from Germany and from
other Axis garrisons stationed in Southern and Eastern
Europe. With British troops spread out all over the globe,
the largest force that could have been allocated to an at-

tack on Western Europe in 1941-2 would probably have amounted to at most six to ten divisions. In addition Britain lacked the specialized landing-craft and particularly the tank-landing craft required for a large-scale assault on defended coasts. Indeed, with shipping losses to Axis submarines and surface raiders at a very high figure, Britain was perilously short of shipping even to provision itself and supply its forces in the Middle Eastern, Indian and Far Eastern theatres.[5]

What American historians have called 'Britain's peripheral strategy' was, in 1940-41, largely therefore a matter of 'Hobson's Choice'. It is an error to attribute it to a mere whim of Churchill's, or of the British Chiefs of Staff. Such a strategy was indeed in keeping with the whole tradition of the British conduct of continental wars up to that of 1914-18; and the experience in the 1914 war of committing large armies to a continental war of attrition had not been such as to encourage a repetition. Faced with a more powerful enemy, operating on interior lines, the obvious course for a country with global commitments and resources thinly spread all over the world was to use its superior naval power to launch surprise attacks on the more vulnerable parts of enemy-occupied territory; harassing the enemy and keeping him constantly on the *qui-vive*, while at the same time encouraging the subjugated peoples of occupied Europe to rise in resistance. Such attacks would take the form of mere raids at first. Eventually, however, a combination of enemy weakness and local resistance might enable a more permanent lodgement or lodgements to be made, from which would develop gradually a sustained campaign against the enemy armies, gathering up local forces of resistance as it went along. As a preparation for that eventual outcome, the enemy should be worn down by the traditional weapon of naval blockade and the newer weapon of massive air bombardment: in this way both his morale and his resources might be weakened to a point where a successful large-scale lodgement and 'break-out' was ultimately feasible.

This was the strategy which Britain had pursued in the Napoleonic wars: it was the strategy which Churchill had wished Britain to pursue in the First World War at Gallipoli and Lloyd George had also advocated at Salonika. It was, in fact, the only strategy which made sense or promised any hope of victory, so long as Britain stood alone. The acquisition of a powerful ally might certainly change the whole picture, if that ally could be relied upon. But Britain had had much painful experience of the collapse of apparently powerful allies, most recently in 1940. Some hesitation in this respect was therefore natural. It is fair to say, too, that Soviet military capacity had been consistently underestimated in the West ever since the army 'purges' of the nineteen thirties, in a sense indeed, since the Russian collapse of 1917. But so long as Russian resistance hung upon a thread, as it appeared to do throughout much of 1941 and again in the summer and autumn of 1942, it was not entirely unreasonable to think of the Soviet part in Allied grand strategy as being largely a case of reinforcing the effects of blockade and air bombardment, by keeping large enemy forces tied down and gradually wearing out German resources. Soviet resistance, in fact, seemed likely in this period to constitute no more than a part – if the most important part – of the war of attrition against Germany, which would eventually make possible a British or Anglo-American assault against the Continent and ultimate victory. But such a possibility did not then seem very likely before 1943 at the earliest.

There was one theatre, however, where large British forces had of necessity to be maintained, and where some of these forces were in contact with the enemy. This was the Middle East, with Egypt and the large Suez Canal base as its focal point. From 1940 onwards therefore British hopes of immediate and striking success had largely been pinned to the possibility of exploiting the presence of these forces to defeat whatever Axis troops were in the field against them; and to take over and occupy the Italian colonies in Libya and East Africa. The latter objective was achieved in 1940-41, but the former was more important. Mastery of the Libyan coastline would increase British control of the Eastern Mediterranean, providing greater security for Allied shipping throughout the area and greater security and relief for hard-pressed Malta. From Libya in turn attacks could be mounted against Sicily or Southern Italy, where Axis airbases were always a menace both to Malta and to British naval forces in the area: still more to British convoys through the Mediterranean, which indeed were virtually impossible at this stage of the war. Finally the presence of British troops on the Tunisian frontier might encourage the Vichy Government's political and military leaders in North-West Africa to take the plunge which Britain had long urged upon them; namely to rejoin the Allied camp, inviting British forces in to aid them against any Axis countermove. Alternatively, if old resentments still persisted, dating from the British attacks on the French Fleet at Mers-el-Kebir and against French territory in West Africa and Syria, then perhaps the French could be induced to invite the Americans in instead – a prospect which had some appeal to President Roosevelt and his Secretary of the Navy, Frank Knox.[6]

This was the greatest prize. The successful rallying of French North Africa would then give the Allies control over the whole south Mediterranean coast. It would re-open that ocean to British convoys, obviating the need of the long haul round the Cape and saving a million tons of shipping.[7] In addition it might be expected to have a profound psychological effect on the people of metropolitan France, both occupied and unoccupied, providing a stimulus to resistance movements, which were as yet somewhat tentative, and so paving the way for future Allied landings in France. Conversely the effect on the people of Italy, never exactly enthusiasts for the war, might be expected to weaken morale and soften that vulnerable country up for any projected Allied attack.

It was these prospects which Churchill unfolded to Roosevelt at their meeting at Argentia Bay in August 1941, together with the continuation of British blockade, air-bombardment and commando raids as a prelude to Allied landings in Europe in 1943. He hoped to induce the President either to make a move towards North Africa himself, or alternatively to follow up a US occupation of Greenland and Iceland with the dispatch of three or four divisions to Northern Ireland ('Operation Magnet'), thus relieving an equivalent number of British formations for operations in the Mediterranean or French North-West Africa. Churchill continued to advance these plans in letters to the President throughout the late summer and autumn of 1941.[8]

British hopes therefore were pinned, as so often, to a successful offensive in the Western Desert of Egypt, on which all else depended. After his reverse in the spring of that year Wavell had in May attempted an offensive with inadequate forces and been unsuccessful. Now it was hoped that the reinforced Eighth Army under a new commander, General Alan Cunningham and a new C-in-C, General Claude Auchinleck, would inflict a decisive defeat on the German-Italian forces, and, like Wavell and O'Connor in 1940, advance to Benghazi ('Operation Crusader'). Then, unlike their predecessors, the Eighth Army, in greater strength and unweakened by diversions to Greece or elsewhere, would after only a brief pause advance to Tripoli and occupy all Libya ('Operation Acrobat'). Further exploitation could follow. Depending on the way the cards fell, the British might move to an attack on Sicily ('Operation Whipcord'); or at the invitation of the Vichy French, proceed to the occupation of French North Africa ('Operation Gymnast'). Alternatively the Americans might be induced to join in the latter, converting it into a more powerful Allied move ('Operation Super-Gymnast'): or the French invitation might go to the Americans alone, in which case the British would probably concentrate on 'Whipcord'.

In the event 'Whipcord' was abandoned as a result of opposition from Middle East Command, but 'Gymnast' or 'Super-Gymnast' remained a possibility, as did 'Acrobat', and Churchill gave order for three divisions to be held in readiness in the UK to help in one or the other of those operations. Churchill wrote to the Chiefs of Staff on 2 November 1941: 'We have definitely decided to play the sequence, "Crusader", "Acrobat", "Gymnast". There can be no going back on this.'[9]

All depended, however, on a successful 'Crusader'. The operation was duly launched in November, after much prodding from Churchill, and later than he wished. After a hard-fought battle, in which Auchinleck was forced to relieve Cunningham, success was achieved and the Eighth Army advanced to relieve Tobruk, capture Benghazi and occupy Cyrenaica. There however they were halted, as O'Connor had been a year earlier. Before events could develop any further, on 8 December 1941, Japan struck against the US at Pearl Harbour and in the Philippines and against the British in Malaya. The whole aspect of the war again changed decisively. From this time onwards British prospects were inextricably dependent on and bound up with the actions and fortunes of the United States and Russia, particularly the United States: and it became urgently necessary to try to concert British strategy with both.

(ii) THE USSR

The Anglo-Soviet alliance was an ill-starred one from the beginning. To the British the Russian leaders were often surly, demanding and unable to grasp the simplest facts of amphibious warfare; or perhaps simply unwilling to do so, if they were inconvenient.[10] To the Russians Churchill and his colleagues seemed hostile, grudging and deceitful. From the moment the alliance began, Stalin and his associates bombarded the British (and also the Americans) with demands for help of all kinds – supplies of aircraft, tanks, raw materials, ships; and above all the opening of a 'Second Front' in Europe at the earliest possible moment, to take the pressure off the Russian armies. In addition they required that Britain and the US should recognize all the territorial gains which Russia had made during her

two years' ententes with Nazi Germany – that is the annexation of the Baltic states, Eastern Poland and parts of
Finland and Rumania.

In return the Soviet leaders offered nothing. They felt,
not unnaturally, that they were already playing their part
in taking the full brunt of the Nazi attack. Between June
and September, as we have seen, three German army
groups, comprising over 150 divisions, had overrun Eastern Poland, burst into Russia and reached the gates of
Leningrad, Smolensk, Kiev and Odessa on the Black Sea.
There they were momentarily checked, but in October
the German offensive resumed and their armies pressed
forward to the approaches to Moscow, took Kharkov and
invaded the Crimea. Sebastopol was again besieged after
nearly a hundred years. Only in December was the situation again stabilized.

Stalin did not waste much time in presenting his needs
to his new allies. On 8 July, encouraged by Anglo-
American offers of support, he submitted to Washington
a request for two billion dollars' worth of supplies, including the provision of 6,000 aircraft. On 18 July, in
his first official message to Churchill, he described the
situation on the Eastern Front as 'desperate' and called
for the opening of a 'Second Front' by the British in
France and/or Norway. Churchill replied that Stalin
must understand the extent of the heavy commitments
involved in the defence of Britain, the Middle East and
the Battle of the Atlantic, which made such an undertaking in the view of the British Chiefs impossible. Nonetheless Churchill sent a few hundred aircraft immediately,
and promised supplies of urgently needed raw materials
as soon as possible.[11]

On the supply front Washington, still nominally neutral, was more forthcoming. Roosevelt and his Secretary
of State Cordell Hull were anxious to do what they could
to help. The President's personal emissary and close associate, Harry Hopkins, was dispatched to Moscow at the
end of July and promised Stalin that the US would send
'all possible help', a promise which was repeated in a

message to Stalin on 2 August.[12] Hopkins had returned
with the assurance that Stalin intended to continue the
fight to the end. At the Anglo-American conference at
Argentia which followed, therefore, Churchill and
Roosevelt agreed that British and Soviet requirements for
munitions and other supplies should be coordinated and
that an Anglo-American mission should be sent to
Moscow to deal with the matter. At the end of September
the mission took place, as a result of which promises were
made that tanks should be sent to the USSR at the rate
of 500 a month and aircraft at the rate of 400 a month,
besides other supplies and munitions of all kinds.[13]

Meanwhile, however, Stalin had continued to press
Churchill very hard for his longed-for Second Front.
On 4 September, in a message to Churchill, he asserted
that this alone could save the situation on the Eastern
Front, and asked for an operation which would draw off
at least forty German divisions. The Soviet Ambassador
Maisky, in delivering this message, asked that a British
force of fifteen or twenty divisions should be employed
and at the same time spoke woundingly of the lack of
British efforts. This was not the last time Churchill had
to endure taunts of this kind, which in general he bore
with considerable patience. Nonetheless he felt bound to
point out again that there were more German divisions
available in Europe than we could bring against them,
even if the landing-craft and shipping had been available
to transport a British force of that size. In the opinion of
the British Chiefs of Staff, there was no operation we
could mount at that time which would draw off troops
from the East. However, in accordance with what had
been agreed at Argentia, he promised all possible help in
supplies of tanks and aircraft. When this promise was confirmed in Moscow by the British and US delegates
Beaverbrook and Averell Harriman, the assurance was
also given that Britain would *aid* in the transport of these
materials as far as possible. As was the way with our
Soviet allies, this carefully qualified undertaking was later
to be treated as a binding promise to maintain regular

all-British convoys to the USSR through the Arctic Ocean, whatever the cost and whatever the situation in other theatres of war might be.[14]

Churchill and Roosevelt were certainly sufficiently concerned by the situation on the Eastern Front and the state of Anglo-Soviet relations to make what offers they could, and to consider what else they could do. Churchill was anxious already at the thought that the Soviet Union might be forced into signing a separate peace with Germany, though Stalin had undertaken not to do so. The question was already beginning to loom on the horizon whether, if it were necessary to hold out inducements to the USSR to continue the fighting, such inducements should take a military or a political form – ie Anglo-American recognition of the 1941 Soviet frontiers, including the acquisition of the Baltic states and Eastern Poland. Faced with this problem, the American instinct was that the Western Allies should strain every nerve and take every risk to help the Soviets *militarily*, while eschewing territorial commitments. Churchill, after some initial hesitation, was to take the opposite view. Made cautious by two years of struggle and defeat, the British view came to be that it was better to accept unpalatable Soviet demands in Eastern Europe than to throw away precious lives and material in more Dunkirks, Cretes and Singapores. However harsh the political realities involved, it was a wise instinct. For if Russia lost the war, Germany would occupy Poland and the Baltic States and much else besides; while if Russia won, she would almost certainly be in a position to enforce her demands. In either case the Western Allies would be faced with a *fait accompli* about which they could do very little, save in the unlikely event of an ultimate victory over Germany *after* the collapse and defeat of Russia. But such an outcome was the last thing which was desired by the West. What they feared most of all, in fact was a Soviet collapse.[15]

Nevertheless, the US view was in 1941 still opposed to conceding future territorial settlements of this kind: and when Churchill sent his Foreign Secretary Eden to talk to Stalin in December 1941, Cordell Hull urged him, through the US ambassador in London, not to enter into any secret agreements relating to frontiers. Churchill had already made the point to Eden that Roosevelt's opposition to such proposals made it impossible to agree to them. Therefore when Stalin raised the issue, Eden was forced to reply that Britain could not agree to any future commitments on Soviet frontiers without consulting its Allies. As to the 'Second Front', Eden had to say that the Japanese attack on Britain and the US, which had taken place on the very day he had left Britain, made any immediate operation of this kind even more out of the question because of the urgent necessity of reinforcing the Far East.[16]

In spite of this bleak response the Moscow meetings ended in a friendly spirit, partly perhaps because Soviet counter-attacks and the onset of winter had improved the situation on the Eastern Front; and partly no doubt because Stalin, like Churchill, recognized that the entry of the United States into the war made the ultimate defeat of Germany inevitable. Returning from Moscow, Eden reported to Churchill that 'Stalin seemed fully to understand our inability to create a Second Front in Europe at the present time.'[17] For the moment, perhaps. But the insistent Soviet demand was soon to be heard again and was to loom large over the coming arguments about Anglo-American strategy in 1942. In the end that strategy was to be largely determined by the conflict between the two irreconcilables of the Soviet demand for a Second Front in Europe in 1942 and the equally firm British resistance to it – a dilemma to which only one possible strategic move seemed to offer a solution.

(iii) THE UNITED STATES

When Churchill heard of the Japanese attack on Pearl Harbour on the evening of 7 December 1941, his first reaction was, rightly, to give thanks that now, whatever difficulties and setbacks lay ahead, the ultimate defeat

of the Axis was certain.[18] His second thought was to con-
clude that another meeting with Roosevelt was urgently
necessary to revise and co-ordinate Anglo-American military strategy in the light of the new situation. Within a
week, after cabling to Roosevelt and receiving his invitation, he was en route to the United States on board the
battleship *Duke of York.*

As they reviewed the war situation during the voyage,
Churchill and his Chiefs of Staff were already thoroughly
familiar with US military thinking and the tentative plans
which the Americans had made for the direction of their
strategy if the United States were drawn into the war.
The assumptions of the US War Department and its
planners had been for some time based on the view that,
if the United States were to become involved in any conflict, it would almost certainly be with the Axis Powers –
either with Germany or Japan separately, or with the two
in alliance. In such a conflict it was assumed initially that
not only Britain but also France would be allied with the
United States. The War and Navy Department's Joint
Board, which considered all matters involving Army-
Navy cooperation, had argued from 1939 onwards, and
even before, that in a two-front war – i.e. against enemies
in Europe and in the Far East – the United States should
first put its main naval and military effort into fighting
the European enemy across the Atlantic while standing on
the defensive and holding off the enemy in the Pacific and
Far Eastern theatre. Various possible plans in detail had
been worked out on this theme, bearing the code-name
'Rainbow', derived from the fact that the various
countries involved were identified by the colours of the
spectrum. Of these, 'Rainbow 5' was that which finally
won the approval of the US Army and Navy Chiefs,
General Marshall and Admiral Stark.[19]

Of these two men, Marshall was at this time the more
cautious and Stark the more vigorous in their attitudes to
the possibility of early involvement in a 'shooting war'. In
this they reflected partly the weakness of the US army
in both numbers and equipment, compared with the size

and power of the US navy: and partly the closer relationship and sympathy of views which then prevailed between
Roosevelt, a former Assistant Secretary of the Navy, and
the bluff outgoing Stark, compared with his somewhat
more formal relationship with the reserved Marshall. By
the beginning of 1941 Roosevelt was fully committed to a
policy of 'all aid to Britain short of war'. It was, as
Roosevelt's biographer admits, a negative strategy 'neither
of war nor of peace', but it was as far as Roosevelt felt he
could go in helping the Allied cause in the then state of
US public and Congressional opinion, and immediately
after an election which he had won partly on the basis of
keeping the United States out of the war.[20]

Stark went a little further. Immediately after the collapse of France he had suggested that there should be
some discussions between British and US Service representatives to consider the new situation and the prospects
for the future, and secured Roosevelt's and Marshall's
consent. At these talks, in London in August 1940, it was
first made clear to the Americans that so long as Britain
stood alone it was unlikely that a major offensive in
Europe could be launched unless and until German
strength and morale were considerably weakened. After
receiving this appreciation, Stark set his naval planners to
work to consider what American strategy should be in the
event of US involvement, which now looked the only
likely means by which the Axis could be decisively defeated. The results of their labours were presented to the
President in November in a Memorandum, which outlined various possibilities under the headings (a), (b), (c)
and (d). Of these, (d) – 'Plan Dog' as it came to be called
– envisaged a strong offensive policy in the Atlantic, cul-
minating in a British-American land offensive, while
avoiding major operations in the Pacific. It was this alternative which the Naval planners recommended in the
event of war. Marshall in his more cautious way, pointed
out that for the moment, and so long as the United States
remained neutral, only alternative (a), cooperation with
the British in 'hemisphere defence', was really a possibil-

ity. This however could mean at very least naval co-operation in the Atlantic and US occupation of vital 'neutral' points such as Greenland and Iceland – moves which took the United States measurably closer to war against Germany. Marshall in fact welcomed the emphasis on the Atlantic and European theatres, because it would, if conveyed to the British, encourage them to keep fighting. Thus in effect, as an American military historian has said, Marshall became committed to a policy which would give priority to the European over the Pacific theatre 'a full year before Pearl Harbour'.[21]

There was more to 'Plan Dog' than this, however. In considering possible US action in the event of war, the memorandum appeared to treat the Mediterranean as well as the Atlantic as part of the European theatre; and talked of Africa as an alternative to Europe as a theatre of operations. In this it reflected the interest of both the Navy planners and the Secretary of the Navy in this theatre. At about this time indeed Secretary Knox had discussed with the British Ambassador the somewhat unrealistic possibility of landing large US forces on the north-western coast of French North Africa, in order to forestall a possible German threat in that quarter. Noticing this, Marshall sounded a warning note about the danger of dispersing US strength in a multiplicity of operations.[22] His views, and those of his Army planners, already leaned towards the concentration of US military efforts on one decisive thrust, which should probably be on the European mainland itself. It was a reservation which was to foreshadow much argument to come.

Roosevelt for his part, without explicitly endorsing 'Plan Dog', gave his approval to further exploratory talks with the British, on the basis of a Joint Navy-Army agreement of December 1940 which in effect embodied most of the elements of 'Plan Dog', (including the statement that prevention of Axis entry into North-West Africa was very important). In a meeting with the political and military Chiefs in January 1941, he specifically accepted the concepts of 'Europe First' in the event of war and US convoying of shipping to the UK in the near future, knowing that the latter would inevitably increase the chance of armed conflict with Germany.[23]

Between January and March of 1941, therefore, further prolonged secret talks took place between senior representatives of the British and American Chiefs of Staff in Washington. Although the US Army representatives at these talks, particularly their leader General Embick, reflected their Chief's distrust of what they were already coming to regard as the British 'peripheral strategy', the two sides found it fairly easy to come to an agreement on what could be expected of each other if the US became involved. The Joint Report (ABC 1) they submitted to the President re-stated the general principle of priority for the Atlantic and 'Europe first', and this became the basis of a revised 'Rainbow 5'. It also – and this was to be of great importance for all future operations of the Anglo-American Alliance – recommended that in the event of war there should be much closer integration of Army-Navy Command and of the Supreme Allied Command than had ever been envisaged before. It suggested on the first count that there should be a unified Command Structure – a 'Supreme Command' over all arms – for every major operation: and on the second count that there should be a Supreme Anglo-American War Council. The implications were obvious: an integrated Supreme Command for an Anglo-American operation meant presumably a Supreme Commander, who would have to be British or American and have an inter-allied and inter-service staff; a Supreme War Council would have to have some regular base, if it were to operate continuously, and if so that base would have to be London or Washington: it could not be both. ABC 1 and the new 'Rainbow 5' were not, however, as the American historian Trumbull Higgins has pointed out, quite as clearcut in their strategic implications as the above implies. Inevitably, perhaps, they reflected to some extent a merging of British and American viewpoints. Thus, although they singled out the Atlantic and European areas as the decisive theatres, reflecting Marshall's thinking, they also talked of 'the great importance of the Mediterranean and North African areas', reflecting both a US naval interest and a theatre on which Churchill's eyes had long been fixed. In addition they incorporated the British insistence on an air bombardment, commando raids and support for resistance movements as a prelude to 'the eventual offensive against Germany' which had been for long the staple elements in British grand strategy. The result, Higgins implies, was not so much 'Plan Dog' as 'a dog's breakfast'. From this source and the lack of a 'sharp strategic focus' he traces most of the Anglo-American arguments which were to follow, and the eventual decision to land in North Africa. Whatever one may think of Higgins's judgement on the merits of the North African operation, and the strategy it embodied, it is difficult to dissent from this appraisal of the seminal importance of ABC 1 and the new 'Rainbow 5'. They did indeed predicate both the major strategic arguments to come, and the eventual triumph of the North African strategy.[24]

For the moment, however, both were merely plans on paper. Roosevelt himself had held aloof from the talks and did not formally approve ABC 1, though it subsequently became evident that he regarded it as in the nature of a fairly specific understanding with the British. Taking his cue however from the President's outward posture, and anxious to avoid specific commitments in the light of the Army's unreadiness for war, Marshall considered the talks 'exploratory' and as not imposing binding commitments on either side. By this time, however, he had become convinced that the US would almost certainly be drawn into the war sooner or later, and perhaps that it was desirable in the interests of US security that she should be. No doubt the plans envisaged in ABC 1 for full American participation in escorting convoys in the North Atlantic helped to bring about this frame of mind.[25]

At all events Marshall agreed to send a personal representative, General Chaney, to London, to join Admiral Ghormley, Stark's representative, in maintaining liaison with the British Chiefs; though warning them to avoid commitments. The Argentia conference between Churchill and Roosevelt in August 1941 did not alter the essential picture very much since, insofar as military matters came up, they amounted to no more than a re-statement by both sides of the positions embodied in ABC 1. But one new factor which strengthened the emphasis on North-West Africa in all this was the fact that during the preceding months the French Vichy government had moved closer to Germany and there had been regular though unfounded rumours of a Nazi incursion into Spain and Portugal and/or French North Africa, with the possible collusion of Franco and Pétain.[26] In fact, the German High Command had already the previous winter ruled this strategy out in favour of 'Operation Barbarossa' – the invasion of Russia – thereby committing, in Goering's subsequent opinion, their major strategic blunder of the war.[27] The rumours were sufficiently substantial, however, for the US navy to revive its plans for operations against the Portugese Azores and perhaps French West Africa, which had already figured in the Joint Army-Navy memorandum of December 1940; and for Roosevelt to authorize in May fairly specific plans for the Azores operation. Churchill gave his full support to these proposals, seeing in them no doubt a means of pulling the US towards the African and Mediterranean theatres.[28] The British Chiefs were themselves contemplating an operation to occupy the Azores, and before very long 'Gymnast' was also to become a major element in their planning. Churchill was well aware that in putting such ideas forward he had sympathetic ears in Washington, both in those of Admiral Stark and of the President himself.[29]

As has been noted, Roosevelt had largely held aloof from the detailed planning of potential future Allied strategy, and even from the planning of purely American strategy. He was well aware that too direct an involvement personally in American military planning could be used as a dangerous political weapon against him by his

33

isolationist and 'anti-war' critics. Nevertheless he was of course fully informed of US naval thinking and it was generally considered in Washington that he was very much more 'on the same wavelength' with Stark than with Marshall. Certainly the President showed repeatedly a lively interest in North-West Africa. US naval thinking hardly went beyond a possible move against Dakar, on the extreme Western tip of French North-West Africa, whose strategic significance to American security was obvious enough. But Roosevelt talked also of Morocco and in conversation with the British Deputy Premier Attlee in the autumn of 1941 had even evinced an interest in Algiers.[30] Not surprisingly, Churchill welcomed this interest of the President's and, with 'Gymnast' in mind, did all he could to encourage it. Nor was it surprising that Marshall viewed the rapprochement between the two men with some reserve. The US Army Chief remained convinced that an assault on 'Fortress Europe', with very large ground forces, remained the soundest, and ultimately the inevitable strategy; and in September 1941 he had the satisfaction of getting Stark's agreement to a memorandum to the President which stated that it would probably be necessary for the US to fight in Europe; and envisaged, if the worst came to the worst and both Britain and the USSR were virtually knocked out, that an American army of six million men, over 200 divisions, might be required.[31] Significantly the Army's planners thought that the necessary forces, equipment and shipping for such a massive and predominantly American operation could not be ready until the summer of 1943 – a date which was to assume considerable significance later on.

For the moment, however, the argument remained evenly poised. But it was already evident that Marshall was in effect 'outnumbered', with the US navy planners, the British and the President himself leaning towards the 'peripheral' and 'dispersionist' strategy which he so much disliked. At that precise moment the decisions which hung in the air were precipitated by the sudden onset of war in the Pacific – an event which the British at least feared might render all such arguments anachronistic by calling into question the very principle of 'Atlantic and Europe first' itself.

(iv) THE WAR BECOMES GLOBAL

Throughout the year 1941 the United States had been edging towards war with Germany. In March the passage of the Lend-Lease Act, whereby munitions and raw materials could be virtually given to Britain, though not in the strict sense a breach of neutrality, still less an act of war, was a clear indication of where the Administration's sympathies lay; and it was followed in April by the US occupation of Greenland, and then in July by the occupation of Iceland. In the same month the US navy was ordered to escort merchant vessels to United Kingdom ports. Such a step made some kind of incident between US warships and German surface vessels or submarines almost inevitable at some not too distant date. Meanwhile German and Italian assets in the US had been frozen, and in September Roosevelt took the decisive step of ordering US escort vessels to take the initiative in attacking submarines or vessels threatening merchant convoys. The United States was thus, in effect, though still nominally neutral, fully engaged in the war at sea against Germany. Inevitably, in October 1941 an American destroyer was sunk by German action. All legal restrictions on carrying aid to Britain in US ships was then removed, and a beginning was made in rearming US merchant vessels. What Roosevelt's biographer calls, referring to the early part of the year, 'a strategy neither of war nor of peace'[32] had become by the autumn something very close to full US participation as a belligerent.

By this stage Roosevelt's Chiefs of Staff and many of his administration, including Secretary of War Stimson and Secretary of the Treasury Morgenthau, had with varying degrees of reluctance or enthusiasm come to the conclusion that the United States must in the end join Britain (and, after June, the USSR) in the war against

Germany. Roosevelt, too, by that time had clearly come
to the same conclusion; but having given election pledges
the year before that he would not lead America into war,
was inhibited from the final step. He preferred to wait
for the United States to be attacked.

It is no part of the present study to consider whether
Roosevelt's actions in taking the United States closer and
closer to war were blameworthy, as some of his domestic
critics thought, or praiseworthy, as they naturally seem to
most Britons. What is unquestionable, however, is that
these actions were gradually putting the United States in
positions which increased the likelihood of Germany being provoked into acts of war which could not be over-
looked. As Roosevelt told Morgenthau in May 'I am
waiting to be pushed into a situation.'[33]

In this Roosevelt was supported by his Chiefs of Staff.
Stark had always been strongly pro-Ally and by mid-
summer the more cautious Marshall had also concluded
that war was ultimately inevitable, though he hoped that
it could still be put off for a year or so, to give him the
time he needed to train the scores of divisions created by
the recent conscription acts; and convert the small professional peacetime army into the massive force he believed would be needed. Obviously if this applied to
Germany, it applied even more to Japan. A simultaneous
conflict with Japan and Germany, or even worse a conflict with Japan from which Germany stood aside, might
throw into jeopardy the whole 'Atlantic First' strategy
which the American Chiefs regarded as vital.[34]

The logical course politically, therefore, for Roosevelt
to have followed in 1940-41 would have been one of ap-
peasement of Japan. Such a course had indeed already
been enforced by hard necessity on the British government, which had closed the 'Burma Road', along which
supplies were carried to Chiang-Kai-Shek's Chinese Nationalist forces, the previous autumn. The Roosevelt government, however was inhibited from this line of policy
by the degree of sympathy for China in Congress and
amongst the American public, as well as by a desire to

protect US economic interests in China. *Pari passu,* therefore with the moves against Germany, limited steps were being taken against Japan. In 1940 embargoes had been placed on the vital US supplies of aviation fuel and scrap-iron to Japan, and conversely aid on a fairly large scale was sent to Chiang-Kai-Shek. In July 1941 Japanese assets in the US were 'frozen', as German and Italian assets had already been. The Japanese war-machine and the entire Japanese economy, already strained by years of warfare, and heavily dependent on trade with the US and the British Empire, was hard-pressed by these moves. Originally the Japanese preference had been to finish off the China war, and then to turn against Russia, against whom she had already conducted fairly large-scale military operations in the 'undeclared war' of 1938-9. In the latter year, however, the signing of the Soviet Non-Aggression Pact with Nazi Germany put a different complexion on matters, and the eyes of the Japanese Chiefs of Staff turned southwards, to the oil and rubber and other commodities of the European Colonial possessions in South-East Asia. The collapse of France and the Nazi conquest of Western Europe in 1940 made this prospect more inviting. France and Holland were in no position to protect their Colonies in Indo-China and the East Indies, nor indeed were the hard-pressed British in Malaya. In July 1940 therefore the Japanese Cabinet took a provisional decision to advance southwards, as opportunity presented itself. The first step was taken almost immediately. Without much difficulty the Vichy government of defeated France was compelled to agree to the movement of Japanese forces into the northern half of Indo-China. The following spring similar concessions were extorted from the government of Thailand and negotiations begun with the Dutch East Indies. Meanwhile the Japanese safeguarded themselves doubly by signing a Non-Aggression Pact with the USSR and adhering to the Tripartite Pact with the Axis powers, which imposed on Germany and Italy the obligation to join Japan in any war with a third party in which she became engaged. This it was hoped might serve to deter the United States from continuing to stand in the Japanese path. In June the Nazi attack on the Soviet Union presented the Japanese with a double opportunity, either to join the Axis in an advantageous two-front war against the USSR, or to take advantage of the removal of any Soviet threat in the north and west to move south. Despite German blandishments, the final decision was taken in favour of the southern strategy – a bland ignoring of German wishes which makes the later German willingness to be dragged into war by Japan all the more astounding.[35]

The Japanese, however, still hoped that they would be left to pluck the easy fruits of conquest in South-East Asia without actually having to engage the United States. But American aid to Chiang-Kai-Shek and economic pressure against Japan made it seem imperative that one way or another the American capacity to interfere should be diminished. Either the Americans must be bullied and cajoled by negotiation, therefore, or their striking power decisively crippled by a surprise attack. Accordingly in November 1941 negotiations were opened with Washington. But there was never any possibility of agreement. The minimum US terms for calling off their measures against Japan were a total evacuation of China and an end to Japanese aggression against that country. The most the Japanese were prepared to offer was the evacuation of Indo-China and a promise of no further aggressive action in the South Pacific, in return for the end of US aid to China and US economic sanctions. Neither side moved from their positions and the failure of the negotiations therefore was a foregone conclusion.

The US Administration knew well enough that the breakdown of these negotiations would inevitably produce some aggressive military countermove on the part of the Japanese. But they did not know what form it would take. They feared – and the British government feared still more – that the riposte would be an invasion of Malaya and moves against the Dutch East Indies, leaving American forward bases in the Pacific in the Philippines,

Guam and Wake Island severely alone.[36] Indeed common-sense and elementary prudence would have dictated such a course. The British government had long been exercised about this possibility, and had received scant comfort from Roosevelt's emissary, Harry Hopkins, when he visited London the previous winter. Hopkins had said he could not guarantee US action in the event of a Japanese attack on British possessions, though indicating, correctly, that Roosevelt's preferences were all in favour of vigorous US action in such a case.[37] But the actual declaration of war was not in the President's hands: it rested with Congress, in which there was still a substantial 'isolationist' and anti-war element. Rather later in the year the extent of US moves against the Axis and the stubborn US resistance to Japanese demands led the British Foreign Secretary Eden to take a more optimistic view of probable US actions. But there was still uncertainty; and Cordell Hull, the US Secretary of State, was cautious in his words to the British Ambassador as late as November.[38]

All of these anxieties were needless. That the Japanese would launch a direct attack on the main American naval base at Hawaii, thereby making an American declaration of war inevitable, had been considered the least likely possibility. Indeed, although warnings of a possible surprise attack had been sent from Washington to all Pacific bases, this had been somewhat negated by the rider that an attack on Hawaii itself was unlikely. Yet this was precisely the decision which the Japanese had already taken in October, as the inevitable consequence, if negotiations with the US should break down. By the beginning of December the Japanese government had concluded that the negotiations were deadlocked, and dispatched the appropriate orders to its naval units. A last-minute appeal and warning by Roosevelt to the Mikado, strongly urged on Washington by Churchill, failed to have any effect. Cordell Hull had already reported to the US War Council that 'there was practically no hope of agreement with Japan'. On 7 December the Japanese struck. 'It was', Roosevelt said to Hopkins, 'a great relief'.[39] The hard decision whether to come to the aid of Britain if she alone were attacked had been taken out of his hands. So, as an American historian has put it 'Having moved steadily towards belligerency in the Atlantic, the United States found that war came instead in the Pacific.'

I

The Significance of French North Africa

(i) THE MILITARY AND STRATEGIC ARGUMENTS

'For over two years', Roosevelt's biographer writes, 'he had shown remarkable consistency in keeping the African option open.'[1] During the latter half of 1940 and for the whole of 1941 the US administration had maintained its connexions with the Vichy government of Marshal Pétain, not only as a means of preventing that weak vessel from handing over its North African colonial possessions to Germany or permitting German forces to use its facilities, but also in order to prepare the ground among the North African civilian and service chiefs for a possible US or British operation in that quarter.

During the same period Churchill's mind had been intermittently concentrated on the same thought. In the immediate aftermath of the Fall of France he had tried to encourage the setting-up of a rival French government in North Africa, and to induce French commanders, notably Noguès and Weygand, to declare for the Allies. At various times too he had suggested to Roosevelt that the Americans should act to forestall a rumoured Axis threat to occupy the area. Such a plan – a move through Spain into North Africa, taking the British base at Gibraltar en route – had been seriously considered by the Axis High Command in 1940. It had been turned down by Hitler in the end, mainly because the Spanish dictator, General Franco, demanded too high a price for collaboration in the enterprise, a price moreover that would be paid largely at the expense of France. Anxious at this period to retain the goodwill of the Pétain government, and aware of Churchill's blandishments, Hitler decided against the move and in favour of a two-pronged offensive towards the East. German troops were to move through the Balkans and to reinforce the defeated Italian armies in Libya: then the main thrust was to be launched against Russia.[2]

Hitler's decision did not in fact prevent similar rumours of a German move into North Africa from surfacing from time to time during 1941. They were used repeatedly by Churchill to support his advocacy with Roosevelt of an American or combined Anglo-American move in that area. Roosevelt and the US Navy Department were certainly not totally unresponsive to these arguments. As early as May 1940 such rumours had prompted the President to consider sending 100,000 US troops to Brazil to offset this possibility, and he again considered it in 1941, this time making a definite offer to the Brazilian government. On the main issue, however, of a US move against North-West Africa, he was cagey, conscious that US military weakness virtually ruled out such a possibility. Indeed, as Hull pointed out to the then British Ambassador, the US had virtually no power to intervene in that quarter. All that could be done was to issue clear warnings to the Germans and the Vichy Government that the United States considered her vital interests were engaged. President Roosevelt himself had put the point explicitly in a speech on 15 May 1941, when he said 'The delivery of the French Colonial Empire [to Germany] would be a menace to the peace and safety of the Western Hemisphere.'[3]

What then were the basic reasons which led both Roosevelt and Churchill to attach such importance to North West Africa? In the last analysis it is probably true, as many historians have argued, that the reasons for the ultimate decision to launch the North African invasion were as much political as military. But this is not to say that the persistent US belief that Churchill's support for the operation was prompted mainly by a wish to secure British interests in the Mediterranean and Middle East rested on any very substantial foundation. There were in fact perfectly sound military and strategic arguments for the operation and for the view that North Africa was of vital importance to the West.

These reasons, however, were seen with slightly different perspectives from Washington and London. It would be fair to say that the US leaders looked at North-West Africa more with an Atlantic and the British more with a Mediterranean viewpoint. From Washington, Axis control of West Africa was seen as a major threat to US lines of communication with the UK and Latin America. From the French West African naval base at Dakar, only 1,600 miles from the nearest point on the Brazilian Coast, German submarines, surface raiders and aircraft could harass Allied convoys far out into the Atlantic. Theoretically it was even possible for Axis troops to be airlifted from there to Latin America. German use of Dakar had been described by Secretary Knox in April 1941 as 'a disaster to US hemisphere safety and a threat to the Monroe doctrine'. Therefore projected US operations in this area – never going beyond the tentative planning stage – had focussed exclusively on Dakar and to some extent Casablanca.[4]

The British viewpoint was different. The major objective for Churchill and the British Chiefs of such operations was to 'clear the Mediterranean'. Control of the North African coastline would enable Allied convoys to move again freely from east to west, shortening the supply lines to the Middle East and India by thousands of miles and, as the Chief of Imperial General Staff put it, 'saving a million tons of Allied shipping'. Conversely it would be possible, through the use of French naval bases at Oran and Bizerta, to harass Axis communications across the Mediterranean with Rommel's forces in Libya and relieve hard-pressed Malta. The use of North African airfields would also be a major advantage, bringing Axis bases in Sicily and Southern Italy within range. As an incidental advantage 120,000 poorly equipped but well-trained French troops might join the Allies for operations in the Mediterranean and Middle East, together with various French naval and air units. Given the right political outcome – the rallying to the Allied cause of the French civil and military 'establishment' in North Africa

– the great prize of the French main fleet at Toulon might even be gained. Rommel's forces in Libya could then be threatened and, it was hoped, defeated by a pincer movement from Egypt and Tunisia.[5]

There were political gains to be hoped for also from the operation, most of all in terms of influencing French opinion. If French North Africa rallied to the Allied cause, and especially if it did so voluntarily and wholeheartedly, the morale of the whole French people would be affected, and the nascent resistance movements would receive a powerful boost. If, as was to be expected, Axis forces occupied the whole of France, the effect would be that much greater, since the *raison d'être* of the Pétain government would then largely disappear. Conversely Italian morale would be adversely affected, and the Italian people, never very enthusiastic for a war in which they had so far gained little but lost much, might be expected to turn more towards the prospect of a negotiated settlement with the Allies. Air raids on Italian soil and the possibility of an invasion of Italy from North African bases might be expected to sharpen this reaction. Further east, Turkey might be encouraged to move closer to direct participation in the Allied war effort, an event which Churchill, probably erroneously, regarded as a major gain for the West.[6]

Some of these British arguments appealed to Roosevelt at least, if not to his military advisers. But in the main the US view before Pearl Harbour saw the significance of North Africa in Atlantic terms: and while Marshall accepted that large-scale operations *inside* the Mediterranean would probably have the incidental effect of drawing some troops away from the Eastern Front, he still considered that objective could be better served by a full-scale thrust across the Channel; a strategy which would also provide the best hope of a quick victory over the Axis.

There was one powerful argument, however, in favour of a North African operation which was difficult to contradict; and that was the simple fact that, through the accidents of colonial rivalries, large British and Axis forces were already established in the Mediterranean theatre and engaged in operations against each other. It seemed logical to make use of that fact and treat a successful campaign in Egypt and Libya as a springboard for future Allied operations, rather than leave it as a mere cul-de-sac. Certainly American troops would have to be safely convoyed large distances to participate in African operations. But, as Churchill put it to Roosevelt, these troops would in any case have to be transported almost as far to the UK, in order to take part in an invasion of Western Europe, and would then require a further lift to put them on shore in France. To transport them directly to a fighting front was certainly a more economical use of scarce shipping resources.

In the minds of the British there was also a further argument in favour of making the North African venture the first major Anglo-American operation – but one that it would have been tactless to stress, though in fact Marshall and other US commanders were far too realistic not to be aware of it. This was the plain fact that inevitably the American troops who would participate – and their commanders – would be green, unseasoned formations, without battle experience. Far better that such troops and their leaders should gain experience against opposition that it was hoped would be relatively light, and in an operation that might be virtually unopposed, than that they should be flung straightaway against the Germans in Western Europe. Within a year or so of Pearl Harbour the Dieppe Raid and the Battle of Kasserine were to provide in their different ways ample justification for this view.[7]

(ii) VICHY AND FREE FRANCE

Whether the hope of an unopposed landing in French North Africa would prove to be justified or not depended on the tangled complexities of French politics, both at Vichy and in North Africa itself. The roots of the North

African political problem lay in the events of 1940. Following the collapse of French resistance the Pétain government, which had come into existence in order to negotiate armistice terms with Germany, had set itself up at Vichy; and had since remained there, exercising relatively independent control over the two-fifths of French soil which had remained unoccupied. This government had been voted full powers by the French Parliament and had gradually transformed itself into an authoritarian regime under the aged marshal, pursuing a policy of hesitant collaboration with Germany – though it had indeed little choice in the matter. Whatever views might be held about the honour and dignity of its role, or the moral basis of its authority, its legal claim to be the government of France was difficult to disprove.

At the same time an unknown major-general, Charles de Gaulle, had come to England and called on all Frenchmen who wished to continue the fight to join him. He had been welcomed, encouraged and given financial and other assistance by Churchill and the British government. From those beginnings the Free French movement had been created. Some French territories, notably in Equatorial Africa and the Pacific had rallied to de Gaulle, providing him both with additional land, sea and air forces, and with a territorial base. Gradually his strength had increased, and increasingly the forces of resistance in France itself looked to him for leadership. There had been some setbacks, notably an abortive attempt by Free French forces to win over Dakar and French West Africa in September 1940; but the movement had grown in strength and by mid-1941 looked a more valid contender to the claim to represent the 'true' France, as de Gaulle argued, than had been the case a year earlier. To the Vichy government he and his movement were of course anathema. De Gaulle himself had been pronounced a traitor and stripped of his rank. He faced summary court-martial and a firing-squad if he returned to France.

The British government, as the patron and protector of the renegade, was hardly less detested by Vichy and its adherents, including most of the civil and service chiefs in French North Africa. In the immediate aftermath of June 1940 the Churchill government had attempted to maintain some links with the Vichy government, hoping to influence it against too overt a policy of collaboration with the Germans: and believing too, as has been noted, that it might still be possible to encourage some leading figure in the Vichy government – notably General Maxime Weygand, then Resident-General in North Africa, to rally French North Africa to the Allied cause. These hopes proved illusory, however, and the British decision to attack French warships at the Oran naval base in July 1940, in order to ensure that they should not fall into Axis hands, led Vichy to break off relations with Britain. Not surprisingly it also caused a bitter resentment in French governmental and service circles, particularly on the part of the French navy.[8] Though feelers were still occasionally put out to Vichy after this time, essentially the British government was now wedded to the cause of General de Gaulle. The latter's Council for the Defence of the French Empire, later to be called the National Committee was recognized by the British government as representing the cause of Free France and as the *de facto* administering authority in all those French territories which had joined the Allied camp.

Relations between Churchill and de Gaulle, and therefore between Britain and Free France were never easy and often very difficult. Elsewhere I have compared them to 'a fever chart'.[9] Both were proud and masterful men. In addition de Gaulle was profoundly pessimistic and cynical in his assessment of human nature and national policy, deeply suspicious of what he regarded as the inevitable tendency of the British government to take advantage of French weakness in order to supplant French influence wherever she could; and equally determined to resist all such encroachments and to defend the independence and sovereignty of France against all comers. It was a role that came easily to him, since he was by nature obstinate and obdurate to the point of perversity, once he had made up his mind. It was also a role – and the perspective of thirty-five years makes it easier to acknowledge the fact – that it was essential for a French leader to play at that time, if French interests were to be fully taken into account: but it did not ease the task of negotiation with him. Tension and acrimony were in fact inherent in the nature of the Anglo-French partnership at that time. A relationship involving patronage on one side and dependence on the other is almost certain to be characterized by both. The personalities of the two leaders were not therefore the crucial factor. They merely contributed to making it worse.

Nonetheless, the relationship held throughout 1940 and 1941, and in fact achieved much. Not only were French Equatoria and Oceania won over, but in a brief but skilful campaign by British and Free French forces in the summer of 1941 Syria and the Lebanon also. Meanwhile Free French forces had grown in strength and the resistance in France had begun to stir its head and to look to some extent to de Gaulle and his movement for leadership and support.

Unfortunately, the Syrian campaign made relations between Britain and Free France particularly acrimonious. General Wavell, the Middle East C-in-C, had not wished to undertake the Syrian campaign with his limited resources, and was anxious to persuade the Vichy regime in Syria to negotiate an armistice as soon as possible. In these difficult and delicate negotiations the Free French, with their demands for participation and recognition, were a vexatious complication. Other British commanders and civil officers in the area took their tone from the C-in-C. In the negotiations with General Dentz, the Vichy commander, de Gaulle felt that he and Free France had been slighted; and he was further affronted by the British promise of independence to Syria and the Lebanon after the war – a promise that he felt only France could give.[10]

Not surprisingly, relations between Britain and Free France deteriorated sharply in the latter half of 1941. Nor was it surprising that Churchill was wont to say that 'the heaviest cross he had to bear was the Cross of Lorraine'.[11]

A further and damaging complication in these relationships was provided by the Americans. Churchill made no secret of his view that victory depended above all on the maintenance of the closest and most harmonious relations with the United States generally and with President Roosevelt in particular. This meant, since Churchill was realist enough to acknowledge that the United States was potentially the stronger partner of the two both economically and militarily, that he would often have to defer to Roosevelt's wishes, even when he considered them mistaken. Unfortunately the American attitude to de Gaulle and his movement was just such a case. Characterized at first by indifference and scepticism, that attitude turned, at the very moment when the Anglo-American alliance came to fruition, into active hostility and mistrust.[12]

For this de Gaulle himself was considerably to blame. He had resented the American attitude, but had done very little to improve matters. It is only fair to say that in the cause of better relations with the United States he was little helped by the ostentatious dissociation from his cause of certain well known and influential Frenchmen in the United States, including Jean Monnet and André Maurois. The entry of the United States into the war might have produced a better and closer relationship, as Churchill certainly hoped it would, but de Gaulle chose that very moment for one of his worst displays of intransigence and folly. In defiance of the wishes of both Britain and the United States and contrary to undertakings which he had given, he ordered his forces to seize the islands of Saint Pierre and Miquelon off the Canadian coast. By so doing he antagonized the governments of his two most powerful allies. The US Secretary of State, Cordell Hull, never forgave him, and the incident rankled with Roosevelt also, though he regarded it at first as a minor matter. Seldom can so much have been put in hazard for such a trivial cause.[12]

The United States had in fact, from the outset, taken a different path in relations with the French from that followed by the British government. The collapse of France had come as a shattering blow to the Americans, as it had to the British; and Roosevelt thereafter regarded France as a spent force in world affairs, unlikely ever to rise again to any kind of international status. This contributed to Roosevelt's unwillingness to take de Gaulle's pretensions seriously. But it did not mean that France could be ignored altogether as a factor in the war situation. French collaboration with Germany could only assist the Nazi war machine. The Germans already controlled the French Atlantic coast and had full use of French naval and air bases there, for use both against Britain in invasion or air bombardment, and against Allied shipping in the Atlantic. They must not be allowed to gain the use also of the French Mediterranean ports and bases in unoccupied France, or in the North African or West African colonies. In addition the French fleet at Toulon must be kept inviolate. But it was the government at Vichy which controlled these assets, not General de Gaulle: it was the Vichy government therefore which the United States deliberately chose to cultivate between 1940 and 1942, and it was this government – a reactionary, corrupt and defeatist government – which came to symbolize France to the Americans.[14]

Space does not permit a lengthy consideration here of the tortuous course of American relations with Vichy during the period before Pearl Harbour, relations which have been fully and exhaustively dealt with elsewhere. American policy was designed to strengthen the enfeebled will of Marshal Pétain and his government against any policy of collaboration with Nazi Germany going beyond the minimum limits dictated by the Franco-German armistice terms of 1940. The prospect of American economic assistance both to unoccupied France and to North Africa was held out as an inducement to good behaviour: American good offices could also be used with the British government to bring about some lifting of the British blockade in this direction. As part of the bargain which Robert Murphy, Roosevelt's representative in North Africa, negotiated with General Weygand, the United States was permitted to establish a dozen or so consular posts in North Africa, ostensibly to monitor the passage of American supplies and to see that none of them ended up in Axis hands. In fact these officers became part of an intelligence and news-gathering service, and were also used to establish contacts with Vichy civil and military officials sympathetic to the Allied cause. Hull and Murphy were rightly to claim later that these activities had laid a useful foundation for future collaboration in the North African landings.[15]

The influence which the United States, and Britain also, most feared at the court of Marshal Pétain was that of Pierre Laval. In a long and chequered political career, during which he had been both Prime Minister and Foreign Minister and had contrived to move from the extreme left to somewhere near the extreme right of French politics, Laval had acquired an inveterate distrust and dislike of 'perfidious Albion', which he felt had let him down on a number of occasions in the thirties, notably over the so-called 'Hoare-Laval Plan' of 1935. He had long felt that French interests would be best served by participation in a 'Latin bloc' consisting of France, Spain and Italy; and by a Franco-German rapprochement. He accepted the defeat of France in 1940 as final and conclusive, and indeed almost welcomed it as ridding France of the incubus of the British alliance and paving the way for the policies which he himself favoured. The fact that these policies meant allying republican France with three authoritarian regimes worried him not at all, since he had long ceased to believe in the parliamentary system of the Third Republic. He had gladly played his part in bringing about the collapse of that system in 1940 and helping to instil the authoritarian regime under Pétain. Even more gladly he accepted the rewards of office in that regime.[16]

Laval's key position, therefore, in the Vichy government, in which as vice-premier and Pétain's designated successor he was the second most powerful figure, was a source of constant anxiety to the United States and Britain immediately after the Fall of France; an anxiety increased by the knowledge that Laval was negotiating with Otto Abetz, the German representative in Paris, for full French partnership in Hitler's 'New Europe'. Pétain's dismissal of Laval in December 1940 came as a corresponding relief. His successor as deputy premier and heir-presumptive, however, though less pro-German than Laval, was if anything even more anti-British. Admiral François Darlan was a career naval officer who had been brought into the government by Pétain as Navy minister as well as naval C-in-C, and now became Foreign Minister and Minister of the Interior as well. He had devoted his life to the creation of the French navy, and felt the British attack on his ships at Oran as a personal affront. Moreover, until the United States entered the war, he was as convinced as Laval or any of his Vichy colleagues that Germany had already won the war. He took up Laval's policy of collaboration with the Germans with almost equal enthusiasm and, ignoring American pressure, negotiated in May the so-called 'Paris Protocols' with Hitler, granting the Germans facilities in Syria and West Africa. US pressure and the opposition of Weygand proved more effective with the aged Marshal, however, and the latter repudiated the agreement. But it was clear that Darlan would try again, when opportunity presented itself. In the meantime he remained the second most powerful man in the government until Laval's return to power in April 1942, though somewhat diminished by Pétain's repudiation of his policy and the British conquest of Syria, which had been provoked by the abortive Paris agreements. Darlan was in fact at a later stage to play a leading and totally unexpected role in the final dénouement in North Africa; but this was something which probably neither he nor the Americans could have foreseen in 1941.[17]

Churchill had watched the progress of US-Vichy relations with a cautious but on the whole sympathetic eye. In May 1941 he wrote to Roosevelt: 'With regard to Vichy, we are more than willing that you should take the lead, and work out how to get the best from them by threats or favours.' Churchill could see the value of maintaining some kind of hold over Vichy, with a view to safeguarding the North African colonies and the French Fleet. He recognized, too, the value of the American 'listening-posts' at Vichy and in North Africa. His principal worry in this connexion was the prickly de Gaulle, who disapproved equally of US links with Vichy and of the British tendency to acquiesce in the American line. The realistic strain in de Gaulle's personality recognized that Churchill had very little choice, but he resented it just the same. Unhappily these clouds were to persist and grow darker as the North African strategy came more and more to the forefront of Allied war plans. It had been the essence of de Gaulle's position all along that French territories, as they returned to the Allied camp, should be united under one French authority, not divided into separate categories, some inclined more to Vichy, some to the Free French, some mainly under British influence, some under American. He believed that only he and his movement could provide the necessary impetus and centre for such unity. As events were to show he was justified in this belief. None of the alternatives put forward by Churchill or Roosevelt at different times – Weygand, Noguès, Darlan, Giraud – combined as he did commanding abilities with a reputation uncompromised by any truck with Vichy.[18]

Washington, however, did not see it this way. To Roosevelt and Hull de Gaulle was simply a relatively unknown and quite unrepresentative figure with arrogant and unjustified pretensions and possibly dangerous political ambitions for the future. As to the political role of the General, they took the not unreasonable view that the future position and the rights of the French people should not be preempted by the recognition of the Free French Committee, or anyone else as a provisional government: as to the military role of the Free French, they considered that whatever military value its forces might have, was more than counterbalanced by its poor security and political unreliability. Moreover in any operation involving Vichy-held territory, events in Dakar and Syria had already shown that the use of Free French forces was likely if anything to provoke even stronger resistance. It was already clear therefore that if the North African strategy became a reality, American opinion would be most unfavourable to Free French participation, either in the planning or the execution of the enterprise: and equally clear that de Gaulle would feel his exclusion from operations in North Africa – the largest and most important of French colonial possessions – more keenly than in relation to anything else. The seeds of much future trouble were already present in this irresolvable dilemma.[19]

II

The Creation of
an Allied War-Machine
and an Allied Strategy:
the 'Arcadia' Conference
December 1941-January 1942

(i) THE ANGLO-AMERICAN RELATIONSHIP

As Winston Churchill and his party of service and political chiefs made their way to Washington on the battleship *Duke of York,* their minds – and Churchill's most of all – were pre-occupied with the new problems confronting them, now that the Anglo-American alliance had become a reality. That alliance gave an assurance of ultimate victory; but in the short run grave problems and the prospect of many set-backs and disappointments were inevitable. The immediate problems were firstly to make the alliance a reality, in the sense of creating an inter-allied machinery for the conduct of the war, the allocation of munitions, shipping and raw materials etc; and secondly to formulate an Anglo-American strategy to which both partners could subscribe and to which the vast and as yet largely untapped resources of the United States could be harnessed.[1]

Three problems were therefore in the forefront of Churchill's mind. So far as the machinery of the Alliance was concerned, there was the question whether in all spheres – both the purely military and the vast field of economic co-operation – the machinery to be created should be one of close and intimate inter-allied partnership, with decisions being taken by Anglo-American representatives at all levels, only major disputes being referred to the highest levels of government; or whether the war should be conducted largely by dealings between the two governments, Britain and the United States going their own way through their own national machinery, subject to broad agreed directives only from the top. Churchill wished to establish the closest working relations with the Americans, though he recognized that the relative economic and industrial strength of the two partners must mean eventually the acceptance by British representatives in all bodies of the status of junior partners. But he felt nonetheless, and rightly that the method of close cooperation at all levels would give the British point of view more influence and of a more continuous kind than would otherwise be the case. No doubt too he expected that in the crucial initial stages of policy formulation, the advantage of two years' experience of war would give British counsels in practice more weight, whether the Americans consciously deferred to them or not.[2]

To forge the instruments of Allied war-making in this manner, certain pre-requisites clearly needed to be present. There had to be a minimum foundation of mutual trust and confidence and understanding – in the most literal sense of being able to comprehend the minds of one's partners – and a willingness on both sides to make the effort involved in sacrificing nationalistic prejudices, and looking at problems from the viewpoint of the common cause. Fortunately though some Americans viewed their new partners with some suspicion these foundations were on the whole present at the highest level. There was on the American side an admiration of the way Britain had continued the fight in the face of an apparently hopeless position, and a personal regard and respect for the character of the British war-leader; and on the British side a gratitude for the help already given by the Americans, without which the war could not have been continued; and again a personal feeling of respect and affection for Roosevelt who had been a staunch friend when Britain most needed friends.

On the personal level the meetings which had already taken place between British and US representatives at the Argentia conference, in the staff talks earlier in the year and on occasions such as the two visits to London in 1941 of Roosevelt's special representative, Harry Hopkins, had already forged some valuable links. Most important of all, Churchill had set himself from the beginning of his premiership to establish, through correspondence, a close and friendly relationship with President Roosevelt; and to a large extent had succeeded. The two men had a bond in common in their associations with and deep interest in naval matters. But above all they were both heart and soul devoted to the Allied cause and conscious of the fact that they shared with Stalin a unique status in the Allied war effort.

There is not space here, nor is this the occasion, to go at length into a relationship which has been widely explored in innumerable books. It need not be questioned that there were occasions when they differed, both over politics and strategy, or times when momentary irritation overcame habitual friendship and liking. For two men, however congenial, who laboured under the burden and strain of conducting a global war over a period of many years, this is hardly surprising. Temperamentally they were different and Roosevelt had not entirely escaped those occupational hazards of all who occupy for any length of time the lonely eminence of the Presidency – vanity and over-confidence. He was capable of occasional pettiness in his relations with Churchill, just as Churchill could sometimes be crotchety and difficult with him. Moreover his liberal, internationalist view of world affairs was far removed from Churchill's old-fashioned imperialism, which Roosevelt not only disapproved of but felt to be sadly out of date. On occasions, particularly over India, this led to clashes between the two men. At such times Churchill fiercely rebutted what he saw as American attempts to interfere in matters which they did not understand, as on the well known occasion when he stated emphatically that he 'had not become His Majesty's First Minister in order to preside over the liquidation of the British Empire'. But in general Churchill, magnanimous by nature, and realistically conscious of the dependence of Britain on the United States, did not allow these ar-

guments to have a lasting effect on his real regard and
gratitude towards the President, nor did Roosevelt waver
from his general liking and respect for Churchill.

Again Roosevelt, rightly or wrongly, felt that the obvious conflict of interests and views between Britain and
the Soviet Union, which he thought did not exist between
the United States and the USSR, placed him in a unique
and favourable position to mediate between Churchill and
Stalin. This too sometimes caused friction and resentment
on Churchill's part in later stages of the Alliance. But
these were not the cause of lasting breaches in the friendship of the two men, and there is no reason to doubt that
the general spirit of the relationship is summed up by
Roosevelt in one of innumerable friendly messages they
exchanged over nearly five years – 'It is fun to be in the
same decade as you' – nor to question Mrs Roosevelt's
judgement that 'it was a fortunate friendship'. Churchill
for his part clearly was sincere when he wrote to the War
Cabinet 'I have formed the highest regard for the President – his breadth of vision, resolution, and loyalty to the
common cause.'[3]

The relations between Churchill and Roosevelt were
clearly of paramount importance to the successful welding
of the alliance. In this relationship Hopkins played a key
part, both in his ability to reflect accurately Roosevelt's
views to Churchill and in his ability to interpret Churchill
to Roosevelt. He had for a large part of the war the complete confidence of both men; Roosevelt's because he
knew that Hopkins had no prior interest other than to
serve him, Churchill's because he recognized Hopkins' integrity and straightforwardness and uncompromising determination to defeat the Axis powers. Churchill recognized, too, the penetrating mind and will-power concealed
behind the unlikely façade of Hopkins' frail body and
cynical manner. Finally, he saw that Hopkins had the
respect and confidence both of the President and of
General Marshall.[4]

Beyond and below the political relationships at the
highest level of government lay the field of direct military

co-operation between the service Chiefs. In this sphere the
commanding figures, both by reason of their personalities
and the positions they held, were George Marshall and
Alan Brooke, respective heads of the US and British
armies. Marshall's position was now to become even more
important, with the replacement as Chief of Naval Operations of the friendly and co-operative Stark by Admiral
Ernest King. King was a tough and able naval officer, but
he was also crusty, narrow-minded, and a poor co-
operator. His eyes were fixed firmly on the Pacific, where
his own service could largely conduct its own war, un-
embarrassed by the necessity of co-operation with allied
states, or other unfriendly powers such as the US Army.
His services to his navy and the US war effort need not
be questioned, but from the viewpoint of Anglo-American
co-operation his appointment was not helpful. The third
member of the US Chiefs, the Army air leader Arnold,
though friendly and co-operative, was also somewhat
limited in his strategic vision and not particularly knowl-
edgeable outside his own sphere.[5]

Much therefore devolved upon Marshall. Fortunately
he was a man of commanding ability, great patience and
magnanimity, and broad vision. His dignity and unshake-
able integrity commanded respect not only from the President, who soon came to rely almost unquestioningly on
him, but also from his colleagues on the Chiefs of Staff
committee and throughout Washington. From the point of
view of allied military co-operation it was no less essential
for the British to forge close links with him than with
Roosevelt.[6]

On the British side General Alan Brooke, the newly-
appointed Chief of the Imperial General Staff, was
soon to stand in much the same position in relation to the
British war effort. Universally acknowledged to be the
ablest soldier in the British Army, a man of forthright
opinions and great moral courage, Brooke also concealed a
sensitive nature under a mask of iron self-control which
rarely slipped. Like Marshall he commanded respect even
from men like Churchill and Montgomery who found it

difficult to defer to anyone. His colleagues on the British Chiefs of Staff Committee were Admiral Dudley Pound, at this period of the war an ageing and soon a very sick man and Air Marshal Charles Portal. The latter was a man of wide vision whom the American Chiefs both liked and respected; but inevitably it was to the head of the British Army that Churchill largely turned for strategic advice; the more so since now, for the first time since 1940, it seemed certain that neither the Battle of the Atlantic nor the air war against Germany, but large-scale military operations would dominate strategic planning. The relations between Brooke and Churchill were often tempestuous. From the latter's fertile brain and capacious mind plans, injunctions, memoranda flowed in a ceaseless stream and it was Brooke's thankless task to sort the wheat from the chaff and his disagreeable role to say which was which to Churchill. Nonetheless Churchill recognized his outstanding capacity and perhaps also the importance of having someone in this position who was not afraid to stand up to him. Their partnership continued unbroken throughout the remainder of the war.[7]

Unfortunately Brooke and Marshall were not to hit it off when they encountered each other for the first time in April 1942. Both at first underestimated the other. Marshall was disconcerted by Brooke's abrupt manner and Brooke irritated by Marshall's failure, as he saw it, to grasp strategic and logistical realities, especially in relation to cross-Channel operations. It was important therefore that there should be in Washington, as representative of the British Chiefs of Staff, someone who could command Marshall's confidence and interpret the two men to each other. By a fortunate chance such a man was found at precisely this moment, in the person of Sir John Dill, Brooke's predecessor as CIGS. Dill had already made a favourable impression on Marshall at the Argentia conference by his tact and courtesy as well as his obvious high professional capability. Sensing this, Churchill decided to leave Dill in Washington at the end of the conference as British representative on the newly-formed

Combined Chiefs of Staff. He soon established the closest relations with Marshall, which continued till Dill's death in 1944. Dill's importance as a link between London and Washington was to be perhaps second only to that of Hopkins.[8]

Therefore through a combination of shared objectives, good personal relationships in key positions and clear mutual understanding, much facilitated by a common language, there did exist the basis for an Alliance that was to be unique in its closeness and integration. Churchill was ready, for the reasons already given, to accept such integration. By chance it was also what the Americans, and particularly Marshall wished. Marshall was the apostle of Supreme and Unified Command for all major military operations and major theatres – the concept of one Supreme Commander over all arms involved in the operations and by definition over all the forces, of whatever nationality. Such a Commander, whether American or British, must needs be responsible to some unified and inter-allied body at the higher levels of command. As a concept, therefore, the idea of a Supreme Commander led directly to the creation of such a body – the Combined Chiefs of Staff. Before the Washington Conference broke up, this body was to be created and the first Supreme Commander appointed – General Wavell for South-East Asia. Wavell's ABDA[9] command had in fact an impossible task and before many months had passed into limbo. But the precedent had been set, and was to govern all future Anglo-American operations, including those in North Africa.

As important in Churchill's mind as the creation of inter-allied machinery for the conduct of the war was the formulation of an Allied grand strategy. Here he had two principal concerns. One was to ensure that the Americans stuck to the principle of 'Germany First' or 'Atlantic First' embodied in 'Rainbow 5' – that is the principle that the main Anglo-American effort should be devoted to the defeat of Germany, while that against Japan took second place. There was considerable anxiety on the

British side that the shock of Pearl Harbour and the popular fury and indignation which it had aroused might create pressures for the main US war effort to be directed against Japan, pressures which Roosevelt would find it impossible to resist. The second main point was to secure US agreement to a joint North African operation which should have a high priority, leaving the assault on 'Fortress Europe' to some future date. Churchill felt more strongly than ever with US entry into the war that the prospects and the urgency in this respect were great. On the one hand the fact of US participation in the war against the Axis might be expected to sway many wavering French minds, both at Vichy and in North Africa itself, towards the Allied cause. Surreptitious feelers had indeed already been put out by Darlan towards the Allies. On the other hand the Germans, temporarily held in Russia and driven back in Libya, might themselves decide to descend on North Africa unless forestalled by the Allies. Both considerations prompted Churchill to hope more fervently for US agreement to 'Super-Gymnast'.[10]

In fact Churchill was to be assured of his first aim – US commitment to 'Germany First' – without argument, and from the outset of the conference. The second aim, however, was not to be achieved without months of tedious argument. At the Washington conference Roosevelt was to give the North African plan his qualified approval: but the hard necessities of war and in particular the need to try to prop up a crumbling position in the Far East, together with severe setbacks in the Western Desert, soon afterwards pushed the possibility of such an operation into the background. The consequent hiatus enabled Marshall and Stimson to revive again in full force the arguments for a cross-Channel assault as the first major Anglo-American operation. At the 'Arcadia' conference itself Marshall had been cautious in his remarks about 'Gymnast', but the War Department's position had been made quite clear already.[11]

(ii) THE IMPACT OF PEARL HARBOUR

The Anglo-American representatives who assembled at Washington in December 1941 had then the task in effect of creating almost from scratch an Allied war-machine and an Allied strategy. But in relation to the latter, as always, short-term considerations were at war with long term planning. Churchill had wished to see the conference devote all immediate Anglo-American efforts to the achievement of his Mediterranean strategy: Marshall wished those same efforts to be concentrated wholeheartedly on preparations for a cross-Channel assault in force. But over all long-term plans for the future loomed the immediate impact of Pearl Harbour and the immediate need to improvise some means of checking what looked like being an irresistible Japanese tide in the Pacific.

The immediate reaction, as has been noted, on both sides of the Atlantic to the news of Pearl Harbour was in effect one of relief. The die was cast, and neither Churchill nor Roosevelt doubted that victory over the Axis powers was now certain in the long run. In particular the German and Italian decision to declare war on the US – 'a gratuitous act', as Eden called it – had removed a cause of anxiety from British minds as to what might happen to the strategy of 'Europe First' if the US had found itself at war with Japan but not with Germany; just as the Japanese attack on the United States itself had removed the British fear of finding themselves facing Japan alone, and relieved Roosevelt of the unpalatable necessity of deciding between US entry into the war by deliberate choice, or leaving Britain to her fate.

As the full consequences of Pearl Harbour and the Japanese 'follow-up' measures sunk in, however, these first Allied reactions were swiftly superseded by fears and worries as to what the immediate future would bring. Most severe were the effects on Anglo-American naval power. Four US battleships had been sunk at Pearl Harbour and three others severely disabled: within a

week the only two British capital ships in the Pacific –
the *Prince of Wales* and the *Repulse* – had also been sunk
by Japanese air attack. With these two blows 'mastery of
the Pacific', as Churchill put it, 'passed into Japanese
hands'. With it, in effect, went temporarily control of the
Indian Ocean also. The disaster was compounded by the
fact that at the same time the Allies lost naval and air
control of the Mediterranean, where three battleships and
an aircraft-carrier were sunk or put out of commission in
the space of a month. As a result of these events Allied
naval power, in terms of capital ships, had been suddenly
cut by half. The effects in the Mediterranean were almost
as calamitous as in the Pacific. Rommel's supply lines
could no longer be menaced, and the simultaneous transfer
of a German Air Corps from the Russian front to Sicily
meant that the British had lost control of the air in the
Central Mediterranean also. The effects on Auchinleck's
offensive in Libya, which at that moment was going well,
and on Rommel's ability to counter-attack were bound to
be considerable in the not too distant future. The demands
for immediate reinforcements for the Far East were also
bound to affect the prospects for the Middle East adversely. Yet on the successful exploitation of the 'Crusader' offensive depended to some extent the prospects for
'Gymnast' also. There could hardly be a better demonstra-
tion of the way the various fronts were inter-connected,
and how the course of events in one affected the prospects
for the other.[12]

The Japanese were quick to exploit the advantage
gained. Within a few days Hong Kong was attacked and
the Philippines were invaded; landings in the Dutch East
Indies soon followed. The Japanese forces made rapid
progress. In London the future of British possessions in
the Far East was viewed in gloomy, if realistic terms.
Brooke thought that Hong Kong might last a fortnight,
Malaya a month. There was not much hope of saving the
great naval base of Singapore itself. All efforts should
probably be concentrated on saving what could be saved;
namely India and Burma. Churchill too knew that 'severe

64

punishment awaited us', in the light of the loss of naval power. Brooke foresaw that there would be an immediate demand for reinforcements to the Far East at the expense of the Middle East, which could not be entirely resisted in the circumstances. Indeed Churchill had already cabled to this effect from the *Duke of York*. As Brooke afterwards put it 'I saw my hopes of carrying on with the reclamation of North Africa look more impossible every day'.[13]

In Washington the mood was equally sombre. The Americans had not expected that the Japanese would be so bold as to strike directly at the main US Pacific naval base. Certainly none of their war plans had envisaged an immediate naval disaster on so great a scale. It had been assumed that if the US possessions *were* directly attacked, the first blow would fall on the Philippines and the US forward island bases alone; and that the naval base at Hawaii and the powerful US Pacific Fleet could then be used as a secure foundation for the relief of these points. Now much of the fleet was lost and with the loss of Anglo-American naval supremacy the Philippines and the island bases at Wake, Guam and Midway were immediately at risk, just as Malaya and the East Indies were. All was not lost certainly. The US aircraft carriers had escaped, and by a fortunate chance the British carrier *Indomitable* had also not yet reached Singapore; events were later to show that the day of the battleship was almost over, and carriers of far more importance. But for the moment things looked very black indeed, while at the same time domestic pressures to try to relieve hard-pressed US forces in these exposed positions was bound to be considerable. What Dill and Brooke judged to be unrealistic plans to attempt to defend the Anglo-US-Dutch position in South-East Asia were in a sense forced on the US government, despite the War Department's injunction not to reinforce such points as the Philippines at the expense of the Atlantic theatre. It was politically impossible simply to write off the whole of this vast area without making some effort to hold it. Washington too foresaw the impact of all this on other theatres. US battleships were recalled from the Atlantic, and Lend-Lease shipments momentarily halted, pending Allied decisions on the priorities for supplies as between the Far East, the Middle East and aid to Russia. It was clear to the Americans as to the British that some hard immediate decisions might have to take precedence at the Washington conference over long-term strategic plans.[14]

(iii) ORGANIZATION FOR WAR

It would be true to say that of the three leading personalities in the Conference which assembled in Washington on 22 December 1941, each had different priorities. Marshall, as one American historian has put it, 'was more concerned with organization than strategy'. Aware of the US Army's weakness, and anxious lest his carefully laid plans for a prolonged period of training of a mass army followed by a large scale cross-Channel offensive should be pre-empted by Churchill's 'peripheral strategy', he preferred to concentrate on '*how* to fight the War': '*where* to fight it could be worked out later'. Roosevelt for his part was aware of the necessity for an allied command structure and an agreed strategy to be worked out, and equally an agreed plan for the allocation of munitions. But the first of these were matters largely for the military men, and the second for the supply experts. His eyes were fixed on 'Declaration of War Aims' which the US, Britain, the USSR, China and all their allies should sign. The US had been drawn into a war which few of its citizens wanted, and it was essential that they should at least have a clear idea of what they were fighting for – not for the British Empire, or for Communist Russia, but for 'life, liberty and independence, human rights and justice', in the words of the Declaration. Only so could he take a united nation into war. Churchill alone was preoccupied almost entirely with the strategic questions before them – the broad principle of 'Atlantic First' and, within that general framework, the decision for North Africa.[15]

Since these three men were the dominating figures at the conference, by reason both of their characters and the positions they held, it is not surprising that each obtained to a large extent what they wanted. Roosevelt's Declaration was signed at the White House on New Year's Day 1942 by the representatives of twenty-six Allied nations. Noble as these ideals were, events were to show that it is difficult to enforce the observance of ideals which are not fully shared by all who theoretically subscribe to them. Of more immediate importance was Marshall's pressure for 'Unity of Command' both between the various services and between the various Allied nations. By the time the Declaration was signed, he had already won this battle. It was a two-pronged concept. For each major theatre there should be a Commander-in-Chief or 'Supreme Commander' over the armies, navies and air forces of all Allied nations in the theatre. Since it was the Far Eastern areas which were most immediately threatened, and it was also there (more than in the Middle East for example) that so many different allied forces – British, American, Dutch, Australian – were involved, it was in this area that the principle should first be applied. But who was to give such an Allied Supreme Commander his orders? To whom should he report? Obviously an Allied Commander could only report to an Allied body. So the creation of a permanent unified Allied directorate or 'Supreme War Council' also followed from the acceptance of this proposal.[16]

Marshall had long believed in this concept. The difficulties of obtaining adequate US Army-Navy co-operation through the rudimentary joint liaison available had first perhaps convinced him of the need for someone who had authority over all arms in the field. The history of the difficulties of coalition warfare throughout the ages made it a logical step to apply this principle to all Allied forces in one theatre. On Christmas Day, at one of the first meetings of the Conference, Marshall put his argument for unity of command in the Far East to his British counterparts. 'With differences between groups and between services, the situation is impossible . . . I am convinced that there must be one man in command of the entire theatre – air, ground and ships.' As he spoke, Marshall was making use of and going beyond arguments prepared for him, appropriately in the light of the future, by an officer in his War Plans Division – Brigadier Dwight D. Eisenhower.

He had much opposition to overcome. The British Chiefs were at first dubious about the new concept. The US Navy Department, as always, was hostile to any proposal which might limit the right of its admirals to conduct their own war in their own way. Churchill for his part was doubtful about the concept of one commander with authority extending over such vast areas. That the first of these new supermen was to be, if Marshall's proposal were adopted, an Englishman, General Wavell, was gratifying but carried with it the danger that he might become the British scapegoat for the inevitable setbacks that lay ahead. Undeterred, Marshall instructed Eisenhower to draft a proposed letter of instruction to a future Supreme Commander. He had, as always, the loyal support of his political chief, the US War Secretary, Henry Stimson, with whom he had much in common and a relationship of mutual trust. The Navy's grudging acquiescence was obtained through Knox, King and Stark. Most important Roosevelt, as was so often to be the case in the future, was convinced by Marshall's vigorous and clearly expressed arguments. Hopkins, whom Churchill trusted, took it upon himself to put a timely word in the latter's ear, supported by Lord Beaverbrook, an old friend and associate whom Churchill had brought with him to the Conference to discuss supply matters. Beaverbrook saw the advantages of the close and intimate involvement of the two allies at all levels which such a proposal would bring and advised Hopkins to arrange a meeting between Marshall and Churchill. Churchill, anxious to please the President, ultimately agreed, and on 29 December cabled to the War Cabinet in London that he had accepted the appointment of a Supreme Commander, Wavell, for the so-called 'ABDA' area – American, British, Dutch, Australian – embracing Malaya, Burma, the Philippines and the East Indies. It was, as he put it, 'necessary to defer to US views on this'. In response to their doubts he pointed out the necessities of the new alliance – 'we are not now single, but married'. Neither Churchill nor Wavell, when he accepted the command, had any doubt that the latter was taking on a forlorn cause. 'It was', Churchill says 'certain that he would have to bear a load of defeat'. Wavell took the post as a newly-appointed captain might take over a ship which was already sinking under him. In effect he was the sacrificial victim on the altar of the Anglo-American Alliance and Marshall's insistence on unity of command. The sacrifice was not in vain. The principle was established, and was to be the mainspring of success in all future Allied operations, including that with which this book is concerned. Marshall regarded it according to his biographer as 'one of his major contributions to winning the war'.[17]

As we have seen, the creation of a supreme Allied war directorate followed logically from this decision. In his message to the War Cabinet, Churchill had also reported that he had accepted the arguments for such a body. 'He [Wavell] would receive orders from an appropriate joint body responsible to me and the President.' This meant that in some way the British and US Chiefs should continue to act together to provide such a body. The British Chiefs, foreseeing that if there was only one such body, its seat would inevitably be in Washington, and fearing that the war would be run from there, proposed that there should be two bodies, consisting of the US Chiefs in Washington and the British Chiefs in London, maintaining constant transatlantic communication. Such a system would, however, clearly have been cumbersome, if not unworkable. When this proposal went from the allied Chiefs of Staff to the President on 29 December Roosevelt revised it drastically. There should be one body in Washington with the three US Chiefs, Army, Navy and Air Force, and three representatives of the British Chiefs of equal

rank, also from the three services. As Hopkins put it, 'a
hell of a row' followed. Neither Churchill nor the British
Service Chiefs liked the stark fact with which they were
now confronted – that the price of the Anglo-American
alliance was the acceptance of the status of a junior partner. But the logic was irrefutable – 'If the principle of
unity of command was valid for each theatre it was all
the more valid for the top command of the entire US-
British effort.' The British gave way gracefully, even accepting that the various Allied Boards for the allocation
of supplies should be responsible to this body; and the
new body, named the Combined Chiefs of Staff – 'in fact
if not in name a Supreme War Council' as Lord Ismay
put it – began to function.[18]

In London the new Chief of the Imperial General Staff,
Brooke, concluded sourly that this meant in effect that
British experience was to be subordinated to American in-
experience; but time was to show that this was too gloomy
a view. Having gained his point, Marshall was too wise and
magnanimous a man not to recognize that the Americans
could learn from the two years' hard-won experience of
their allies; that experience in fact counted for a great deal
in the early meetings of the CCS and the presence of Dill
on the Combined Chiefs of Staff ensured that the British
Chiefs' views would be ably presented and sympathetically
received. Moreover, the US Chiefs were often to journey
overseas to meet directly with their British opposite numbers or the British Chiefs to come to them – nearly half
of the actual meetings of the 'Combined Chiefs of Staff'
were ultimately to take this form, rather than meetings in
Washington of the US Chiefs with simply *representatives*
of the British Chiefs. Both Brooke and Churchill were to
judge in retrospect that the creation of this body was one
of the most important constructive achievements of the
'Arcadia' conference, and represented an advance on all
previous forms of inter-allied military co-operation. These
two decisions, in fact, – the acceptance of 'unified command' and the creation of the CCS – were to provide both
the instrument through which British views were to prevail

in the first major Anglo-American strategic decision; and the command structure which greatly contributed to the successful translation of that decision into effect. In short they were the foundation of the success of the North African landings.[19]

(iv) 'GERMANY FIRST' AND
'SUPER-GYMNAST'

Marshall had got his way on the means and machinery to be adopted for victory. Churchill and the British had made many concessions in these areas in the cause of Allied unity. The latter felt, and rightly, that it was essential to gain Roosevelt's and Marshall's whole-hearted confidence, to make them feel that the British were co-operative, and forthcoming. But what Churchill cared for even more than the *machinery* was the organization of a grand strategy for the Alliance. Having made so many concessions in the organizational field, he was in a strong position to ask that his views on strategy were given considerable weight. Essentially, as has been shown, these consisted of three main points, namely: 1) The previously agreed decision to concentrate the main Allied effort on the defeat of Germany while standing on the defensive in the Pacific should be re-affirmed. 2) The main Allied operation in 1942 should *not* be against the European mainland but should be aimed at the occupation of North West Africa and the control of the whole of the North African shore plus the Atlantic Coast of West Africa. 3) The landing of large-scale Anglo-American forces on the European mainland in 1943 should be the object of all other preparations in the European theatre during 1942. The second of these proposals represented in effect the merging of the British plan for 'Operation Gymnast' with previous tentative American plans for a landing on the West African coast, the new plan now being code-named 'Super-Gymnast'. The third proposal involved the preparation of the operation or operations against Europe which was soon to be given the code-name 'Round-Up', preceded by an extensive build-

71

up of US forces in the European theatre, code-named 'Bolero'. As part of the 'Bolero' build-up, Churchill revived the 'Magnet' proposal for the despatch of four partly-trained US divisions to Northern Ireland, relieving an equivalent number of British troops for operations in North Africa.

But all of this depended on the American re-affirmation of the cardinal principle of 'Germany and Europe First'. The British, as has been noted, had felt considerable anxiety that the American leaders, under pressure from an aroused public opinion calling for revenge against Japan, might go back on this principle. These anxieties, however, were soon set at rest. At the first meeting of the US Chiefs with their British counterparts on 23 December 1941, and again at a meeting on Christmas Day, Marshall and Stark made it clear that they had not changed their view that the defeat of Germany meant the inevitable defeat of Japan, whereas the converse was not true. Therefore the Allies should give priority to the defeat of Germany.

The US paper presented at this first meeting set out the principle clearly in two paragraphs:

(1) It had been agreed that Germany was the predominant member of the Axis powers and consequently the Atlantic and European area must be considered the decisive theatre.

(2) Our view remains that Germany was still the prime enemy, and her defeat the key to victory.

At the same time the US Chiefs accepted the proposed British agenda, which put the emphasis on the Atlantic rather than the Pacific theatre. Roosevelt had no hesitation in accepting this recommendation, courageously ignoring considerable Congressional and public pressure. Indeed he had already approved, on 21 December, a US Joint Board memorandum reaffirming 'Rainbow Five' with its priority for operations against Germany. He never wavered from this view. In a sense therefore this battle was won before the first shots were fired.[20]

It is one thing, however, to affirm a principle; it is another to see that it is adhered to in the face of continuing adverse pressures. Two such pressures were soon to be felt. One was the influence of Admiral King, shortly to succeed Stark as Chief of Naval Operations. Whatever King's head might say, it may be doubted if his heart ever wholly assented to the principle of absolute priority for the European Theatre. But in fairness to King it must be said that far more decisive was the inexorable demand on troops, ships and supplies generated by the needs even of a defensive war in the Pacific, and the attempt to halt or at least delay the advancing Japanese. Logic might dictate that the Allies should cut their losses and not waste valuable resources attempting to defend the indefensible. But in practice no American President could fail to make some attempt to aid hard-pressed US forces in the Philippines and British and Dutch allies in Malaya, Burma and the East Indies. Churchill was well aware how easy would be a gradual erosion of the agreed principle by a piecemeal process of robbing the Atlantic Peter to meet the needs of the Pacific Paul. He felt it necessary therefore, even after the first round of talks had taken place and the principle had been re-affirmed, to draft a memorandum for the Americans in which he again stated 'It is generally agreed that the defeat of Germany will leave Japan exposed to overwhelming force, whereas the defeat of Japan will not bring the war to an end.' He had the satisfaction in the last plenary meeting of the Conference on 12 January 1942, of seeing the record state 'The Staffs are agreed that only the minimum of forces necessary for the safeguarding of interests in other theatres should be diverted from operations against Germany.' No more could be done by way of affirming the principle. The rest lay with the future course of events.[21]

A British historian subsequently recorded his view, that 'The real achievement of the "Arcadia" conference was the decision to make the Pacific War a "holding" war'. Others may well agree with Churchill's and Marshall's judgement that the creation of the Combined Chiefs of

Staff as an allied instrument of victory was at least as important. But the enunciation, or rather the reaffirmation of the principle of 'Germany First' was certainly a crucial decision nonetheless. If the United States had had a President more fearful of popular pressure or a Chief of Staff less firm in his pursuit of strategic priorities the result might have been very different.[22]

The first point gained, Churchill's next main objective was to secure, within this broad strategy, the particular priority in Allied operations of his projected North African landings. His arguments ranged over familiar ground, but the fundamental one was clearly the securing again of free passage for Allied shipping through the Mediterranean. In three papers for the Conference, prepared on board ship, he had set this out first as the object of Allied strategy in the West for the coming year; turning second to the need to fight a defensive war in the Pacific and third to the planning of a campaign against Europe in 1943. The order was significant, and the dating made it explicit. It ran clearly counter to Marshall's views. The question was whether the President could be persuaded in this instance to do what in other matters he consistently refused to do – overrule his Chief of Staff.

Churchill had reason to hope that this might prove to be the case. He knew that the President was favourable to the idea of operations in North Africa. What influenced Roosevelt more than anything in this direction probably was his desire that US troops should join in active operations against the enemy as soon as possible. He felt that American public opinion would demand it, and moreover that it might well be impossible to maintain the momentum behind the strategic principle of 'Germany First' unless both the public and Pacific minded admirals could see that US forces were committed in that theatre. Moreover, there was the continuous pressure from Moscow for a 'Second Front in 1942', and the fear still that without some such reassurance and relief the Russians might abandon the struggle, or indeed be forced to do so. Thus both domestic political needs and the political needs of the Alliance pointed to the urgent necessity of a sizeable American operation in 1942. Marshall's programme of a slow steady build-up of overwhelming US forces for, perhaps, an operation against Western Europe in the spring of 1943 failed to provide for these political necessities. Churchill's proposal appeared to do so.[23]

In taking this view Roosevelt could hark back to the US Chiefs' own memoranda of February and a more recent one of 11 September 1941, which, reflecting both Stark's thinking and the influence of the joint talks with the British in Washington and at the Argentia conference had said, *inter alia,* 'In the Middle East and North West Africa the effort the German forces can exert is only a fraction of what they can put forth in Europe. Yet severe German defeats in these regions might affect the stability of the Nazi regime.' Here was the germ of the further argument for North African operations which Roosevelt was probably not afraid to face – that it might be better to employ green American troops and inexperienced leaders in the first instance against positions which might be undefended and where German troops could only be brought gradually and in relatively small numbers into action, rather than against substantial German forces entrenched in prepared positions on the European coast.[24]

It was true that the American planners, unlike Churchill, looked at the question more from an Atlantic than a Mediterranean viewpoint, and talked more of the security of hemisphere communications through control of West Africa than of the re-opening of the Mediterranean. Roosevelt was aware too that this line of thought reflected Stark's and the Naval planners' view and to some extent that of Arnold and the Air Force more than it did those of Marshall and the War Department, who believed that it would be necesssary to come to grips with the Germans on the Continent, and that any diversion from this aim would merely be 'dispersionist' and serve to prolong the war. Nevertheless, Roosevelt could point to the fact that there was some opinion in favour of North Africa among his own advisers.

It was probably not the case therefore, as Roosevelt's biographer Burns suggests, that Roosevelt was merely being 'the polite host' when at the first main meeting with Churchill, Beaverbrook and the British Ambassador Halifax on 22 December – a meeting from which his military advisers and even Stimson were absent – he appeared to favour the plan 'with or without an invitation from the French'. Certainly, however, after the President had been reminded, or had reminded himself, of the War Department memorandum of 21 December, which suggested that US participation in Mediterranean operations would have relatively little effect, Roosevelt was less encouraging in subsequent meetings. The position at this stage was that the US Army was unconvinced by the arguments for 'Super-Gymnast', and the Air Force was moderately sympathetic but not disposed to give it a high priority. Only the Navy really favoured it – and that with an eye to Dakar and the Atlantic rather than to Algiers and the Mediterranean. Churchill's plan, on the other hand, envisaged three or four British divisions employed *inside* the Mediterranean and about the same number of US divisions aiming not so much for Dakar as much farther north towards Casablanca; and a date for such an operation perhaps as early as 25 May 1942.[25]

Faced with this multiplicity of counsels, and with news of Pacific setbacks coming in thick and fast, the President wavered. Although sympathetic to begin with he felt obliged to point out that the War Department classified Africa and the Middle East as 'subsidiary theatres'. But the American historian who has said of the ultimate outcome 'Super-Gymnast was far from abandoned' is much nearer to the truth than Burns, who comments that 'Gymnast was strangled by the rush of events [in the Pacific].' In terms of what was actually to happen during the next three or four months the latter judgement has much truth in it. The pressure of Pacific needs, combined with a setback in the Western Desert and heavy shipping losses, pushed the North African operation further into the distance. In terms, however, *of the actual decisions agreed at the Conference* the North African operation remained very much on the agenda, and it was Marshall's preferred operation 'Round-Up' which tended to be lost from sight. The latter had been, as we have seen, included in Churchill's original strategic plans for the Conference. In his memoirs Churchill stresses how this shows that he was not, as has sometimes been suggested, both then and later, irrevocably opposed to the idea of 'an assault on Europe'. The truth is, however, a little more complex than this simple statement implies. Both in these papers and in previous discussions at Argentia, Churchill had always used language which left it open whether the policy envisaged was one of a *number* of landings at different points, or one decisive thrust. The language of this 'Arcadia' paper itself, which spoke of forces being 'landed in several of the following countries, namely Norway, Denmark, Holland, Belgium, the French Channel Coasts as well as in Italy and possibly the Balkans', certainly accords more with Churchill's 'dispersionist' strategy rather than Marshall's single, concentrated cross-Channel attack. When, therefore, Churchill talks of his own 'earnest desire that the crossing of the Channel and the liberation of France should take place in the summer of 1943', he is obscuring a vital difference which persisted between himself and Marshall, even in their attitudes to an eventual attack on Europe.[26]

Whichever form this ultimate assault on Europe was to take, however, the truth is that by the time of the final plenary meeting of the Conference on 12 January there was little enough left of it, except a much attenuated 'Magnet'. This operation, or series of operations, – the transport of partly trained US divisions to Northern Ireland – appealed to both Marshall and Churchill since it could be reconciled with both of their strategic conceptions. For Marshall it represented part of the 'Bolero' build-up in the UK in 1942 as a prelude to an invasion of North-West Europe in 1943; for Churchill a means whereby trained troops in the UK could be relieved of their duties in the defence of Britain against possible

German invasion in order to participate in an operation against North Africa. It had been agreed early in the Conference that 'Magnet' should be begun straightaway and the Staffs prepared provisional plans for the transport of about 40,000 US troops to Iceland and the UK during the coming January and February. By the end of the Conference, however, the pressing needs of the Far East had led to these numbers being almost halved, in order that the equivalent of a division could be sent to the Far East. The significance of this decision was that if the movement of US troops to the UK continued at no more than this rate, the 'Bolero' build-up could only lead to the presence of something like three or four US divisions in that theatre by the late summer of 1942 – a small enough contribution to a proposed assault against twenty-five German divisions in Western Europe. Not surprisingly, the agreed record of the Conference, conflating Churchill's and Marshall's strategy, says merely that 'In 1943 the way *may* be clear for action across the Mediterranean from Turkey into the Balkans, *or* by landings in Western Europe'. Churchill was afterwards to write that 'Round-Up' in 1943 which he had wished for was made impossible by the course of military events in that year, and that in his view this was all for the best, since the Germans were far stronger in Western Europe in 1943 than in 1944, and the American troops and commanders less experienced then than they would be later. Many military men and historians, particularly on the other side of the Atlantic differ from this view, and regard it as a major misfortune that the cross-Channel attack was *not* carried out in 1943. The US air commander General Spaatz as well as Marshall certainly held that view, but it seems doubtful if an attack on Western Europe could have been carried out with the same success in 1943 as it met with in 1944. Whatever view one holds on this crucial question, it is clear that at the 'Arcadia' conference the commitment to such an operation was left very 'open-ended' and imprecise.[27]

The position was rather different with regard to North

Africa, though all the participants to these decisions, including Churchill, were well aware that any projected operation of war is subject to the effects of future setbacks in other areas. The status of 'Gymnast', however, or rather 'Super-Gymnast' at the end of the 'Arcadia' Conference was quite clear. The preliminary Combined Staff studies had been made, and envisaged something more like twelve British and US divisions, rather than Churchill's original proposal of six or seven, being employed. It was recognized that any military operation, including this one, would normally take three or four months to mount, and the decisions already taken to reinforce the Far East meant that shipping in any case would not be available for this period. The date for such an operation could not therefore be earlier than April or May 1942.

It had always been agreed between the British and Americans that if possible such an operation should be undertaken with the consent, and indeed at the invitation of the Vichy government. Roosevelt had kept up continuous contact with Pétain, Darlan and Weygand through Admiral Leahy, Robert Murphy and others, and at this time felt the outlook was quite promising. Darlan indeed had put out quite definite feelers to the United States, as indeed he was to do again later. Roosevelt, therefore, was quite content with the delay which would give him more time to bring these delicate negotiations possibly to a successful conclusion. Churchill for his part cared less for the prospects of securing Vichy collaboration, which he had always considered doubtful, but on the other hand he regarded 'Gymnast' as very dependent on the continued success of Auchinleck's offensive in the Western Desert, which at that moment was bogged down. A few months delay would perhaps enable Auchinleck to resume a successful offensive, and permit the other half of the Allied pincer to close on the German-Italian armies in North Africa. He too therefore was prepared to wait, provided the decision in principle was taken for the operation.[28]

This in fact was what was done, though it could be argued that the final record of the conference left it a little uncertain whether the operation should still be undertaken if Vichy consent was not secured. Roosevelt's final comment, however, at the meeting on 12 January, seems clear enough – 'We will make Beaverbrook and Hopkins [the principal negotiators on the supply side] find ships, and will work on "Super-Gymnast" at the earliest possible date.'[29] This was in fact as far as it was possible for anyone to go at that moment. Whether the operation would indeed prove possible in May, in September or November depended on the fast-moving events in a global war being waged in numerous theatres at that moment.

As he flew away from the Conference, Churchill had good cause to feel pleased. He had established a most satisfactory relationship with Roosevelt and seen a closely-knit machinery of Anglo-American co-operation established which, if not precisely what he had wished for, offered good prospects that the British view would be heard at all levels of decision. He had seen plans made for a vast expansion of the US munitions programme. Above all, in the field of strategic planning he had seen the Americans voluntarily re-affirming the principle of 'Germany First' and agreeing to study his preferred operation 'Super-Gymnast' as a major strategic priority for the very near future. He could not have expected or wished for more, and moreover he had noted that in this alone Roosevelt had not always agreed with or supported his Chief of Staff. If Marshall *were* to return to the attack on 'Super-Gymnast' at a later date, there was at any rate some prospect that Roosevelt might continue to agree with Churchill.

III

The Protracted Argument
January-July 1942

(i) A CONFLICT OF OPINION

If Winston Churchill looked back on the results of the 'Arcadia' Conference with satisfaction so too did Marshall, but for different reasons. Marshall had been concerned at that meeting to establish a sound organizational structure for Allied war-making and in this he had succeeded; in the process, incidentally, ensuring that the supreme direction of the Allied war effort should be centred in Washington. The next requirement from his point of view was to get his political chief and the British leader to accept a sound basis for Allied ground strategy – a 'sound basis', that is, as he and his associates saw it. This involved in his view the principle of concentration of resources on one decisive operation against the main enemy, Germany. Ideally such an operation should aim at the heart of the enemy by the shortest possible route. It should be preceded by a methodical build-up of overwhelming forces, and not carried out until certain of success. In the meantime subsidiary operations which might drain away resources piecemeal from the main objective should be avoided like the plague.

As applied to the problem of waging war against the Axis the logic of such principles pointed to an attack across the Channel through France into the Ruhr, the industrial heart of Germany. The danger in Marshall's eyes lay in the penchant of both Roosevelt and Churchill for what he and Secretary Stimson regarded as 'dispersionist' operations of the kind that might drain resources away from this central purpose. In this category they included all operations in North Africa and the Mediterranean, and therefore the proposal discussed at the 'Arcadia' Conference as 'Super-Gymnast'.

The difficulty of course was that theoretically an Allied strategy *had* been agreed at 'Arcadia', and it included at least a certain US commitment to 'Super-Gymnast'.[1] From Marshall's point of view it was necessary to get this embarrassing commitment removed. This in fact did not prove difficult, because the onrush of events and the weight of disasters which fell on the Allies in the early months of 1942, both in the Far East and the Mediterranean theatre, enforced on both Roosevelt and Churchill the recognition that the North African operation would at least have to be postponed. Even at the time of that conference the effect of the disaster at Pearl Harbour and similar naval losses off Malaya could be foreseen to some extent and it was recognized that the Allies would be hard-pressed to hold not only the Philippines and Malaya but also the East Indies and Burma. India and Australia even might be threatened. Looking ahead to the pressures there would undoubtedly be from US public opinion to do something to help the threatened US and Allied forces, and from the governments of Australia and New Zealand for protection, Marshall must have felt that all longterm strategic planning at this time must be tentative and provisional. This clearly applied to the nominal commitment to 'Super-Gymnast', which most Americans regarded as no more than a promise to give serious study to planning such an operation. No doubt this was why Marshall let it pass. As he probably foresaw, in the next two or three months the forces which might have been set aside for a North African operation rapidly had to be allocated to the Far East, and even the plans to send substantial forces to the UK under 'Magnet' were temporarily abandoned. First two US divisions, then four, were rushed off to the Pacific and Australasian theatres during these disastrous months, as Malaya and the Philippines, then the East Indies and Burma fell, as had been feared, into Japanese hands. By contrast no US forces of any size had reached the United Kingdom under 'Magnet' by April of 1942. There was therefore no possibility of a substantial American relief of British forces in the UK for North

Africa, still less of an American contribution to such an operation in May 1942, as Churchill had originally hoped. By this stage indeed it had already been agreed by Churchill and Roosevelt that Gymnast could not be carried out 'for several months at least'.[2]

There was, in fact, as will by now be clear, a wide difference between the British approach to the strategy of war against Germany and that of Marshall and his War Department planners, a difference that could not easily be reconciled. The British approach was designed, as Churchill put it, to 'close the ring' around Germany and Italy by obtaining mastery of the Atlantic, the Mediterranean and the Middle East, as a prelude to launching a series of operations against Europe – in the Balkans, Italy and Norway as well as France and the Low Countries. This strategy was dubbed by Marshall and Stimson 'dispersionist' or 'peripheral', and ran counter to the strategy of the 'direct approach' outlined above.[3]

At the 'Arcadia' conference this difference was to some extent fudged and obscured, a process which not infrequently happens in the conduct of allied or coalition warfare, especially when the politicians superimpose their ideas on those of the military men. The latter are accustomed in their sphere to reaching clear-cut decisions and then giving orders which must be carried out. Politicians are much more accustomed to the necessities of compromise between differing viewpoints. Faced with the necessity of reaching agreement with his allies, both British and Russian, Roosevelt was sometimes inclined to resort to this process of blurring the edges of differences, in the hope that time and the pressure of events would resolve the difficulties: as indeed it often did. He was to apply this technique later in dealings with Stalin over contentious political issues, not always with fortunate results. Churchill too sometimes resorted to somewhat similar tactics. A notable instance in the political sphere was his apparent agreement to the so-called 'Morgenthau Plan' for Germany at the Quebec conference in 1944, when he clearly expected that the logic of events would in fact compel the abandonment of the plan at a later date.[4] Marshall himself was shortly to experience similar tactics in the military sphere, when he came to try to sell his preferred strategy to the British. On this occasion, as at 'Arcadia', apparent agreement concealed in fact irreconcilable differences of view; and just as Marshall had allowed forms of words to pass at 'Arcadia' because he did not expect them to be translated into reality, so Churchill was to do the same at the London conference with Marshall and Hopkins in April 1942.

(ii) THE MARSHALL MEMORANDUM

The prelude to this conference had been several months of disaster in the field and of strategic re-appraisal in Washington and London. Meanwhile Marshall and Stimson had not waited long before re-opening the basic question of strategic priorities. During the month of January and the early part of February desperate attempts had been made to get together forces for the Pacific; in the course of which as we have seen both 'Gymnast' and 'Magnet' had been completely emasculated. By the end of January, however, Marshall, Stimson and Eisenhower, the newly appointed head of the War Plans Division, had already begun to worry about the lack of a clear strategic plan for 1942, and particularly about the effect of these piecemeal and emergency rescue operations on the cardinal principle of 'Germany First'. It was time to reassert that principle, before the effects of Far Eastern needs and Admiral King's powerful presence – who, as Eden remarked 'had more of his way in *executing* Allied policy than in formulating it' – combined to rob the principle of any meaning. As early as 22 January Eisenhower, reflecting clearly Marshall's views, was writing, 'We must quit wasting resources all over the globe . . . we must launch a land attack in Europe as soon as possible.' In mid-February Marshall asked Eisenhower to prepare an outline of general strategy along these lines to put to the President and the Combined Chiefs of Staff. The result of this request was a memorandum by Eisenhower, dated 28 February, in which he came down firmly on the side of devoting all Allied efforts to a build-up for a cross-Channel attack. The arguments for this strategy were clear and logical. The transport of US troops to the United Kingdom for such an attack would be fairly inexpensive in the use of scarce shipping resources – and the Allied shipping losses to submarine warfare in the early months of 1942 had been the heaviest yet. Furthermore there were already large British forces in the United Kingdom. Then the use of British airfields would enable the Allies to obtain air-superiority for the necessary period over the Channel coast – a superiority which could not be easily obtained anywhere else. The build-up of US forces in the UK to sufficient strength would certainly take time, but the very fact of the build-up, which would certainly become known to the Germans, would compel them to keep substantial forces in Western Europe and so indirectly relieve the Russians. Finally, once the Allied Expeditionary Force had been established in North-Western Europe, it would have the benefit of an excellent communications network, and would be poised to strike at the heart of Germany by the shortest route.[5]

The logic was irrefutable and the strategic principle was undoubtedly sound. It suffered from only one disadvantage, as an American historian has conceded, namely, that it could not be carried out in 1942! The truth of this proposition was soon to be demonstrated when the prospects of such an operation were exposed to critical British scrutiny in London. But it was probably moderately obvious to Marshall and Eisenhower at that moment. At the very most, and if all went well, no more than ten or twelve US divisions could be transported to the UK by the *end* of 1942, and weather conditions in the Channel made it unlikely that a cross-Channel operation could be carried out after mid-September. By that time only a handful of US divisions could possibly be both available and reasonably well-trained and equipped, to add to the half-dozen or so British divisions which were likely to be actually available for such an operation. Moreover there were as yet few landing-craft constructed of the type that would be required to land both troops and tanks on a defended coast.[6]

Yet it was clear that Roosevelt was determined that US troops should go into action against Germany in 1942, and Churchill had made it equally plain that he would look askance at any strategic plan which envisaged large US and British armies standing idle for the whole of 1942. It was necessary therefore to embark on a somewhat tortuous process of argument, which was to lead Marshall and his associates into what was bound to be in the end a losing battle. In order to win Roosevelt's acceptance of the broad cross-Channel strategy it was necessary to add to the main proposal of a cross-Channel attack in 1943 ('Round-Up') and a prolonged UK build-up in 1942 ('Bolero') a possible small-scale attack in 1942 – the operation which was soon to be called 'Sledgehammer'. The latter certainly was hedged around with reservations: it was suggested that it should only really be undertaken if the Germans became very much weakened – which in 1942 seemed unlikely; or alternatively as an emergency measure, if the collapse of the Russian armies seemed imminent. Having sold the package to the President on this basis, however, it would then be necessary to sell it to the sceptical British, who in the event had little difficulty in showing that 'Sledgehammer' was an impracticable suggestion.[7]

At this point, however, Marshall did not perhaps fully foresee where his arguments would lead him. On 5 March, at a meeting at the White House with Roosevelt, he put the arguments of the Eisenhower memorandum to his chief, supported by Stimson. It was a favourable moment. The day before Churchill had written to Roosevelt accepting that the need to reinforce the Far East partly from Middle East resources, and the consequent need to replenish the Middle East, had imposed on them both a 'Shipping Stranglehold'. This meant that a North African operation ('Gymnast') was ruled out for the time being and that the transport of US troops to the UK ('Magnet') was also in question. Thus the President was well aware of the effects the emergency measures of the past two months had already had on the strategy postulated at 'Arcadia', including the whole doctrine of 'Germany First'. He was in a mood receptive of any suggestion which might reinstate this principle and offer effective plans for bringing US troops into action against the Germans. After hearing Stimson's and Marshall's arguments, he asked them to instruct their Joint Planners to prepare a detailed scheme for the cross-Channel attack, and replied to Churchill that he accepted that the North African operation must be temporarily shelved, but that he himself was 'becoming more and more interested in the establishment of a new front this summer on the European continent, certainly for air and [commando] raids'. The language is worthy of note. The qualification attached to the 'European Front' might mean that Roosevelt envisaged no more than an extension of the old British strategy of massive air-raids on Germany and larger-scale commando raids. 'Gymnast' was not completely disposed of, but merely 'temporarily shelved'. It was clear that the President was by no means fully convinced yet that North Africa should be abandoned; though he was still 'determined to stand firm for the strategy of "Europe First" '.[8]

Indeed when Stimson and Marshall returned to the charge on 25 March with the planners' report they found that Roosevelt was disappointingly inclined to talk at large about operations in various parts of the world, in particular the Mediterranean. It required strenuous efforts by the two, supported by Arnold, King and Knox to pin the President down firmly to the cross-Channel operation. He eventually agreed, however, that the War Plans Division (now called the Operations Division) should produce further studies – a more or less 'final blueprint' – which Hopkins then urged should not be referred to the Combined Chiefs, but go with Roosevelt's approval straight to Churchill, and not by means of transatlantic messages but via a high-powered mission to London.

Again it is interesting to consider the reasons for Hopkins' initiative. He knew Roosevelt's mind better than anyone and was well aware a) that Roosevelt still hankered after the North African strategy but b) that the latter was as heart-and-soul committed to the principle of 'Germany First' as Marshall. On that principle certainly the two were fully agreed, and it was threatened at that moment from many quarters and many pressures – by King's preference for the Pacific, by MacArthur's demands to give his theatre priority, by the Australian government's urgent appeals, even by Churchill's own anxieties for India. Hopkins saw that it was urgently necessary to get the European strategy moving again, and that the difficulty lay partly in the British caution in relation to the direct attack on Europe – the one operation Marshall most cared about. At this stage the British were still inclined to discuss the invasion of Europe as a possibility even in 1943 only if Germany was considerably weakened. A very much qualified and imprecise 'Round-Up' would, as Hopkins saw, be insufficient to stand up to and prevail over the 'Pacific Firsters'. The British must be committed more definitely than this to 'Round-Up'. If this was Hopkins' line of reasoning he was undoubtedly right – and he probably envisaged that he himself would be asked by Roosevelt to go with the mission and put the argument to Churchill. This indeed is what happened; and it is probable that it was Churchill's knowledge that Hopkins so faithfully reflected Roosevelt's mind and that Marshall's military judgement counted for so much with Roosevelt which alone induced the Prime Minister not to reject the American proposals out of hand, but instead give them a qualified acceptance.[9]

At all events Roosevelt at a final meeting on 1 April approved the draft OPD plan envisaging an assault on the Boulogne – Le Havre area in April 1943 with an Anglo-American force of over forty divisions; and for 1942 a possible small-scale landing in the Calais area with perhaps seven divisions – if the Russian situation became desperate or, as was in fact very unlikely, Germany became much weakened. The OPD planners pointed out that in 1942 the US contribution would be minimal – two or three divisions at most – and even early in 1943 the majority of the forces initially engaged might well have to be British. It was clear therefore that British consent was essential. Roosevelt asked Hopkins to accompany the US Chief of Staff to London to secure that consent, and wrote to Churchill 'What Hopkins and Marshall will tell you has my heart and mind in it'. It seems that the President was convinced – for the time being.[10]

A factor which must not be forgotten in all this was of course, as has been indicated, the Russian front, and the constant pressure from Moscow for aid – first ever-increasing supplies but second, and above all, a 'Second Front in 1942'. There was a direct link here with the Soviet demands for Anglo-American recognition of their frontiers of 1941 and the territorial gains these embodied, particularly the annexation of Polish territory. Churchill, after reacting at first very strongly against these demands, was beginning to come round to the view that it might be necessary to concede them, in order to encourage Russia to stay in the fight. Hopkins, however, reflecting Roosevelt's views, specifically saw the promise of definite military help as an alternative to conceding Soviet territorial demands – and said so to the British.[11]

A further factor which cannot be ignored is the underlying US suspicion that behind much of the strategic arguments for Mediterranean operations put up by Churchill and the British lay a political rather than a military motive – namely a desire to safeguard and further the British position in the Central and Eastern Mediterranean. Some historians have gone further, and reasoned backwards from Churchill's later concern over Soviet ambitions in the Balkans to the conclusion that in 1942 he was already looking to military operations in North Africa as a springboard for a further move towards Italy and the Balkans *for political reasons*. There is no real evidence for this latter conclusion, whether put forward as a criticism or as a vindication of Churchill's foresight. Indeed all the evidence suggests that far from foreseeing the Soviet threat in that quarter, in the early months of 1942 Churchill's main concern was the fear that Russia might collapse; and that he thought that at the end of the war 'the balance of power will favour the Anglo-Americans, and the Russians will require our help more than we theirs'.[12]

All statesmen, of course, in a world of sovereign states pursue, consciously and unconsciously, their country's national interests; and Churchill was well aware of the dictum 'war is a continuation of politics by other means'. This was equally true of Roosevelt and the Americans, and certainly the American post-war position in the Pacific was as carefully looked to and adequately provided for by the military and political policies pursued as was the British position in the Mediterranean. But this is not to say that political considerations were uppermost in the minds of either when they argued about strategy. The natural predisposition of the British to the 'peripheral strategy' needed no particular political stimulus, and in-sofar as other motives than strictly strategic ones may have subconsciously influenced Churchill, it is probable that Lord Moran is right to see his doubts about the cross-Channel attack as reflecting a deep-seated and wholly admirable desire to avoid another 'blood-bath' like that of 1914-18. Perhaps, also, Eisenhower may be right in thinking that a subconscious desire in Churchill's mind to vindicate his own 1914-18 strategy in the Dardanelles may partly have contributed to his belief in Mediterranean and particularly Balkan operations. But neither motive much influenced Brooke, for example, who in general, and over the long period shared Churchill's preference for the North African operation and his resistance to any pre-mature and ill-conceived assault on Western Europe.[13]

(iii) THE LONDON AGREEMENT

When Marshall and Hopkins came to London in April 1942 the real Anglo-American argument about strategy began. Ironically the situation which had obtained at 'Arcadia' was now reversed. At that conference Marshall had been confronted with a plan for an operation which he had disliked, in the shape of 'Gymnast'. He had supplied Roosevelt with the necessary arguments against it, only to see the latter give it in the end his qualified approval. 'Gymnast' had then been swept aside by the tide of events, as Marshall perhaps had foreseen it would be. Auchinleck's set-back in the desert, the adverse changes in the naval and air balance of power in the Mediterranean and the frightening shipping losses of the period had completed the process which the demands of the Pacific theatre had begun. This had enabled Marshall to re-open the question of strategic priorities and he now sought to put as first priority what Churchill at Arcadia had put third – the build-up and launching of a major cross-Channel assault. The arguments in favour of this strategy – 'Bolero' and 'Round-Up' – were as we have seen convincing enough. Marshall's Achilles' Heel in relation to the whole case was 'Sledgehammer' – the proposal for a possible limited invasion in the autumn of 1942, as a prelude to the major assault in 1943.

The case for 'Sledgehammer' was ostensibly that it was necessary to have a plan ready to be put into operation in the event of two contingencies. Firstly, if the Russians showed signs of collapse at the end of the coming German summer offensive, it might be necessary to undertake some desperate measure in order to relieve the pressure on them. Secondly, in the unlikely event that it was Germany which showed signs of weakening, there should be some plan ready to take immediate advantage of the situation. Later it was also suggested that it might in any case be useful to establish a bridgehead on the Continent in 1942, for full-scale exploitation in 1943. In Marshall's mind, the proposal probably served even more importantly the purpose of meeting Roosevelt's insistence on a plan for the use of American troops in 1942 and enabling both Marshall and his Commander-in-Chief to stave off the champions of 'Pacific First' in Washington.

If this was the purpose, then it worked. 'Sledgehammer' with its more important companions 'Bolero' and 'Round-Up', held the field throughout the spring and summer of 1942, and conditioned, as Marshall intended they should do, all American decisions as to troop movements, production and supplies which were made during this period, providing a greater degree of urgency for the 'Bolero' build-up in the UK than could be supplied by 'Round-Up', and keeping American eyes fixed on Europe. Though in the end it had to give way to a revived 'Gymnast', it had served its purpose.[14]

'Sledgehammer' and 'Gymnast' were in a sense the two opposite sides of a coin, the point-counterpoint of Allied strategy. So long as there was any possibility of a landing in North-Western Europe in the autumn of 1942, troops, shipping and supplies would have to be kept in reserve for that and could not be found for a North African operation. Similarly, if 'Gymnast' was to take place in 1942, no provision could be made for 'Sledgehammer' – and, more important, Marshall feared that 'Bolero', the build up in the UK, might be so weakened that 'Round-Up' also might be imperilled.

Marshall therefore had to try to sell 'Sledgehammer' to the British as well as 'Round-Up'. It was the British in fact who were now confronted with a proposal for an operation which they much disliked, though in this case the objection was not based, like US objections to 'Gymnast', mainly on grounds of broad strategic principle, but on the sheer impracticability of the operation. The troops available in 1942 would, they argued, not be adequate, the specialized landing-craft would not be available, and the Germans had more than enough forces in Europe to contain such an attack and probably destroy it. The result would be at best a useless and expensive bridge-head or at worst a disastrous defeat which would set-back all Allied plans for at least a year.

Faced with an unpalatable proposal, the British Chiefs' reaction was not dissimilar to Marshall's at 'Arcadia'. Having failed to strangle it at birth because of the unwillingness of their political master to say a flat 'No', they had to consent grudgingly to the plan being studied, in the confident expectation that the logic of facts and events would eventually dispose of it. This proved to be the case. Just as one can follow the fortunes of 'Gymnast' in Washington in the early months of the year, from Roosevelt's confident assertion in January 'We will make Beaverbrook and Hopkins find ships and will work on "Super-Gymnast" at the earliest possible date', to his regretful ' "Gymnast" cannot be undertaken' in March, so the progress of 'Sledgehammer' can be followed after the Marshall-Hopkins mission through the War Cabinet minutes and those of the Chiefs of Staff Committee. Between April and July 1942 one can read the whole story of its decline and fall.[15]

At first, however, it seemed that the American view had largely prevailed. Although Churchill at the first meeting with Marshall and Hopkins re-stated all the British Chiefs' objections to cross-Channel operations with inadequate forces and inadequate preparation, he implied that nonetheless he might overrule their objections and accept the broad American plan. Churchill had not exaggerated the British Chiefs' views. When Marshall put these plans to them on the following day and in subsequent discussions, he found that all were more or less opposed to an attack on France in 1942; and doubtful about such an assault even in 1943, unless the Germans were then much weakened. Churchill had already pointed out to Marshall that none of his advisers had been able to produce a satisfactory plan for such an operation before 'the late summer of 1943'. Brooke, as was his way, was more forthright. He took the first opportunity to indicate to Marshall that he had many misgivings, about a 1942 operation particularly; and during the next few days confided to his diary that the proposal was apparently too little thought out, and indeed Marshall had apparently no clear idea what the strategic plan for exploitation of a successful landing would be. The whole idea seemed to Brooke 'fantastic' and an American 'castle in the air'.

Marshall in fact conceded that the implications of the 1942 landing had not been thoroughly studied. As has been noted, the 'Sledgehammer' concept had in fact been added to the main proposal for 1943 operations largely to make the package more acceptable to Roosevelt, and it was not the part of the plan Marshall himself most cared about.[16]

A prolonged battle between the British Staffs and Marshall seemed likely. It came therefore as a surprise to the Americans and indeed to some of the British that at the crucial meeting with the Defence Committee on 14 April Churchill appeared to give his full approval to the plans outlined in the US memorandum, which Marshall and Hopkins had brought with them. As Marshall put it to his deputy, McNarney, in a telephone call that evening 'He virtually accepted our proposals *in toto*', while Hopkins cabled Roosevelt in similar terms. The record of the meeting shows that this was no exaggeration. Churchill indeed concluded by saying expansively 'Our two nations are resolved to march together in a noble brotherhood of arms.'[17]

A large question mark hangs over this remarkable series of meetings. One question is the extent to which Churchill consciously misled the Americans, or at any rate allowed them to go away from the Conference with a false impression. On this point there are differences of opinion. Among American authorities Burns certainly implies it, as does Stimson, who later commented 'The agreement [of April 1942] held for only two months,' and Sherwood who entitles the chapter of his book dealing with the later reversal of this agreement, 'The Decision is Changed.' On the other hand Averell Harriman does not think Churchill was devious, in that he was in fact in favour of 'Bolero' and 'Round-Up' and made his doubts about 'Sledgehammer' clear. On the British side Lord Ismay has recorded his view that it would 'perhaps have been better if the British had expressed their views more frankly' – a reflection which was unfair perhaps to the British Chiefs, if not to Churchill. The latter had said at the meeting on the 14th that he 'cordially accepted the [US] plan' and that there was 'complete unanimity on the framework'. Brooke himself recorded in his diary 'We accepted their proposals for 1942 perhaps and 1943 for certain.' In addition Churchill had cabled to Roosevelt that 'the campaign of 1943 is straightforward' and 'the proposal for the interim operation [Sledgehammer] has met the difficulties in a sound manner'. The last remark comes closest to a blurring of the truth, since Churchill himself concedes in his memoirs that at this time he thought that rigorous examination of the 'Sledgehammer' proposal would in fact probably rule it out as impracticable, and that his prefered strategy remained what it had been at 'Arcadia' – namely in 1942 'Gymnast' *and* a build-up in the UK of US forces, followed by a major assault on Europe in 1943. Yet 'Gymnast' was not even mentioned at these meetings; and Churchill's conception of 1943 operations against Europe was, as we have seen, different from that proposed in the US memorandum.[18]

Churchill says frankly that he did not feel it was politic at this time to reject plans which meant so much to the Americans. Hopkins probably contributed to this diffidence on Churchill's part by reminding him how much importance Roosevelt attached to putting American troops into action against the Germans in 1942 and by the same means aiding the Russians in their desperate struggle. Indeed Roosevelt, like Churchill, was under constant pressure from Stalin for a 'Second Front in 1942' and had already invited the latter to send a mission to Washington to discuss the US proposals to 'relieve your critical Western front'. Hopkins had reminded Churchill too of the continuous pressure on Roosevelt from King and MacArthur to devote more resources to the Pacific. Churchill therefore was fully aware of the necessity of strengthening the President's (and Marshall's) hands in maintaining the principle of 'Atlantic First'. Brooke indeed had also divined that some such considerations perhaps lay behind Marshall's advocacy of the European offensive plan. (He might in fairness have added that what he saw

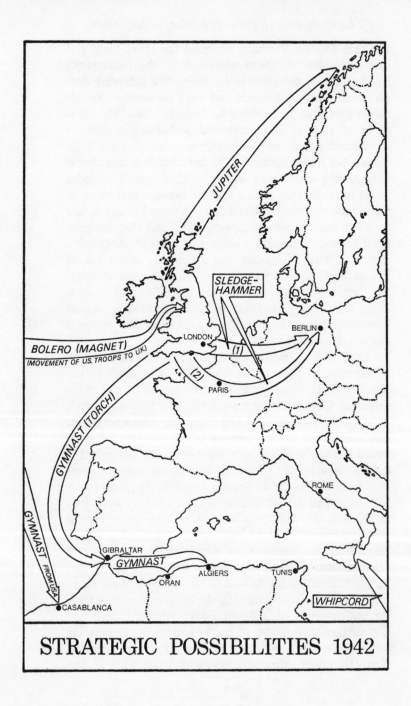

JUPITER

SLEDGE-
HAMMER

BOLERO (MAGNET)
(MOVEMENT OF U.S. TROOPS TO U.K.)

LONDON

BERLIN

(1)

(2)

PARIS

GYMNAST (TORCH)

ROME

GYMNAST
FROM U.S.A

GIBRALTAR

GYMNAST

ALGIERS

TUNIS

ORAN

WHIPCORD

CASABLANCA

STRATEGIC POSSIBILITIES 1942

as 'strategical weakness' in Marshall's thinking may have been more a sense of political realities.) Churchill, indeed, argues that he himself did not totally rule out the possibility of an operation against Europe in 1942: he had in fact earlier toyed with the thought of such an operation. His position at this moment was that he felt it would *probably* prove impracticable; rather than that he was irrevocably opposed to it. He therefore felt that he could give his consent to the study of such an operation, to see if a workable plan could be devised.[19]

It may be questioned how far Marshall, once he had had time to think it over, was in fact the victim of any illusions on this score, fostered by Churchill. He was fully aware of the British Chiefs' reservations and had written to McNarney the day before the decisive meeting that these reservations made 'continued firmness necessary to avoid dispersions', ie peripheral operations such as North Africa and the projected operation against Norway, code-named 'Jupiter', which Churchill also advocated. Two factors must be borne in mind in this connexion. One was that Marshall cared not so much for 'Sledgehammer' as for the 'Bolero'-'Round-Up' strategy – that is a major build-up of US forces in the UK in 1942 and the launching of these forces against North-West Europe in 1943. At the decisive meeting indeed he had spoken of 'Sledgehammer' in qualified terms, talking of 'the *possibility* we might be *compelled* to launch an emergency operation' and adding 'if such an operation *were made necessary* by development on the Russian Front' (ie if there was a likelihood of a Russian collapse). The 'shock' he experienced which his biographer refers to, when the British later revived the possibility of a North African operation, was probably more due to his firm conviction that such an operation would prejudice 'Bolero' and rule out 'Round-Up', rather than because of a belief in 'Sledgehammer' as a vitally necessary operation of war. But Churchill for his part did not believe that the North African venture ruled out the possibility of an assault on Europe in 1943; and if, as he then hoped, the North African campaign had been brought to a successful conclusion by the end of 1942, this consequence need not have followed.[20]

The second point which is relevant to this question is the fact that the 1942 operation had been specifically presented by the Americans as one that would take place *only* if there was a complete collapse on the Russian front, or alternatively if Germany appeared gravely weakened. In the arguments about whether or not Churchill was completely straightforward, it tends to be forgotten that his acceptance of 'Sledgehammer' was an acceptance of a proposal qualified in this way. Since neither of the conditions specified actually arose in 1942, there was no breach of faith in not carrying out that particular operation.

(iv) THE MOLOTOV MISSION

Ironically it was now the turn of the Americans themselves to become involved in dealings, this time with the USSR, which would subsequently lead to charges of bad faith. President Roosevelt himself was the major figure in this affair, and it must be said in his defence that he had not yet experienced the tendency of Soviet leaders of that period to interpret a qualified statement of intentions as a binding promise. Equally it must be said that Roosevelt, against Marshall's advice, did commit himself fairly definitely, though it is certainly possible to query the exact nature of the commitment.

A few weeks after Marshall and Hopkins had returned happily from London the Russian mission which Roosevelt had invited arrived. Between 20 May and 12 June the Soviet Foreign Minister Molotov visited London, then Washington, returning to Moscow via London. He had two objectives which have already been described, namely to secure Anglo-American agreement to a treaty which would ratify the Soviet territorial gains of 1939-41; and more important, because more urgent, to obtain a binding promise of Anglo-American military action in 1942 on a scale which would bring relief to the hard-pressed Russian armies and implement the indication Roosevelt had given that the United States had plans to do so.

Molotov had little satisfaction from his first round of talks with the British. Aware that American opinion was still strongly adverse to any ratification of Soviet territorial demands, Churchill and Eden made it plain that they could not at that time sign such a treaty, though Churchill himself had come to the conclusion that these demands ought to be conceded, at least so far as the Baltic States were concerned, and had so informed Roosevelt. The US position remained unchanged, however, and Churchill felt he had to go along with it. Molotov eventually therefore had to be content with a Twenty-Year Treaty of Alliance with Britain which made no mention of frontiers. Eden's view was that Molotov and Stalin probably thought it politic not to be too demanding on such matters in the hope of getting satisfaction on the more pressing need of military help. The British, however, were no more forthcoming on this issue than on the political questions. Churchill would have been willing to make political concessions if he had had a free hand, but was determined not to be trapped into any binding commitment of a military nature which might prove difficult or impossible to fulfil. Indeed at the time of the Molotov visit he had told his Chiefs of Staff that in view of their grave doubts about the feasibility of a landing in Europe in 1942 he was not prepared to give way to the 'popular clamour for a Second Front [in Europe]'; and added that he thought from a military point of view an operation in Norway ('Jupiter') would be more attractive than 'Sledgehammer'. He took advantage of the Molotov visit in fact to try to educate his visitor in the realities that controlled the practicability of amphibious operations, particularly the need for air superiority, the shipping shortage, after the heavy losses of the previous three months, and the lack of sufficient landing-craft to put a powerful force ashore in the first assault. It may be doubted if the Russian visitors regarded these arguments as anything more than an evasion, or indeed understood the technicalities. Molotov after all was not a military man, and in any case the Russians had no experience of amphibious operations. Churchill, however, had made his position clear, and cabled to Roosevelt that he had been careful to avoid a positive commitment to a Second Front in 1942. Molotov therefore departed for Washington, where he hoped for a more forthcoming attitude.[21]

He was not disappointed. The American attitude in fact was the exact reverse of the British. They were not prepared to make political concessions to the Russians, but were anxious to aid them militarily. They felt indeed that a firm promise of military help would enable them to resist Soviet political demands more effectively. Since so far as they were concerned the April agreements with the British still held, the Allied programme for 1942-3 continued to be 'Sledgehammer' and 'Bolero' in 1942, and 'Round-Up' in 1943, and they saw no objection to saying so to the Russians. Moreover, the situation on the Eastern Front was particularly discouraging at this time, and both Roosevelt and Marshall feared a Soviet collapse or near-collapse. They therefore felt that the condition stipulated for 'Sledgehammer', namely a situation so grave as to justify an Anglo-American 'suicidal' operation, was likely in fact to arise and that the Allies would be forced to undertake it. Molotov not unnaturally or unjustifiably did his utmost to reinforce this impression.

In the first meeting with Molotov, Roosevelt had turned to Marshall with the query 'Can I say we are preparing a Second Front in 1942?' and had received the latter's 'Yes'. Roosevelt had then told Molotov to inform Stalin that a Second Front could be expected that year. Marshall was more cautious in his language, telling Molotov only that the United States was making *every effort* to bring about the conditions which would make the creation of a Second Front possible, thus slightly diminishing the effect of Roosevelt's remark.

The President, however, was clearly even more worried about the situation on the Eastern Front after Molotov had described it in sombre terms, and also about the general state of Soviet morale. He told his Chiefs of Staff that he would have to give Molotov a more specific answer (clearly of an affirmative nature) on the Second Front; and cabled Churchill that he was 'more anxious than ever' that some kind of attack on Europe should be undertaken *in August*. The following day, 1 June, Roosevelt told Molotov that the Americans 'expected to establish a Second Front' and a few days later agreed to a public communiqué which included a reference to the subject in the form which the Russians wished: 'In the course of conversations full understanding was reached with regard to the urgent tasks of creating a Second Front in Europe in 1942'. Though slightly ambiguous, these words were taken by the world at large, and certainly by the Russian people, to indicate a firm intention on the part of the Americans; and Molotov himself could be forgiven if he took Roosevelt's agreement to them, coupled with his words of 1 June, to indicate the same thing. Moreover, Roosevelt overrode Marshall's and Hopkins' objections to the mention of specific dates both in the communiqué and in the cable to Churchill.[22]

Not surprisingly, Churchill and the British received this news with some consternation. Only a few days before Churchill had told the Chiefs of Staff that he accepted their doubts about the practicability of 'Sledgehammer', and had cabled Roosevelt that he had asked Lord Louis Mountbatten to go to Washington to 'explain the difficulties of 1942'. In this message he had put forward the possibility of a landing in Norway and added 'We must never let "Gymnast" pass from our minds' – his first reference to North Africa for some time. It seemed at the time that this message had had little effect on Roosevelt. On the contrary, the latter had committed them both very fully, in language which, as Eden records, the British would certainly not have agreed to. Churchill hastened to repair the damage when Molotov returned to London. He pointed out that such an attack must be launched with air superiority. This limited the possibilities to a relatively small area of the French coast, extending from

Cherbourg to the Pas de Calais. The Germans were clearly well aware of this. Equally the shortage of landing craft made it unlikely that a very powerful assault could be mounted. The picture Churchill painted, therefore, was of an operation which could not in fact possibly draw off any German divisions from the Russian Front, and which indeed could easily be contained and probably destroyed by the twenty-five German divisions then available in Western Europe – an outcome which, as he pointed out, would benefit neither the Russians nor the Western Allies. Against the background of this deluge of cold water, Churchill's assurance that he would certainly put into effect any 'sound or sensible' plan to take the weight off the Russians can have been little comfort, though in fact it was sincere, and in Churchill's mind clearly meant the possibility of the North African or Norwegian ventures. As a further safeguard Churchill agreed to the communiqué only in conjunction with an aide-mémoire which was handed to Molotov at the same time. This document stated that, while preparations for a landing in August or September 1942 were being made, it was impossible to say at that time if its *execution* would prove to be feasible or not. Therefore the British *could give no promise* in the matter. Whatever may have been Roosevelt's intentions, therefore, Molotov was left in little doubt about Churchill's views. He would have been even more discouraged if he had known that on the very day the communiqué was issued the War Cabinet had agreed with Churchill and the Chiefs of Staff that there should be no landing in Europe in 1942 unless there was a good prospect of a permanent lodgement and unless also the Germans were 'demoralized' by setbacks in Russia.

The Chiefs of Staff had already indicated their view that the first condition was unlikely to be fulfilled. As for the Germans, they were advancing in the Kharkov sector and to the capture of Sebastopol, and at that moment were clearly the very reverse of demoralized. Not surprisingly Churchill records in his memoirs that ' "Sledgehammer" fell of its own weight', adding with slightly less accuracy that he had not had to argue against it.[23]

As with the Marshall-Hopkins talks with the British in April, a number of questions hang over these encounters between the Western Allies and the Russians. The issues which arise are firstly, 'Did the West fail to honour its legitimate obligations to its Russian allies?' and secondly, 'Did the failure to carry out a landing in Europe in 1942 in fact constitute a breach of faith on the part of the Americans, if not the British?'

It is impossible not to sympathize with the Russian viewpoint at this time. They were bearing the full brunt of the Nazi war machine – there were two army groups in the southern sector alone. Their casualties and the sufferings both of soldiers and civilians in the besieged cities were on a heroic scale. By contrast the Western Powers seemed to them to be doing very little against Germany. There was an element of unfairness in this view, certainly. The Soviet leaders blandly ignored the vast resources and manpower which the British and Americans were devoting to the war at sea and the war in the air. Both constituted a drain on resources from which the Soviet Union was largely exempt. The Russians also tended to ignore the fact that, unlike themselves, the Western Powers were at war with Japan and large British and American forces were fighting in the Pacific, where a second naval war was also in progress. But, caught as they were in the fearful catastrophe of total war and near defeat, the Russian attitude was understandable.

The question whether there was any moral obligation involved is debatable. Interest might dictate that the Soviets should be helped and certainly saved from collapse, but it may be questioned whether there was a real duty to do so. The Soviet Union had not entered the war out of a desire to help the Allies, but because she had been forced to do so. For two years the Soviet leaders had stood calmly by while France was destroyed and Britain brought to the brink of defeat, gaining what advantages they could in the meantime. The West had every reason to be glad that the Russians were defending their homeland so fiercely, but had no particular reason to be grateful, since they were not doing so for the benefit of the West. This, as he makes clear, was certainly Churchill's view and also that of Brooke, who in fact begrudged the despatch of aircraft and tanks to Russia which British forces badly needed, at the cost of heavy losses in equally scarce shipping resources.[24]

The question of bad faith is a little more difficult to assess. It can hardly be levelled against Churchill, who made his position crystal clear. Soviet historians do not on the whole make this charge against him, but instead criticize him for his persistent opposition to a Second Front in Europe in 1942 and his alleged lukewarmness towards the opening of such a front even in 1943. Roosevelt's language on the other hand had been encouraging to say the least, and moreover, though informed of the British aide-mémoire, he had not sought to associate himself with it. Even after he had talked with Mountbatten, who had given him a full picture of the British Chiefs' reservations and 'conveyed the disturbing impression that there might be some question of the revision of the "Round-Up"-"Sledgehammer" agreements made by Marshall and Hopkins six weeks previously', Roosevelt did not seek to halt the publication of the agreed communiqué on the 'Second Front'. Most American authorities certainly hold the view that something of a 'public pledge' was given to the Russians.[25]

Yet Roosevelt acted with the best motives. He wished to encourage the Russian people by assuring them that they did not stand alone.[26] So far as the specific operation – 'Sledgehammer' – was concerned, he recognized certainly that the British, who would have to supply the bulk of the forces had in effect the power of veto – and Molotov had appeared to understand this – but so far as he knew the British were still bound by the April agreements, and the condition of an imminent Russian collapse seemed quite likely to be fulfilled. Moreover, neither Roosevelt's conversations with Molotov nor the language of the communiqué actually bound Roosevelt to a specific operation such as 'Sledgehammer'. The pledge as it stood could be redeemed by an operation elsewhere; and, appearances to the contrary, Roosevelt had told Mountbatten that he had in fact taken note of Churchill's reference to 'Gymnast' in the message of 28 May.[27]

Ironically, the result of the undertakings given to Molotov was in the end to swing the President back to 'Gymnast'. In his anxiety to secure a Second Front Molotov had demanded a categorical assurance of an operation against the Germans in 1942, and in his desire not to send him away empty handed, Roosevelt had given it. But if the British vetoed 'Sledgehammer', how was the undertaking to be redeemed, except by an operation in 1942 in some other quarter? This was soon to emerge as the irrefutable logic of the situation.

(v) 'SLEDGEHAMMER' GIVES WAY TO 'GYMNAST'

The War Cabinet's decision, that a landing in Western Europe should not be attempted unless conditions obtained which it was clear were very unlikely to arise, made 'further and early consultation with the Americans inevitable'. Rommel's resumed offensive in the Western Desert and the disastrous battles in early June, which effectively destroyed Auchinleck's armoured capacity, reinforced this necessity. Churchill for his part was already convinced that Roosevelt's pledge to Molotov of an Anglo-American operation in 1942 had created a situation which could only be resolved by face-to-face talks, leading to a clear understanding of strategic and logistic realities – namely that a European landing was out of the question and therefore the President's pledge could only be redeemed by some other means. It was necessary, as he told Brooke, to convince the President of this.[28]

It was in order to prepare the ground that Churchill had despatched his Chief of Combined Operations, Lord Louis Mountbatten, to Washington at the beginning of

June. Mountbatten, he knew, was considered by both Marshall and Eisenhower to be the British commander who most fully understood the problems of amphibious operations and of assault on a defended coast. They respected his knowledge and were likely to regard his arguments about the possibility of 'Sledgehammer' as more authoritative than those of anyone else.[29]

In a cable to Roosevelt just before Mountbatten's departure, Churchill described the purpose of the latter's visit in discreetly neutral terms. 'Dickie [Mountbatten]' he said 'will explain to you the difficulties of 1942 when he arrives.' But it is clear what Churchill and Brooke expected of this mission, and Mountbatten himself had no doubt about his purpose. His task, he was to say years afterwards, 'was to try to persuade Roosevelt and his advisers that our entire strategy needed re-thinking.'[30]

The two men met without the accompanying presence of the American Chiefs of Staff, it seems by Roosevelt's deliberate decision, and rather against Mountbatten's own wishes. He fully appreciated the danger of seeming to go behind Marshall's back to the President. He had no hesitation, however in putting his case strongly to Roosevelt. The shortage of landing-craft alone made it impossible to mount a European landing in 1942 powerful enough to draw off troops from the Russian Front. The German forces already in France were sufficient to contain and probably destroy the Allied forces, which could not amount to more than six or seven divisions at the most – and it might take three weeks to land even a force of that size with the craft available. The whole purpose of such a landing and therefore the case for it was destroyed by these arguments. Roosevelt reminded him of the agreement to make a 'sacrificial landing' to relieve the Russians if their situation grew desperate, even as late in the year as December if necessary; and mindful of his commitment to Molotov, reiterated the importance of getting American troops into action in 1942. For that reason if 'Sledgehammer' were impossible he preferred some such operation as 'Gymnast', which Churchill had so recently revived, to the mere despatch of an equivalent number of US troops to the United Kingdom under 'Bolero', releasing British forces for active operations elsewhere. There was no disloyalty to his Chiefs of Staff in all this. Roosevelt had put their case – the case which had always been argued for the 1942 cross-Channel operation – with its two limiting conditions. Having done so, he was bound to take notice of the unpalatable fact, which was clearly being put before him, that the British, who had an effective veto over this operation, were likely to exercise it; and therefore to consider what alternatives there might be. Unfortunately, from Marshall's point of view, of the two alternatives left when 'Sledgehammer' was ruled out, 'Bolero', the American build-up in the UK, did not meet the requirement of putting US troops directly into an active theatre of operations, while 'Gymnast' did.[31]

Mountbatten put the same case to the US Chiefs themselves before leaving for home. The message was clear, even though the Americans seem to have thought, quite wrongly, that Mountbatten was expressing Brooke's views rather than his own. Stimson and the Chiefs of Staff were now well aware that Churchill would make every effort during his own forthcoming visit to Washington to have the 1942 cross-Channel attack abandoned, probably in favour of the North African plan. The question was, 'Would the President be persuaded?' It was already clear he was wavering as a result of Mountbatten's arguments. This was made apparent at a White House meeting with Marshall and Stimson on 17 June. They then made a further attempt to reinstate the 'Sledgehammer-Bolero' concept in full force for 1942, arguing that 'Gymnast', if revived, would rule out a cross-Channel attack in 1942 *and* 1943. A memorandum conveying their views was drawn up and forwarded to Roosevelt at his country home at Hyde Park. But it may well be that in Roosevelt's mind the die was already cast. On the one side his commitment to Molotov and the mounting public pressure in the US for a 'Second Front in 1942' – on the other, Mountbatten's clear indication that these could not be met in 1942 by a cross-Channel attack, Admiral King's obvious dislike of the overriding priority Roosevelt had agreed should be given to 'Bolero', Churchill's obvious preference for 'Gymnast'. These formed a pattern which was difficult to ignore, and which made him for once disposed to overrule his Chief of Staff.[32]

Taking all the evidence into account, it is difficult to dissent from the view that Roosevelt's interview with Mountbatten on 9 June 1942 may well have been one of the most decisive moments in the development of Allied Grand Strategy. Mountbatten himself thought that at that moment Roosevelt grasped 'the inexorable realities' of the situation and the need therefore to think seriously again of the North African operation. If that be so, he is not exaggerating when he describes his visit to Washington as 'probably my most important task of the war'.[33]

It was time now for Churchill himself to follow up the advantage that had been gained. He arrived in the United States on 18 June, and flew to Hyde Park to see Roosevelt; on the 20th both men returned to Washington to continue the conference with their military advisers, who had already conferred together the previous day. On that very day, however, the news of the British disaster at Tobruk was received, and imposed on all the participants the need once again to concentrate for the moment on the immediate emergency and to postpone a decision on the fundamentals of long term strategic planning.[34]

The outcome of this second Washington Conference was then indecisive, and Churchill was not able, as he had obviously hoped, to obtain a clear decision against 'Sledgehammer' and in favour of 'Gymnast'. The reasons are not far to seek. Churchill himself subsequently felt that the news of Tobruk in itself so weakened his position that he could not hope at such a time to impose his views over the objections of the President's most trusted advisers – and Marshall and Stimson had certainly not at this stage given up the fight. It is impossible to be absolutely certain what was in Roosevelt's mind. It is pretty clear he was gradually moving towards the acceptance of the North African strategy, which both Churchill and Stimson believed he had always been drawn to, but he too probably felt that until the immediate crisis had been weathered, all options should be kept open. At that moment it must have seemed that Cairo might be lost, and with the German armies also moving forward into the Caucasus, the spectre of the Germans overrunning the entire area and even joining hands with the Japanese in India could not be entirely discounted, unlikely though it seemed. But then a month before Pearl Harbour the disasters which fell on the Allies in the first three months of 1942 would also have seemed unlikely.

Then, too, Churchill's arguments were not at this time wholly supported by his own principal adviser. Certainly Brooke made it clear to the US Chiefs that he considered 'Sledgehammer' out of the question. But with the Eighth Army in full retreat, he was doubtful if the Allies should contemplate any operation such as 'Gymnast' capable of absorbing resources which might be needed for the reinforcement of the Middle East. Consequently he was content for the moment to support Marshall along the lines that the US build-up in the UK should continue, with the possibility of a cross-Channel attack in 1943 at least kept open. Here was something on which he and Marshall could agree. It had always been the attraction of the 'Bolero' policy that, precisely because it did not commit the Allies definitely to either the European or the Mediterranean strategy, it could be accepted as a temporary compromise acceptable to both the British and Americans. At their meetings on 19 and 20 June, therefore, while Churchill was at Hyde Park, the Combined Chiefs agreed that 'Bolero' should continue to be pushed forward with a view to 'Round-Up' in 1943 and that there should be no immediate plans for 'Gymnast'. Having made his point that he thought it unlikely a practicable plan could be developed, Brooke even accepted that planning for 'Sledgehammer' should continue for the moment. It is not surprising that Marshall was much relieved, nor that Brooke was able to record in his diary the at first unlikely comment that he and the American Chiefs were 'pretty well agreed'. Meanwhile, however, Churchill's efforts at Hyde Park had not gone entirely unrewarded. The President was still anxious to keep the North African option open and unwilling simply to rely on the cross-Channel strategy for 1942. Churchill's arguments, like Mountbatten's, had made it only too plain that whatever might happen to 'Round-Up', 'Sledgehammer' was in fact unlikely to materialize. The outcome of the final meeting between the political leaders and their military advisers on 21 June was, therefore, that the Combined Chiefs' recommendations were accepted, insofar as they recommended the continued pursuit of the 'Bolero-Round-Up' policy, but the important rider was added that it was essential that British and American forces be prepared to act offensively *in 1942*. 'Sledgehammer' planning should still continue and, if a practicable plan could be devised, it should be put into effect; but again the rider was attached that if it proved impossible to devise such a plan, there must be some alternative *for 1942*. Finally, and following precisely the logic of Churchill's own arguments, the Chiefs of Staff were instructed to explore carefully the possibilities of French North Africa, with the specific implication that if that operation were decided upon, the US forces for it would be those which would otherwise go to the UK under the 'Bolero' plans. Marshall's feeling of relief must have been short-lived.[35]

On the face of it, then, this conference was indecisive, or to put it in a way which accurately reflects what happened, the outcome of this round in the long-drawn out contest between Marshall's and Churchill's strategy was a draw. A final decision between them was once again postponed. But Marshall was only too well aware that the President's acceptance of the renewed possibility of 'Gymnast', combined with the evidence of unalterable British opposition to 'Sledgehammer', meant that he had lost ground, even though 'Bolero-Round-Up' remained the agreed and primary strategic plan. Churchill for his part no doubt felt that, if he had not been able to obtain a decisive verdict for North Africa, he had probably succeeded in administering the knock-out blow to 'Sledgehammer'.

(vi) THE DECISION IS TAKEN

As Churchill records, he had now to secure final American agreement to the North African operation, at precisely the moment when he was at his weakest, politically and militarily. Britain had sustained a major defeat in the Middle East, losing ultimately over 30,000 men, and by 28 June the Eighth Army had retreated to El Alamein. At the same time Allied shipping losses had risen to 400,000 tons in one month. Paradoxically, these facts helped rather than hindered his cause. The urgent need to reinforce the Middle East and the fact that the shipping 'stranglehold' was worse than ever inevitably slowed down the movement of US troops to Britain, and even, thanks to a generous gesture by Marshall, deprived some of the US troops intended for 'Bolero' of modern weapons they had only just received. Eisenhower, who had just been sent to take over command of US troops in the United Kingdom, had noted that the 'Bolero' build-up was already behind schedule. Now further delays were necessarily imposed, delays which were more damaging to the prospects for a cross-Channel attack in 1942 than to the North African venture. It was the general view that weather conditions would make amphibious landings across the Channel too hazardous after mid-September – and it was now already July. The North African operation, however, could be carried out in October, or even November. Moreover, for a North African operation some of the US troops involved could be transshipped directly from America to the theatre of operations, whereas for a cross-Channel attack they had first to be transported to the United Kingdom. Events, as Churchill well knew, were forcing the issue in his direction.[36]

The first essential was to kill off 'Sledgehammer' once and for all. The British Chiefs of Staff had been considering this operation now for two months – longer, in fact – and had always come back to the same conclusion, namely that it was doubtful, given the forces and landing craft available, if it had the smallest chance of success; and even if successful, it would not serve the major purpose of drawing troops – or air forces – from the Russian front. Instead it would merely delay and weaken the full scale assault in 1943. On 2 July the Chiefs of Staff reported that the conditions for 'Sledgehammer' laid down by the Prime Minister and War Cabinet a few weeks earlier were unlikely to be fulfilled. As Churchill puts it, 'The moment had come to bury "Sledgehammer", which had been dead for some time.' On 8 July he cabled Roosevelt repeating what he had said to him at Hyde Park, namely that no British commander was prepared to recommend 'Sledge-hammer' as a practicable operation for 1942 or could devise a workable plan for it. Whether a failure, as was probable, or a success, in the sense that a permanent lodgement was obtained, it would certainly delay 'Round-Up' in 1943. The latter was an argument that Churchill no doubt hoped would appeal to Marshall and Stimson, who cared so deeply for 'Round-Up'; but in using it Churchill was perhaps a little disingenuous, since he was proposing to substitute 'Gymnast' for 'Sledgehammer' and that might equally weaken and postpone the cross-Chan-nel operations – as in fact it did. To this Churchill would have probably replied that if all went well and North Africa were occupied quickly with the connivance of the Vichy government or the French North African estab-lishment, then 'Round-Up' in 1943 would still not be much affected. Indeed the saving of shipping consequent on the opening of the Mediterranean would ease some of the problems of the US build-up in the UK. At all events he had no hesitation in again recommending 'Gymnast' (or rather 'Super-Gymnast') as the best method of re-lieving the Russian front in 1942, and urging that it should be undertaken even without the connivance of the Vichy government – which originally had been the American condition for this operation.[37]

In Washington Marshall and Stimson received the news of this message with a mixture of anger and despair. 'Sledgehammer' for them represented the British commitment to the cross-Channel strategy, and they were firmly convinced the North African operation would inevitably drain off Allied resources in 1943 as well as 1942, thus making 'Round-Up' also impossible. One can sympathize with their feelings. They had seen their strategic plans at first apparently agreed to and then gradually eroded; and they felt their British allies, if not guilty of bad faith, had at least been less than candid with them.[38]

Marshall had one last card to play. With the approval of Stimson, he persuaded his colleagues of the Joint Chiefs that they should ask Roosevelt to say to the British that they must either accept 'Sledgehammer' or the United States would concentrate all its efforts on the Pacific war. This, as both Marshall and Stimson subsequently admitted, was an attempt to bluff Roosevelt and Churchill. Neither of the two Americans had suddenly become convinced that the arguments in favour of 'Germany First', which they had always accepted, had suddenly become invalid. Roosevelt in fact had no difficulty in seeing through this ploy and replied that he would have none of it. He told them that he was opposed to abandoning the strategy of 'Germany First' and was still determined to get American troops into action in 1942. That meant 'Sledgehammer' if possible, but if not 'Sledgehammer', then something else. North Africa was one possibility or – and here one detects a Rooseveltian ploy – would the Chief of Staff prefer to send US troops to the Middle East, to fight in the battle there? Marshall reacted to this suggestion as though he had been stung. 'That' he said, precisely as Roosevelt no doubt expected, 'Would be worse than North Africa'. It would indeed, for it would mean putting his cherished and carefully trained new divisions under British command. Ungenerous though it may seem, his attitude cannot altogether be blamed – the record of the British command in the Middle East had not recently been a glorious one. At all events, Marshall knew he was beaten, and reported to his colleagues that the President would in his view probably insist on the North African operation. At a final White House meeting on 15 July Roosevelt made it clear to Marshall and King that he was not prepared to threaten Churchill; and that evening he told Hopkins that if the cross-Channel attack in 1942 was not possible, he preferred the North African operation to any concession to the idea of 'Pacific First'. He instructed Marshall, King and Hopkins to go to London immediately and secure a new agreed plan with the British for 1942 and 1943. They were to press for 'Sledgehammer' one last time, but if the latter proved 'impossible of execution' they were to 'determine upon another place for US troops to fight in 1942'. For 1943, he added, 'Round-Up' should still hold the field – cold comfort to Marshall who, as we have seen, feared that an operation elsewhere than across the Channel could reduce 'Round-Up' to the status of a 'residuary legatee'. It was perhaps as well he did not know of Roosevelt's remark to Hopkins that the 'Bolero' build-up might be weakened for *three months* by a decision for North Africa. The envoys were given one week to reach agreement.[39]

Historians differ as to the precise moment when the North African operation became 'the inevitable decision'. Formally that decision was not taken until 24 July. There can be little doubt, however, that the decisive day was probably 14 July when Roosevelt rejected the Chiefs of Staff's suggestion that he should threaten the British with the reversal of 'Germany First'. From that moment it was clear to Marshall, as it equally was to Roosevelt, that there was no possibility of overcoming the British veto on 'Sledgehammer' and therefore if there was to be an Allied operation in 1942 it must probably be in North Africa. One American historian concludes bluntly that 'Sledgehammer' was dead before even Marshall, Hopkins and King arrived in London. One cannot quarrel with that judgement.[40]

The formalities, however, had to be completed, and the US delegation travelled to London for the obsequies, arriving on 18 July. Marshall, as his biographer says, did not expect to succeed in resuscitating 'Sledgehammer'. However, he duly consulted the American commanders in England, Eisenhower and Clark, finding that they shared his fears about the effects of a decision for North Africa on the whole cross-Channel strategy, but equally that they felt the British were unalterably opposed to 'Sledgehammer'. Eisenhower, who had served under Marshall in Washington and been deeply influenced by him, was as much wedded to the cross-Channel strategy as his Chief, but at this point it was not his views which were decisive.[41]

As instructed by Roosevelt, and in accordance with his own convictions, Marshall made one last attempt to save the 1942 cross-Channel attack. At successive meetings with the British Chiefs of Staff on 20, 21 and 22 July he urged a revised 'Sledgehammer' plan, aiming at an attack on Cherbourg and the Cotentin peninsula. But it was not a very plausible case he had to argue, and he was too good a soldier not to know it. The operation would take two months to prepare, which would mean it could not take place till the end of September, thus placing it in a period when weather conditions in the Channel would be extremely uncertain and probably unfavourable. It would take place only on a narrow front with one division in the first assault, and the United States itself could only supply three divisions for the follow-up, compared with a possible six or seven British. But on such a narrow front the difficulties of holding on to and expanding the bridgehead, so as to permit the landing of more troops, were bound to be formidable. Moreover his own Army Commander, Eisenhower, estimated the chances of a successful landing at five-to-one against.[42]

Not surprisingly the British Chiefs remained unresponsive to this proposal, as indeed they would probably have been to a much more convincing one. Marshall conceded defeat and on 22 July Roosevelt was informed that there was no possibility of agreement on a cross-Channel attack in 1942. The latter replied on the same day reiterating his previous instruction to obtain agreement on some alternative operation, and indicating that they should choose between 1) a North African operation either by Anglo-American combined forces or by US forces alone; 2) an operation in Norway and 3) the despatch of US troops to the Middle East; at the same time he wired Churchill that he was 'influencing his Chiefs' in favour of North Africa. Eisenhower, who called this 'the blackest day in history', adding quite accurately, that he 'was back where he had been on December 15th', urged Marshall to suggest sending one US division to the Middle East, as a means of staving off 'Gymnast' and saving 'Round-Up' in 1943. But Marshall rejected this suggestion. He knew that it would not stop at one division. Neither man could see anything to be said for the Norwegian proposal, and Eisenhower was aware that the British Chiefs themselves disliked it. Inevitably, therefore, they came back to North Africa as the best among a number of infinitely bad jobs. Eisenhower conceded that it might well result in reopening the Mediterranean and strengthening naval control of the Atlantic, with much saving of Allied shipping, besides, if all went well, threatening Rommel's rear. As opposed to this, it might bring Vichy France and/or Spain into the war against them: but most objectionable of all, it would weaken the build-up for a successful cross-Channel attack in 1943. This was the crux of the matter, but the two men saw no alternative, particularly when Roosevelt cabled again on the 23rd that he definitely favoured the North African operation. On the 24th the US Chiefs accepted that this operation, rechristened 'Torch', should be the first priority. Marshall was able to secure, as he thought, one final concession – that though preparations should be made for 'Torch', a final decision should be postponed until 15 September and then only made in favour of North Africa if it was then clear that 'Round-Up' could not take place before July 1943. Hopkins, however, loyal as always to Roosevelt's wishes, saw to it that Roosevelt immediately named a date for the North African operation – 30 October. This really clinched the issue.[48]

The long-drawn out argument was at last over, and a crucial strategic decision had been made which, as Churchill rightly said, was to dominate the next two years of the war. For it did in fact mean that the cross-Channel invasion of Western Europe was postponed till 1944, just as Marshall had feared. It inaugurated a North African campaign which was to continue until the spring of 1943 and lead inevitably to the subsequent Italian campaign in that year. Whether this was for good or ill will be considered later. It is clear, however, that it was a decision which had to be made, unpalatable as it was to the US Chiefs. Roosevelt certainly knew when he framed Marshall's and Hopkins' instructions that this was so. 'Sledgehammer' or an alternative for 1942 meant in fact North Africa, since it was already clear that the British would veto 'Sledgehammer'; and other alternatives were even less palatable to Marshall than North Africa. Stimson sums up the matter succinctly when he says 'The decision was the result of two rulings, one by the British, the other by the President.' The British ruled against a cross-Channel attack in 1942, Roosevelt ruled that some other operation must be undertaken by US troops in that year. Together these two made 'Torch' inevitable.[44]

IV

From Decision to Action:
August-November 1942

(i) PROBLEMS OF COMMAND

The British and American Governments were now committed to an operation which was disliked by all the military advisers on the American side, and which was to be entrusted to a commander – Eisenhower – who was himself extremely lukewarm about its strategic value and prospects of success. It was to be the most ambitious amphibious operation ever attempted, involving the movement initially of about 75,000 men 1,500 miles from Britain, and a further 35,000 men, with more to follow, across the Atlantic from the United States. The assaulting troops would be using new and experimental landing-craft, with little time left to train them in their use – and there were still pitifully few of these. They would be landing and conducting operations on terrain with which none of the commanders were familiar. Air cover would be minimal inside the Mediterranean, since it would be dependent on the highly vulnerable Gibraltan airfield – 500 miles from Algiers – plus whatever aircraft-carriers could be spared for escort, probably no more than three or four. All of this was to be planned and executed in about three months, by a newly created Allied Headquarters and inter-allied staff unaccustomed to working together and under an unknown commander, who had never seen a shot fired in anger nor commanded so much as a company in battle.[1]

There was, however, one major factor in favour of success which would have been lacking in the case of a cross-Channel attack, namely that there was at least a good prospect that the landings would meet only token or moderate resistance. Indeed this constituted the crux of the argument in favour of North Africa as opposed to Western Europe. The former was a fairly hazardous operation in all the circumstances; powerful enemy resistance would have made a cross-Channel attack much more so. But there could be no absolute guarantee at this stage that French resistance would be light, and the fact that the operation was to be carried out against neutral instead of enemy territory added a whole host of political complications to the military ones. There was just as little time to deal with these political problems as with the military factors. Not surprisingly, one American historian has called the operation 'bizarre, doubtridden and unpredictable'.[2]

The effective time available for planning was in fact to be rendered even shorter by the fact that over a month of it was to be consumed in further argument about fundamental aspects of the operation; and until decisions were reached on these matters, effective planning was hamstrung. There were very understandable reasons for this. One was that Marshall and Stimson had accepted the July decision only with great reluctance and profound reservations. Indeed, as Marshall's biographer puts it, 'On no other issue of the war did Roosevelt's Secretary for War and Chief of Staff differ so completely with their Commander-in-Chief.'[3] Marshall had insisted at the July meetings on one last proviso – that although planning for 'Torch', as the North African operation was now called, should begin, preparations for 'Sledgehammer' should also continue, and a final decision between them should not be made till mid-September – and then 'Torch' should only go ahead if it were decided that a cross-Channel attack could not be launched before July 1943. In effect, Marshall had said 'Very well, I will agree to a North African operation, but only when it is absolutely clear that otherwise we shall literally be doing nothing at all to take the pressure off the Russian front during the whole of 1942 and a good part of 1943.' He had added that if the decision were then made for North Africa, it would in his view mean that there would in fact be no cross-Channel attack in 1943. This was a view that neither Churchill nor

Roosevelt were prepared to concede, though the British Chiefs at least privately thought Marshall was right – as he was.[4]

If Marshall was hostile to 'Torch', Admiral King was even less enthusiastic. The US Navy Chief had even refused at first to allow US naval personnel to crew the landing-craft for European operations, until talked round by Mountbatten, who had pointed out to him as one sailor to another that he could not go down in history as the American admiral who refused to allow his men to crew the ships in some of the major amphibious operations of all time.[5] King, however, always remained lukewarm towards European and particularly Mediterranean operations. His attitude towards the naval requirements for 'Torch' throughout August 1942 was extremely unforthcoming, and subsequently he seldom lost an opportunity to bolster his forces in the Pacific at the expense of the Atlantic and Mediterranean theatres.

The US Chiefs, however, soon discovered that whatever the 'small print' of the July agreement, both Roosevelt and Churchill were talking and behaving as though the final decision for 'Torch' had in fact been made. (Roosevelt had showed his hand immediately when, prompted by Hopkins, he had cabled Churchill on 25 July that the date for 'Torch' should definitely be 'not later than October 30th.') For a while Marshall continued to cling gallantly to the September proviso, but by this cable Roosevelt had effectively pre-empted his Chief of Staff, and he made it plain to both men at a meeting on 30 July that his decision for 'Torch' was unalterable. Marshall did not give up easily, but, faced with the clear decision of the President he eventually felt bound to accept it. On 10 August he dissuaded Stimson from making one final protest to Roosevelt, and a few days later wrote to his friend Dill, the British military representative in Washington, that 'US planners would enthusiastically and effectively support decisions made by the Commander-in-Chief', ie that he would give his personal backing to 'Torch'. Dill had himself exercised his not inconsiderable influence with Marshall to good effect, and had even suggested that Marshall should eventually command 'Torch' – a suggestion that Roosevelt and Churchill brushed aside, since both knew full well that Marshall had no desire to command an operation he had always opposed.[6]

By mid-August, therefore, one cause for the lack of thrust behind 'Torch' had been removed. A further cause, however, lay in the fact that for much of August Churchill, the most vigorous proponent of the North African venture, was on his travels once more. Between 2 August and 23 August he was first in Cairo then in Moscow, then back in Cairo again. Though constantly in touch with London and Washington by cable, this was by no means the same as being on the spot in London during the early stages of the planning; and, moreover, his mind was much preoccupied with other issues, notably the question of command in Egypt and Anglo-Soviet relations. Space does not permit more than a cursory reference to these matters, though both were germane to the North African issue, as has already been indicated. In British minds indeed the rallying of North Africa had always from the beginning been associated with a successful offensive in the Western Desert. Churchill's 'Arcadia' plan had envisaged a pincer movement on Rommel's German-Italian army in Libya, a trap closing from two sides at once. The Eighth Army was to advance from Egypt into Cyrenaica and Tripolitania, while the 'Gymnast' forces were to close in from Algeria and Tunisia on Rommel's rear. Auchinleck had failed in his attempt, and been driven back to Egypt, but the conception still remained in Churchill's mind, though he had decided that it would have to be carried out under other commanders. During these visits, therefore, with Brooke's approval, Alexander was appointed Commander-in-Chief Middle East and Montgomery to command Eighth Army. Both of these appointments impinged on 'Torch', since both men had previously been successively appointed to command the British forces in the North African operation. These rapid changes in the Commanders nominated for 'Torch' were unfortunate, since they added to the difficulties of planning, besides giving Eisenhower the feeling that he was being left with the 'second eleven'. Not surprisingly he began to wonder if not only Marshall but even the British were serious about 'Torch'.[7]

As was his wont, Churchill at once began to press his new Middle East commanders to attack as soon as possible. His pressure was firmly resisted, however, by Alexander, and even more firmly by Montgomery, who had no intention of launching an attack before he was ready. Churchill accepted this with fairly good grace, recognizing that the new commanders must be allowed to get into the saddle and decide the actual date, and also that there was much to be said for a Desert offensive just before 'Torch' rather than some time before. Eventually, in September, Alexander informed him that he had concluded that the best date for the offensive would be thirteen days before 'Torch'.[8] On 24 October Montgomery finally attacked. A week later he had broken through and was advancing towards Tripoli.

The Soviet mission was important in the wider context of Anglo-Soviet relations, though not crucial in relation to 'Torch', since the decision had now been made and the Soviet leaders had no power to influence it. It was necessary, however, to inform the Soviet leaders and if possible obtain their approval. The latter, for obvious reasons, was likely to be a difficult task, since essentially Churchill's mission was to tell the Russians that there would be no Second Front in Europe in 1942, as they had persistently demanded – and this at the moment when the Russian armies were particularly hard pressed in the Stalingrad sector and in the Caucasus. It was, as Churchill vividly put it, 'like carrying a lump of ice to the North Pole.' The visit proved no less difficult than expected, with Stalin by turns critical, offensive and at last surlily acquiescent. Ultimately he conceded that there was something to be said politically and militarily for the North African operation, but it clearly fell a long way short of what he wanted. Subsequent Soviet historians have made it plain that this remained his and the official view. As Churchill himself concedes, at such a time of extreme peril the Soviet reaction was understandable. It had the effect of making Churchill even more anxious to press on with 'Torch' as quickly as possible.[9]

On his return to London, therefore, Churchill lost no time in again giving his full attention to 'Torch' and putting his full weight behind the lagging preparations. On 26 August he cabled Roosevelt urging that Eisenhower should be given full authority and that a note should be struck 'of irrevocable decision and superhuman energy'.[10] The goad was necessary, for at that moment the whole apparatus of planning was in danger of being bogged down. Marshall's and King's reservations and Churchill's own absence had certainly contributed to this, but the fundamental cause lay in the necessity of agreement on crucial matters of policy, agreement which was proving as difficult to achieve as the original decision had been. Nor is this surprising. The decision of 26 July had been simply to launch an invasion of North Africa, but there had been no previous Anglo-American planning for the operation, for reasons which will be obvious to readers of this account. The long and painful process had now to be gone through of reaching Anglo-American agreement on the main details of what was to be their first joint operation. Since one of the partners approached the operation with an Atlantic bias and the other with a Mediterranean bias, this agreement was not likely to be easy.

The first hurdle – the appointment of commanders – had been overcome fairly easily. Both sides had agreed that the Commander-in-Chief should be an American, the main reason for this being that it was regarded as important that the enterprise should appear to the French to be wholly American. As will be seen, it was considered that the Vichy French were less likely to resist an American than a British invasion. In addition, Marshall may have felt some reluctance to entrust his precious troops to British commanders who had little but defeat to show for their efforts at this stage of the war; and the British for their part thought, rightly, that an American commander for the operation would help to ensure a greater degree of support for the operation at all levels of the US war machine.

Once it had been made clear that Marshall was uninterested in the command, even if Roosevelt had wished him to take it, the choice almost inevitably fell on the man on the spot – Eisenhower. The latter had been in England since mid-summer as US Commanding-General, European Theatre of Operations, and had been concerned with the operational planning and the training of troops for any operations which might be decided upon by the Combined Chiefs of Staff. He had arrived committed heart and soul to the cross-Channel attack, and was now ordered to switch to planning for North Africa. Marshall's biographer says that Eisenhower's original appointment seems in retrospect 'remarkably casual', but it may be doubted if Marshall often acted casually, certainly in making an important appointment. Eisenhower lacked combat experience, and indeed even experience of peace-time command, since he had held mainly staff appointments, but he had demonstrated to Marshall's satisfaction in Washington that he possessed a clear military brain, that he understood the theory and practice of his profession and that he had the necessary physical and mental stamina. One other major requirement was necessary for high command, namely the ability to shoulder responsibility, and this too Marshall had also established to his satisfaction before he sent Eisenhower to England. For the command of an Allied Headquarters and an Allied Expeditionary Force it was also of prime importance that the new commander should have the capacity to work with and control his British allies, and Eisenhower had already demonstrated his ability to get on with the British, and in particular had established an excellent relationship with Churchill, who thought highly of him. Finally, he was imbued with Marshall's military views, and in particular was wedded to the doctrine of 'unity of command'.

In short Eisenhower, as a number of critics have said,

may not have been the greatest strategist of World War II, possibly not even the ablest American military commander, but at that time and place and with the special requirements of this command he was in many ways the ideal choice. He was supported as deputy commander by an old friend, Mark Clark, also inexperienced in combat and newly promoted, but vigorous and forceful, and as Chief of Staff by Walter Bedell Smith, possibly the ablest staff officer thrown up on the Allied side during the war. Indeed Marshall's agreement to release Bedell Smith from his own staff in early September was in some ways symbolic of his final acceptance that 'Torch' was going to be launched and therefore should be fully supported.[11]

The initial arrangements for Eisenhower's command of the naval and air forces were somewhat tentative and makeshift, and were far from reaching the degree of integration and unity later achieved by Allied Headquarters in South-East Asia, the Mediterranean and North-West Europe. Nominally he had one C-in-C for all naval forces, Admiral Andrew Cunningham, probably the best and certainly the best-known British naval commander of the war; but Cunningham himself felt that his authority over American naval units and their commander, Admiral Kent Hewitt, was somewhat nebulous and unsatisfactory, particularly in the Atlantic. Inside the Mediterranean, however, where the majority of naval units would be British, his authority was more or less unchallenged. For the air forces Eisenhower dealt with two commanders, Air Vice-Marshal Charles Welsh for the British and Brigadier-General James Doolittle for the Americans, an unsatisfactory arrangement, which was later to be replaced by a system of one commander of all air forces. Similarly, for the ground forces Eisenhower had to deal with two commanders, the British General Kenneth Anderson, who was to assume command of all ground forces engaged in actual operations *after* the landings, and the American General George Patton, who was to command the forces coming from the United States for the capture of Casablanca in the western sector of the landings; and thereafter to occupy and control Morocco and continue training for future operations, while keeping a vigilant eye on any threat from Spanish Morocco. In order to preserve the illusion of a wholly American attack, the initial assault forces inside the Mediterranean, at Oran and Algiers, were to be almost wholly American and operate under the American commanders Lloyd Fredendall and William Ryder, with the British supplying the 'follow-up'. All these forces save Patton's, however, were ultimately to become part of Anderson's First Army. The latter was an efficient officer who had commanded a division in France in 1939-40, but his rather dour disposition and lugubrious manner was to make Allied co-operation, as Clark later remarked, 'somewhat difficult'.[12]

It was a complex and cumbersome system, complicated by political factors, nationalistic prejudice and inter-service rivalries. That it worked as well as it did was largely due to the personality of the Commander-in-Chief and his unremitting insistence on the principle of inter-allied unity, with Clark, Cunningham and Bedell Smith all playing valuable parts. Even so, Eisenhower was more successful at first in establishing an inter-allied command than he was in getting a fully integrated inter-service headquarters. As was perhaps to be expected, he had more difficulty with the two powerful and status-conscious navies than with the air forces. The American air forces, except in the case of carrier-borne units, were Army personnel and therefore did not find it too difficult to accept the authority of an Army commander; the RAF, although an independent arm, was ultimately responsible to Portal, whose influence was usually exerted in the interests of Allied unity. On the naval side the problem was more acute, though the prestige and authority of Cunningham and the close friendship which he and Eisenhower soon established smoothed many difficulties on the British side. With the American navy it was different. Reflecting no doubt King's lack of enthusiasm for the whole project, though Eisenhower himself did not think so, the first US naval officers to arrive displayed a markedly unco-operative spirit. It was some time before they began to 'pitch in and do their share'. In the actual conduct of the operation, however, the fact that the US naval commander, Admiral Hewitt, had spent some time working with the British at Combined Operations Headquarters in London – the first fully inter-service and inter-allied headquarters ever created – was of some value in overcoming the difficulties.[13]

One delicate problem which arose was the nature of Anderson's directive. The first draft which was produced was based on the precedents of the First World War, and allowed the British commander to appeal over the head of the Allied C-in-C to the War Office if he thought his army was imperilled by the C-in-C's orders. Eisenhower rightly saw this as potentially destructive of the principle of unity of command and detrimental to his own authority, and was able to secure Brooke's agreement to a change which allowed this right of appeal only after consultation with the C-in-C; and moreover limited it to occasions when 'no opportunity would be lost and no part of the Allied force imperilled' by so doing. This virtually removed the right of appeal, and amounted to a pretty clear directive to Anderson to carry out Eisenhower's orders in almost all foreseeable circumstances.[14]

By mid-August the British and American planners had finally got down to preparing detailed plans for Operation 'Torch' under the direction of General Clark, and in full co-operation with Mountbatten's experts on amphibious operations. Very little progress could be made at first, however, because of the lack of agreement between the British and American Chiefs of Staff on the fundamental problems of time and place involved in the operation. An agreed decision had to be reached on the place or places for the landings and the size of the forces to be used in each area: a date had also to be fixed, but this in turn was dependent on prior agreement as to the places involved. Although Brooke had initially talked of two landings, at Casablanca and Oran – which was the American preference – the British view became almost immediately that there should also be further landings east of Oran, particularly at Algiers itself, and if possible at points east of Algiers. A basic disagreement therefore at once opened up between the two sides.

(ii) PROBLEMS OF TIME AND PLACE

It very soon became evident, during the transatlantic argument that developed, that the British and Americans had now changed places. So long as the main operation projected for 1942 had been one that the Americans favoured but the British opposed, and indeed regarded as suicidal, it had been the former who had seemed bold and ready to take any risks to achieve the required objective, while the British had been cautious, continually urging the difficulties and dangers of the enterprise. Now that the operation envisaged was one which the British supported, while the Americans regarded it with disfavour, the situation was reversed. It was now the Americans who were cautious and aware of the risks, the British who advocated the boldest courses.

How much Marshall and King and their advisers were influenced subconsciously by their dislike of the whole operation, and their reluctance to commit US forces deeply in the Mediterranean area, is difficult to say. They were certainly disposed to attach much greater weight to the risks involved in so doing than their British counterparts. The principal risk involved from the American viewpoint was the possibility that German forces, with Spanish connivance, might enter Spain, neutralize or occupy the naval and air base at Gibraltar, on which so much depended, and close the Straits themselves to Allied shipping. The effect could be to cut off the main supply route to all forces east of Gibraltar and render them dependent on a long and precarious land line of communication back to Casablanca, hundreds of miles to the west. The further east the Allied force went, the greater the risk. The American Chiefs therefore regarded a landing at Casablanca as an absolute necessity, to secure a port on the Atlantic coast and ensure one definite supply line. They wished to have one landing only inside the Mediterranean, preferably at the most westerly of the major ports, Oran. The British Chiefs replied that the only worthwhile objective for the whole operation was the control of all North Africa and, in conjunction with Alexander's drive from the east, of the whole Mediterranean coast of Africa.[15]

This would virtually open the Mediterranean again to Allied shipping. The Allies must land as far east as possible and close on Tunis with all speed. In general, therefore, the British favoured landings at five points – Algiers, Phillipeville and Bône, as well as Oran and Casablanca. To the American argument that the Straits might be cut, they replied that if Franco had not joined the Axis in 1940 when the war appeared as good as over, and only Britain stood in his path, it was unlikely he would now take on Britain and the United States. As for the Germans, why should they embark on the tortuous process of buying Franco's support, or alternatively overcoming Spanish resistance, when they could much more easily pour troops into Tunisia from their nearest bases in Sicily, only a hundred miles away? As an additional argument, they pointed out that on the Atlantic coast the heavy surf made the odds on a successful landing four to one against, whereas inside the Mediterranean the position was reversed.

In each case the military calculations of the two sides were influenced to some extent by their estimate of the political risks involved and the extent to which they felt they had special knowledge of that factor. On this basis the Americans, as a result of their prolonged contacts with the Vichy Government and the North African French, were optimistic of the chances of French collaboration, particularly if the expedition appeared to be wholly American and felt that once in North West Africa in force, Algeria and Tunisia might rally to them voluntarily and resist any German intervention. They were more inclined to worry about the Spanish factor, to them a more incalculable one. The British, on the other hand, as a result of bitter experience of Vichy hostility, were less inclined to be optimistic of the chances of French collaboration, unless the Allies landed as close to Tunisia as possible and in overwhelming force. Otherwise Tunisia might be lost if the Germans acted quickly. Spanish intervention, as we have seen, they felt to be a measurably small risk.[16]

On these issues the British on the whole were right and the US War Department was wrong. On the broad strategic issue, a landing only in North-West Africa would, unless the American calculation was right and the whole of North Africa rallied immediately, run the risk of either locking up Allied forces in a cul-de-sac or compelling them to fight a long campaign over difficult terrain against German forces, and possibly against the bulk of Vichy French forces as well. The latter outcome would not only be militarily expensive but politically highly damaging. The object was to win over the French, not to fight them. Moreover, the larger the initial scope of the operation and the greater the area brought under immediate control, the more profound the effect on Italian opinion and French opinion both in Africa and at home.

Equally the British were right in their calculation of the risks involved, as the event showed. For the Spanish did not move, and the Germans, finding Franco uncooperative, made no attempt to enter Spain, preferring, as the British expected, to enter Tunisia from Sicily. By so doing they also partially justified Churchill's view that the operation would indirectly help the Russian front, since the Germans were forced to accept a further drain on their resources – though it must be conceded that the number of troops involved was small compared to the vast masses engaged on the Eastern Front. Nonetheless, by the end of the Tunisian campaign the number of German troops engaged and finally captured was not insignificant.[17]

Caught between the crossfire of the two disputants, Eisenhower and his Anglo-American planners laboured to find an acceptable compromise. In spite of his original doubts about the operation he was too loyal not to throw himself heart and soul into his task, and too good a soldier not to see that the British were basically right in regarding Tunisia as the prize. He was therefore inclined to take the British side of the argument against his erstwhile Chief. The problem was complicated by the unforthcoming attitude of the two navies, whose initial reaction was that the shortage of shipping and particularly of escorts, aircraft-carriers especially, meant that they could not provide for more than two main landings. It also seemed doubtful if there would be troops and landing-craft sufficient for three or four. Faced with this non possumus, each side attempted to retain what it regarded as essential. The British, with Eisenhower's acquiescence, proposed delaying, or even dropping the Casablanca landings, but retaining those at Algiers and Bône. Patton's force, it was suggested should land at Oran and move back overland to capture Casablanca. Marshall replied that without the Casablanca landings the operation would have less than a fifty-fifty chance of success, and this would be 'an unacceptable risk'. He proposed to retain Casablanca but drop Algiers. It was about this time that Eisenhower remarked to his naval aide that Marshall might be in the mood to recommend dropping the entire enterprise. The latter had indeed already promised Stimson that he would not allow the operation to proceed, if it seemed 'clearly headed to a disaster'. Eisenhower agreed that 'Torch' as so far envisaged was not sufficiently powerful to achieve the task (finally allotted to him in his directive of 13 August) of gaining control of the whole of the North African coast; but urged at the same time that without Algiers the operation would have 'no worthwhile objective'. The answer was clearly for the two navies to find more ships, so that Casablanca, Oran and Algiers could be assaulted simultaneously.

It was equally clear by this stage that only the two heads of government had the authority to impose a compromise on their two sets of advisers who, as Ismay sardonically put it, 'might otherwise have continued their arguments until Doomsday.'[18]

On his return from Moscow Churchill acted immediately. The following day, 25 August, after conferring with Eisenhower and Clark and hearing their woes, he summoned the First Sea Lord and told him to strip other theatres 'to the bone' in order to provide 'Torch' with more escort vessels. Two days later he cabled Roosevelt that he was 'profoundly disconcerted' by the suggestion that the Algiers landings should be dropped, adding that 'the whole pith of the operation will be lost if we do not take Algiers as well as Oran on the first day', and reminding the President that he had promised Stalin in the Moscow talks that 'Torch' would be a substantial and effective operation. Admiral Pound responded to Churchill's orders as requested. Admiral King proved a tougher nut to crack. Viewing 'Torch' as a vexatious distraction from the naval battles in the Pacific, in which his forces were then heavily engaged, he turned a deaf ear to Eisenhower's and Marshall's pleas. Eventually, however, after a further appeal to Roosevelt from Churchill, King capitulated to a direct order from his Commander-in-Chief. On 2 September Marshall was able to inform Eisenhower that the Chiefs of Staff had found after all that the US Navy could provide more transports and escort vessels, and the latter could be used inside the Mediterranean, ie at Oran. At the same time Roosevelt agreed to withdraw sufficient landing-craft and troops from the Casablanca and Oran landings to make possible a simultaneous assault on Algiers *by American troops*. The latter point was important to Roosevelt, who was advised that an initially all-American assault at all three places would have a better chance of meeting negligible French resistance. Churchill, although like Eisenhower less sanguine on this point, agreed to the President's wishes. The British had already accepted an American Supreme Commander and an American deputy. They now accepted in addition that the three assaults should be under American commanders, though Anderson would take over command of the push for Tunisia and any actual operations against the Germans, once the troops were safely ashore.[19]

On 5 September what Eisenhower called 'the transatlantic essay contest' at last drew to a close. Planning could now begin in earnest in the light of the actual targets of assault and the forces initially available for them – about 35,000 at Casablanca, 40,000 at Oran and about 35,000 at Algiers. The Americans were to supply the forces for the Casablanca and Oran landings, the former coming direct from the United States, the latter from Britain: the bulk of the Algiers forces was to be British, after the initial assault by 10,000 American troops.[20]

It was none too soon for effective planning to begin. Probable weather conditions, particularly on the Atlantic coast, made it unlikely that any landings could be made successfully after the end of November. Back in January Eisenhower, sitting at his desk in Washington, had estimated that any operation of the size and complexity of an invasion of North Africa would take between two and three months to prepare. Now, faced with the task of commanding that operation, he had precisely that amount of time left. It soon became apparent that the earliest possible date for the operation was the beginning of November. Churchill for his part was acutely conscious of his assurances to Stalin, and also of the need to relieve Malta, which at this time was under continuous air attack and in danger of being starved out. In the first instance he had hoped for an assault in October and he had continued to press for this, supported by Roosevelt who had originally set 30 October as the latest target date. In all the circumstances Eisenhower and his staff responded well to these appeals. On 8 September he dined with Churchill, in accordance with what had then become their weekly custom, and informed him that the date for the landings would be 8 November – only a week later than Roosevelt's final date, though a month later than Churchill had hoped. The final and most important basic detail had been decided.[21]

In this first major test of the Anglo-American alliance the inter-allied machinery created at the 'Arcadia' conference had creaked and groaned, moved uncertainly by fits and starts and twice seized up altogether. Eventually it had worked, but only, on the two critical occasions, after the personal intervention of Roosevelt and Churchill. Nor was this surprising. Nothing like it had ever been attempted before, between Britain and the United States or between any two nations. As Eisenhower's biographer rightly suggests, the Chiefs of Staff had to learn to trust their commander, and more important, to trust each other. That trust was gradually forged during these long drawn out discussions, in spite of all the disagreements, and bore fruit in the decision-making and planning of future operations. First at the level of strategic planning and then at the operational and combat level the British and Americans learnt many lessons from the North African experience, lessons which had to be learnt and which could be learnt no other way. They and their commanders were now on the eve of the actual operation itself. On the military side everything that could be done with the resources available had been done: but the actual success of the operation depended as much on political as on military factors, and these could not be determined or controlled simply by the decision of the heads of government or the Combined Chiefs of Staff. Success or failure depended to a considerable degree on the attitude of the Franco government in Spain and the Pétain government at Vichy, but even more on that of the Vichy authorities, both civil and military, in North Africa itself. Roosevelt believed that it would be two weeks after the initial landings before the Germans could bring troops into North Africa in large numbers. Whether by that time they would be confronted by a united Anglo-American and French resistance or by an Allied force still locked in disagreement or engaged in actual fighting with the French depended on the decisions of a few key figures in the North African hierarchy and one man whom neither the British nor the Americans had really expected to be involved – Admiral Darlan.[22]

(iii) THE SPANISH COMPLICATION

In the final exchanges on the mechanics of the 'Torch' operation Roosevelt had reminded Churchill that they had decided long ago that the Americans were to handle the French in North Africa, while the British were to handle the situation in Spain. That arrangement had been adhered to, but humanly enough, neither side completely trusted the other's judgement in its own sphere. A short time before the message referred to above, Churchill had told Roosevelt that he thought it reasonable to assume that Spain would not go to war with Britain and the US as a result of the 'Torch' operation. As we have seen, these assurances were not completely convincing to the US War Department, where the possibility of Spanish or joint Spanish and German action against the Anglo-American forces provided one of the principal arguments for retaining the Casablanca landings at all costs, and indeed putting the main weight of the invasion outside the Mediterranean. The British view, however, based on three years of patient diplomacy, proved to be correct.[23]

There was, of course, little doubt where the Spanish dictator's sympathies lay. German and Italian troops had assisted his victory in the Spanish Civil War. His regime was based on a single-party system of the Fascist variety, ideologically fairly close to that of Italy, if not that of Nazi Germany. Moreover, as the leader of an almost wholly Catholic country and in close alliance with one of the more reactionary hierarchies in Western Europe, Franco was as convinced as any German or Italian ideologue that the prime menace to Western European civilization lay in the threat of Bolshevism. He cherished the hope that the German armies would crush the Soviet menace for ever. To that end he had encouraged the formation of a Spanish brigade to fight on the Russian front. From the viewpoint of national interests also his best hopes lay in an Axis victory, with the prospect of rich pickings at the expense of the French and British colonial empires. Gibraltar would certainly fall into his lap, and perhaps part of French Morocco and the Sahara too. It was an attractive prospect. On the other hand from a British victory he could expect nothing.

There was, therefore, a considerable temptation to emulate Mussolini and join the Axis side openly in the war. The ideal moment might seem to have come in the summer of 1940, with the Fall of France and the apparently impending collapse of Britain. At a meeting with Hitler in October 1940 Franco had even gone as far as to agree to enter the war on the Axis side, which would have made possible 'Operation Felix' – the German seizure of Gibraltar and entry into Morocco, advocated by the German naval chief Admiral Raeder. Franco, however, was a cautious man. He was conscious that Spain was still recovering from the dire effects of nearly three years bitter Civil War, and had no desire to become involved in a long and costly struggle. He hedged his undertaking around with conditions, conditions that were difficult for the Germans to meet, since they were mostly at the expense of France, which Hitler also wished to bring fully into the Axis camp. Hitler had already suffered a check in the Battle of Britain and been forced to call off his projected invasion. Then Mussolini's armies suffered a dramatic reverse in Libya at the hands of a far smaller British force. It seemed there was some fight left in the British after all, and the war was not really over. Franco went back on his promise to enter the war, and Hitler, who compared negotiations with the Spanish dictator to a visit to the dentist, dropped the idea of 'Operation Felix' and turned instead to the conquest of Russia. Had the decision been otherwise, Allied landings in North Africa in 1942, at any rate inside the Mediterranean, would hardly have been possible. Since the success of these landings and the confidence they gave to the British and Americans were a turning point of the war, Goering's judgement that the decision not to go ahead with 'Felix' was the biggest German blunder of the war has something to be said for it.[24]

At all events, Spain had continued during 1941 and 1942 to pursue a policy of cautious neutrality. British economic aid, which Spain badly needed, helped to tilt the balance. Churchill had sent a former Cabinet Minister, Sir Samuel Hoare, as ambassador to Spain after the collapse of France and the latter worked hard and unceasingly both at governmental level and amongst influential Spanish leaders generally. His task had been made more difficult when the Spanish Foreign Minister, Beigbeder, a staunch advocate of neutrality, was replaced by Franco's brother-in-law, Serrano Suñer. The latter was both fiercely anti-British and anti-Communist, believed firmly in a German victory and was anxious to take Spain fully into the Axis camp. The German attack on Russia strengthened his hand, and with Spanish troops sent to fight on the Eastern Front it seemed for a time that his policy would prevail. Franco, however, felt able to distinguish between the war against Bolshevism and a war against the West. Although the Allied disasters in the first half of 1942 tended again to reinforce his conviction that the West could not win the war, he still hesitated. Moreover, he suffered from the occupational neuroses of a dictator, was jealous of Suñer and unwilling to allow anyone in his entourage to engross too much power and gain excessive influence.[25]

So matters stood in September 1942 when the Allied plans for 'Torch' were coming to fruition. The question still remained, would Franco be provoked by a move against North Africa into action against Gibraltar and the Straits? Or would he be bullied or cajoled by the Germans into allowing German forces to move against these vital points? It was this anxiety which, as we have seen, prompted the American insistence on the Casablanca landings, and strengthened their reluctance to venture far into the Mediterranean. In spite of his reassuring words to Roosevelt, Churchill, as he admits in his memoirs, had his own anxieties on the matter, which were not entirely assuaged by Hoare on a visit to England in the later summer of 1942. According to Brooke the Ambassador 'painted a gloomy picture' of possible Spanish actions and their effects on the operation. With the wisdom of hindsight Eden subsequently commented that Hoare 'greatly exaggerated the [Spanish] difficulties, for whatever reason'. The implication was that Hoare, like many an ambassador before him, had exaggerated the difficulties of his task in order to claim the greater credit for overcoming them. This seems unfair to Hoare. The dangers were real enough – Spanish heavy guns controlled the Straits, and a Spanish attack on Gibraltar could probably have rendered both the harbour and air-field inoperative in a few hours. Neither the massing of aircraft on Gibraltar air-field, nor the movement of large convoys through the Straits could be concealed from the Spanish, and their attitude still remained uncertain. Nonetheless, Hoare felt able to tell Churchill that the Spaniards would probably not move if the initial operations were a success. Only if there were failures or delays at the beginning was it at all possible that Franco might succumb to temptation or feel unable to resist German pressure. The early capture of airfields in North Africa, from which Spain and Spanish Morocco could be threatened, would be the best insurance against such a possibility. Churchill was strengthened in his view that it was essential to capture all the main North African ports on the first day, and was on the point of cabling his friend Harry Hopkins in Washington that this was the prerequisite for ensuring Spanish inaction, when Roosevelt's final acceptance of the triple landings rendered it unnecessary to do so. But the niggling anxiety remained, and Churchill instructed his Chiefs of Staff to include in their plans some measures to deal with the danger.[26]

It was not wholly unjustified. Sensing that something might be in the wind in North Africa, the Germans at the end of October made a formal request to the Spanish government to let their troops through, if the Allies attacked Morocco. However, a fortunate change in the Spanish government had occurred at the beginning of the previous month and it may have been the news of this which prompted Hoare's cautious optimism in his final advice to the British government, whatever his earlier language may have suggested. The change was in the vital Spanish Foreign Ministry, where Franco had at last brought himself to dismiss Suñer. His replacement, Jordana, was altogether more sympathetic to the Allied cause, and he was able to delay a decision on the German request for just long enough, though he warned the US ambassador that it might be difficult to refuse. A friendly message from Roosevelt to Franco, intimating that the Allies had no designs on Spanish territory, together with the success of the landings, probably helped to turn the scales. Franco held his hand, and there was never again any serious likelihood that he would abandon neutrality. British optimism proved in the event to be justified.

(iv) THE FRENCH PROBLEM

The problem of the Vichy French was more complex, and in fact more fundamental to the success of the operation as things turned out. After Pearl Harbour the Americans and the British had continued to go their separate ways in their dealings with the French, the Americans maintaining their relations with the Pétain government through their ambassador Admiral Leahy and the British continuing to support de Gaulle's movement, in spite of constant difficulties with the prickly Frenchman.[27] The latter relationship was never easy. British tactlessness at the time of the Syrian campaign and the somewhat ham-fisted and occasionally devious behaviour of the British Middle East Command had first poisoned the atmosphere. The Saint Pierre incident had infuriated Churchill as well as Roosevelt and Hull. The Prime Minister was less disposed thereafter to take the Free French fully into his confidence, or to associate them with the conduct of operations that were difficult and dangerous enough without avoidable complications. Doubts about the effectiveness of French security reinforced this attitude. In relation to operations against French colonial territory, the fact that experience in Syria and elsewhere suggested that Vichy troops would fight all the harder if Free French troops were employed against them further strengthened this attitude. Moreover, it was in itself politically undesirable that Frenchmen should have to fight Frenchmen. There were thus plenty of good arguments for excluding the Free French from actual participation in the North African operation, and these were now powerfully reinforced by American pressures. But even before the North African operation, Churchill had ordered the occupation of the French island of Madagascar in a wholly British enterprise; in this case, as later in North Africa, there was virtually no prior consultation or notice to the Free French, let alone the employment of Free French troops. For the latter, as we have seen, there were good reasons; but for the former there was little excuse. The fact that the administration of the island was later handed over to the Free French in November 1942 did little in de Gaulle's eyes to assuage the initial affront.

Roosevelt and the Americans had always regarded de Gaulle as an obscure and minor figure who probably had little support either in France or North Africa. They took their views largely from Admiral Leahy and Robert Murphy, the American representative in Algeria, who in turn took theirs from their contacts with the Vichy government and high-ranking Vichy authorities in both places. Not surprisingly these views were unfavourable to de Gaulle and the Free French. In regard to North Africa in particular, Roosevelt was strongly warned by Murphy that the use of Free French troops would much increase the resistance of the Vichy French. Roosevelt's prejudices against de Gaulle had been much increased by the Saint Pierre incident, and he knew how strongly his Secretary of State, Cordell Hull, felt on the matter. Moreover, Roosevelt shared to the full Churchill's doubts about Free French security. The latter argument it must be said, was a somewhat dubious one to be used by a government which was engaged in constant negotiations with Vichy, since this was almost equivalent to a direct line to Berlin. Indeed, Roosevelt himself had admitted to Churchill much earlier that as soon as he began serious negotiations to try to win the acquiescence of the Vichy government, the Axis would get to know that something was intended in North Africa, as indeed they did. The Americans too underestimated the extent to which the Gaullists were making headway, both in metropolitan France and in North Africa itself; though it is fair to say that in Africa Gaullist supporters were mostly among the civil population and the lower level of the hierarchy rather than amongst the top-level civil and military authorities, whose support counted for most in facilitating the landings.[28]

However unfortunate the long-term effects of the American attitude towards de Gaulle, it remains the case that on the main issue the Americans were right. The attitude of the Vichy government and of a small group of influential North African leaders would be the most important factor during the first crucial days of the North African operation. It was desirable therefore that the Pétain government should give its open or covert approval to the invasion; or failing that, at least that some leading figure acceptable to the North African establishment should come forward to give some semblance of legality to French co-operation with the invaders. For this position there were various candidates. One was General Juin, the French Commander-in-Chief in North Africa, and a known Allied sympathizer. Another was General Henri Giraud, who had recently escaped from a German prison camp and was living in unoccupied France. Murphy's North African contacts had pointed him out as the obvious man – untainted by Vichy associations, yet equally free of commitments to de Gaulle, and therefore, it was thought, likely to be acceptable to the French 'high-ups' in North Africa. A third contender, and as it turned out, the most influential and useful one, was Admiral Darlan himself.

The purpose of the American Vichy policy had always been to try to influence that government by a mixture of

cajolery and threats against going any further in the direction of collaboration with Germany than was required by
the strict letter of the 1940 armistice terms. In particular,
the object of American policy was to dissuade the Pétain
government from allowing the German and Italian forces
the use of French colonial bases or of the French Fleet,
in its harbour in unoccupied France. Just how much was
achieved by this policy is difficult to assess. The Germans
had much more powerful and immediate threats at their
disposal, which were bound to carry greater weight.
Insofar as Pétain resisted these pressures it was probably
more because he did not in fact wish to collaborate any
more closely than he had to with the Germans and because he wished to retain the two best cards he still
possessed – the navy and the French Colonial Empire –
rather than because of anything the Americans did or said.
On the other hand Pétain certainly did not wish to offend
the American government. The precise degree of effect
which the American policy towards Vichy achieved is certainly debatable, though such judgements as that of
Eisenhower's biographer that the policy was 'shortsighted,
often mistaken, ineffective and frequently ludicrous' are
perhaps a little too harsh. Be that as it may, as the planning of 'Torch' drew to its climax, the lines of communication to Vichy were still open.

It was soon obvious that there was little to hope from
Pétain himself. At this period the Marshal was in his late
eighties. He was not senile, but had reached the age when
he could not concentrate on affairs of state for too long
at a time; and he had his good days and bad days. He was,
as he had always been, conservative, authoritarian and tra-
ditionalist in his political views and vain and solitary in his
personal character. He was well-disposed to the United
States but no great lover of Britain. On the other hand
he did not love the Germans either. But these points were
really irrelevant. At eighty-eight the Marshal was too old
and set in his ways to uproot himself, go to Africa and
lead French North Africa back into the Allied camp. It
required a younger and more flexible man to perform that

turnabout. Pétain in fact was advised by a former minister, General Bergeret, four days before the landings, that American action in North Africa was imminent. He refused however to leave France, holding it to be his duty (as in 1940) to stay with his countrymen in their hour of need. In this he was probably sincere. But if Pétain remained in France, he would almost certainly be at the mercy of the Germans and unable to give even passive approval to the American action, let alone active assistance.[29]

Darlan was made of different mettle. He saw that the time had come to change sides, in his own interests and perhaps also – giving him the benefit of the doubt – in the long-term interests of France. He himself was no longer quite the powerful figure he had been, having been superseded by Laval in April 1942 as the dominant political figure in the Vichy government. Nonetheless he remained Commander-in-Chief of all French armed forces, and both in this capacity and in virtue of the fact that he was the Marshal's nominated heir, he was in a strong position to sway the decision of the Vichy authorities in North Africa. It is clear that he was well-informed of the progress of the pro-American conspiracy which Robert Murphy had set on foot in Algeria, and that he was in touch with some of the conspirators. It seems almost equally probable that, like Pétain, he was informed by one of them at the beginning of November that the landings were imminent, and that he then decided to be on the spot. He had told Admiral Leahy in 1941 that he would be ready to change sides if the Americans appeared in overwhelming force. Later he offered to bring over the French Fleet if offered the command of French forces in Africa. At the last moment the Americans, for reasons that will be apparent, drew back from making a direct deal with him in advance of the landings. They had decided to back a different horse. But Darlan's presence in Algeria at the time of the North African landings was probably not accidental.[30]

The man the Americans had decided to back was in

fact General Giraud. Giraud had emerged as the 'chosen man' from the complex negotiations which Murphy and his vice-consuls, together with the American intelligence organization OSS, had been conducting with a group of civil and military conspirators in Algeria. Some of the most prominent of these had been in touch with Giraud since May and had gradually persuaded him to be prepared to come to North Africa and put himself at the head of the movement for collaboration with the Allies. Giraud named as his representative in North Africa General Charles Mast, then Chief of Staff of the XIX Corps in Algeria, but soon to become commander of the Algiers Division. Mast was thus in a key position to assist the landings at Algiers. Another conspirator was General Émile Béthouart who, as commander of the Casablanca Division, was similarly in a position to assist the American landings at that point. Together with Murphy the conspirators made plans to support the landings by seizing radio stations and aerodromes, interdicting military and naval communications and if necessary placing senior officers who would not collaborate under arrest. At a secret meeting in Algeria with General Clark and other officers on Eisenhower's staff they also furnished valuable details about the location of troops, gun batteries, airfields etc at Oran and Algiers and assured the Americans that if Giraud were to appear at the head of the movement they could guarantee French co-operation. Mast asked for only four days notice in order to guarantee little or no resistance from the ground and air forces in his command. In return Murphy pledged that the United States would restore France to full sovereignty and territorial integrity both in metropolitan France and in her empire, would not interfere in the internal administration of her territories, and would re-equip the French North African Army to fight on the side of the Allies.[31]

The French military leaders would have nothing to do with Darlan, who had put out definite feelers to Murphy a few days before. Roosevelt had authorized Murphy to explore the possibility of a deal during the latter's visit to Washington at the end of August and Murphy himself was favourable. In London Churchill was not disposed to be squeamish about using Darlan, if the latter could bring over North Africa *and* the French Fleet. He had been prepared to accept Stalin as an ally; having swallowed a camel he did not see why he should strain at a gnat, though Eden, aware of de Gaulle's probable reaction, was less enthusiastic. Eisenhower, who knew very little about French politics and cared less, was 'mainly interested in finding a Frenchman who could deliver Algiers'. In Washington Marshall was more cautious, feeling that Darlan could not be trusted, but Roosevelt and the State Department at first were willing to go along. Second thoughts prevailed, however. The complications of trying to bring the two men together to co-operate, together with the unequivocal reaction of the North African leaders, and Giraud's own refusal to have anything to do with Darlan, seems to have convinced the Americans that they had better stick to the General. Churchill, who had long agreed to leave the political decisions in dealings with the North African French to the Americans, accepted the decision. Darlan's arrival in Africa may not have been exactly a coincidence, therefore, but it was not pre-arranged with the Americans.[32]

On the face of it, the ground had been well prepared for the North African landings and there seemed good reason to hope that resistance would be slight. A network of sympathizers had been created, much valuable information had been obtained, the assistance of commanders in key positions had been guaranteed beforehand and an unexceptionable figurehead had been provided for renewed French collaboration with the Allies. All should therefore have been well. But there were major weaknesses in the American arrangements, weaknesses which were to become glaringly apparent before very long.

The first weakness lay in the personality and status of Giraud himself. Giraud's attraction for the Americans lay precisely in the fact that he had no commitments either to Vichy or to the Gaullists. Liberal opinion in the United

States and Britain could not object to him on the former ground nor could the North African establishment on the latter. He was well known by repute and respected as a soldier: de Gaulle himself had been heard to refer to him in favourable terms. But this very lack of commitment was to some extent a source of weakness, since it meant he had no obvious nexus of political support to call upon. He had no particular claim either on the loyalty of the Gaullist resistance or on the support of officers who had sworn allegiance to Vichy. In addition he lacked the abilities required for such a difficult task as that which was assigned to him. Politically he was an ignoramus, without any flair or interest in such matters. Indeed he saw himself as coming to North Africa to assume the command of an American-French army for the liberation of France rather than to play a political role. When thrust into such a role he soon demonstrated that he had little capacity and less taste for it. In the crucial early days of the landings he was ineffectual, and in the sequel was easily thrust aside by de Gaulle.[33]

A second major weakness derived from the fact that the Murphy network had only reached up to the divisional level of command in the military sphere and not as high as that on the civil side. Neither the Commander-in-Chief, General Juin, nor his immediate subordinates had been drawn into the plot, nor had the Governors-General of Morocco and Algeria, Noguès and Chatel. The naval commanders at Casablanca and Algiers were also outside the plot. Yet these were the men who would have real authority in a crisis, and while plans had been made to arrest them if necessary, the execution of such plans depended on whose orders the soldiers would obey when it came to the point. The conspirators' net was spread too thinly in the highest places. They had enough men in key positions to create confusion but not to seize control.

Finally Murphy and the Supreme Allied Command weakened their allies in North Africa by being less than frank, and not always truthful with them. They exaggerated the size of the expeditionary forces, equivocated on the question of command and withheld the crucial details until the last minute. True Mast had only stipulated four days' notice of the actual date of the invasion, which was exactly what he was given, but four days was too short a time to make all the necessary preparations. Juin, who had more than an inkling of what was afoot, was in fact friendly to the enterprise and had attempted to sound Murphy out about it, but was only informed on the night of the landings. Having trusted their friends in North Africa so far, it would have been better to have trusted them a little further. In this as in some other respects, the Americans showed poor judgement.[34]

In all the circumstances Mast, Béthouart and their associates did remarkably well. But the odds were loaded against them. Even without Darlan's intervention the Americans would probably have had to turn to men like Juin and Noguès to obtain a quick end to the fighting and a general cease-fire. As it was, they had to turn to Darlan.

In all these negotiations little attention or interest had been paid by the Americans to the wishes or probable reactions of the majority of the North African population – the Arabs. This was a harsh, but from a military point of view, a realistic attitude to adopt. Power lay in the hands of the French military commanders and civil administration, and it was this power which they had to win over. To have meddled in the internal politics of the French colonies or sought to impose at the outset American ideas would have affronted and antagonised the French, as similar British actions did in the Levant. The nationalist movement in North Africa at this time was still weak, the majority of the Arab population quiescent, and by no means all of the nationalist leaders were anti-French. In Tunisia, Bourguiba saw that an Axis victory would probably merely substitute Italian rule for French rule, and though imprisoned by the French he preferred them to the Italians. In Morocco the nationalists also took the view that they had little to hope for from an Axis victory. De Gaulle was an unknown quantity, but the Americans were known to be sympathetic to nationalism and something could perhaps be hoped for from them. The Arab rulers who had been allowed to retain some authority by the French, particularly the Sultan of Morocco, on the whole took the same view. In assuming therefore that the Arab population would accept them if not actually welcome them, and that the important thing in the first instance was to win over the French administration, the Americans were correctly judging the situation.[35]

It is easy to criticize American, and particularly Murphy's judgements on the situation in North Africa and the particular steps to be taken. The latter, however, was very severely restricted as to the extent to which he could exercise his discretion, particularly in divulging information to the French in North Africa; and where so much was at stake it is difficult to blame Roosevelt and his military advisers for their caution. No one could be sure just how reliable any particular Frenchman might be. The major mistake, the choice of Giraud, was made on French advice. What one could say is that between them Murphy and his French associates did go some way towards facilitating the operation that was now to be launched. There is no certainty that any alternative course to that taken, whether in associating the Gaullists with the planning, or bringing more senior North African officers into the plot would have worked better. A prior arrangement with Darlan might have done so. But apart from the political objections, Darlan's behaviour when confronted by a *fait accompli* is no assurance of what he might have done if informed beforehand. The political preparations for the North African landings, indeed, illustrate very well that Wavell's dictum 'War is an option of difficulties' applies equally to the politics of war.

V

The Campaign in North Africa
November 1942-May 1943

(i) 8 NOVEMBER 1942

The North African landings achieved remarkable success
for operations carried out by widely dispersed units, consisting of green troops and led by commanders who were,
with one exception, inexperienced in handling large formations in battle.[1] That they did so was due to the fact
that tactical surprise was achieved and resistance from the
French North African Forces, though heavy in places,
was sporadic and disorganized by internal sabotage and
political confusion. It was remarkable indeed that surprise
was achieved, considering that both the Vichy French and
the Germans knew that an Allied operation in North
Africa was contemplated; and the concentration of aircraft on Gibraltar airfield, faithfully reported by Axis
agents, made it obvious that some major enterprise was
about to take place. German intelligence, however, was
divided between Dakar and Malta or the Middle East as
the likely quarter. When the reports of large Allied convoys passing through the Straits began to come in, on the
night of the 5/6 November, it was clear that action in
the Mediterranean was imminent. Yet neither the Germans nor the French guessed the destination of the convoys correctly. The Germans considered an operation for
the relief of Malta or possibly a landing in Tripolitania to
take Rommel in the rear the most likely possibility. This
also seems to have been the opinion of the North African
French. The Italians alone guessed correctly but they were
ignored. As a result Axis naval and air power was concentrated in the Central Mediterranean and their submarine
force divided between that area and the Atlantic coast of
North West Africa. Enemy U-boats therefore did not interfere with the landings and did not in fact appear off the

North African coast until two or three days afterwards.[2]

The political confusion on shore which was so helpful to the Allied cause in Algeria and Morocco but unfortunately equally helpful to the Germans in Tunisia, was the product partly of the efforts of Mast, Béthouart and their associates, but due even more to the presence of Admiral Darlan. As to the former, Mast and his associates were able to take virtual control of the city for a few vital hours and to give some help to the landing parties west of Algiers in the early stages of the operation, and Béthouart did his best to take control in the Casablanca area and ensure an unopposed landing. Both men, however, failed either to win over or to neutralize effectively their superior officers. Within a few hours of the landings both had been removed from their posts. At Oran, on the other hand, the pro-Allied groups had no officer even as senior as Mast or Béthouart to take the lead. Nonetheless resistance to the landings was comparatively light at first, and in every case the assault parties were able to get ashore without much opposition. When opposition to the landings did develop at all three places it tended to be, so far as the army units were concerned, hesitant and uncertain. The local army commanders in general reflected the attitude of the Commander-in-Chief General Juin, which was that token resistance to the Americans was necessary, partly '*pour l'honneur*' but even more to try to convince the Germans that *some* resistance was being offered. It was hoped that the Pétain government might then be able to dissuade Hitler from occupying the whole of France, or at least from taking revenge on the French population if he did decide to do so. Juin, however, could not impose his will on the naval commanders, who in general exercised direct control over the port and harbour defences and the warships at Casablanca and Oran. Men like Admiral Michelier, the naval commander at Casablanca, still nourished the resentment engendered by the British attacks on the French Fleet in 1940. They were determined to resist any invasion of North Africa from whatever quarter it came. They were not likely to obey the orders of Juin, if

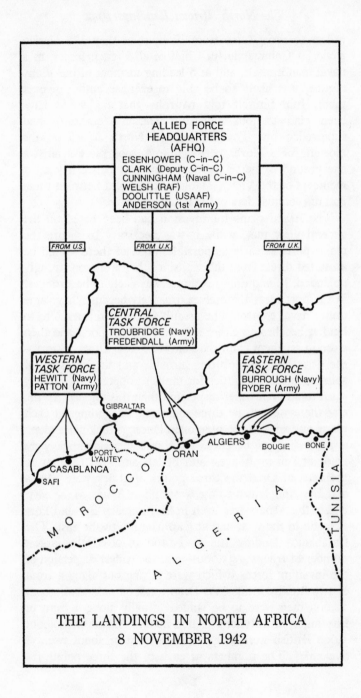

THE LANDINGS IN NORTH AFRICA
8 NOVEMBER 1942

orders to resist came from Vichy – as they did. Darlan alone, as Commander-in-Chief of all French forces, as a naval man himself, and as a leading member of the Vichy regime, was likely to be able to exercise authority over them. Juin himself told Murphy that he would have been glad to join him, but Darlan's authority had superseded his. The landings in North Africa on the morning of 8 November, therefore, took place against a background of fierce political argument between leading members of the Vichy establishment – and between them and the commanders of the invading forces.[3]

The Allied plans for invasion had been based on the general view that, while it was necessary to secure the major ports as early as possible, none of these should be assaulted direct from the sea, since they were too strongly defended. In addition, resistance was likely to be strongest in the port areas themselves, precisely because they came under naval control. The assault forces were therefore to land at beaches on either side of the three ports and then close in on them from the landward side. Other factors – the desirability of securing airfields and the necessity of suitable landing facilities for tanks as opposed to infantry – led to an even wider dispersion than this implied. In the end there were to be three main assault landings at each place, and each of the nine main landings took place along a succession of beaches. At Casablanca landings were made at Safi to the west and Fedala and Port Lyautey to the east; at Oran the three points of attack were Mersa and Les Andelouses to the west and at Arzew to the east; and in the Algiers area itself in Sidi Ferruch Bay and Port Pescade to the west and at Cap Matifou to the east. The Casablanca landings under Patton involved the largest number of troops – 35,000 – and the widest dispersion of the invading forces, which were strung out along a front of two hundred miles. At Oran, under Fredendall, about 22,000 men were to be landed initially along a front of fifty miles; and Ryder's 10,000 men at Algiers with about 5,000 British were to go in on a front of about twenty-five miles. The numbers at each of the three points reflected various factors – the width of the front, the US Chiefs' desire not to commit too much of their forces inside the Mediterranean, and the strength of the resistance expected. On the whole these expectations were borne out by the event. Resistance was not negligible at any of the three points, but it was fiercest and most prolonged at Casablanca, and shortest-lived at Algiers, where the Army Commander-in-Chief was on the spot and naval influence weakest. The pattern of resistance was much the same in both Oran and Casablanca – sporadic or light resistance on the beaches from the French army, gradually developing some strength as orders came from above to resist and the pattern of the invasion became clearer. There was, however, fierce and determined resistance from French warships and naval batteries from the outset. But the overall result was as successful as could have been expected. Morocco and Algeria were won over in three days; the remainder of North-West Africa followed a fortnight later. The cost – 1,800 casualties – was only one tenth of that expected if serious French resistance developed. What was achieved at so little cost was largely due to the unexpected presence of Darlan – 'a curious but highly fortunate complication', as Churchill describes it. Without his authority it is highly doubtful if Juin or anyone else could have brought the fighting in Morocco to an end so quickly against the direct orders of the Pétain government.[4]

(ii) THE FIRST THREE WEEKS

Churchill had cabled to Roosevelt in August 'The first victory we have to win is to avoid a battle'. The means chosen to achieve this end had been the creation of a pro-Allied conspiracy in North Africa itself to ensure the success of the landings; and the provision from outside of a leader of sufficient stature to win over the whole area quickly after the landings had taken place. For this purpose, de Gaulle having been vetoed, Giraud had been chosen. But it very soon became apparent that the pro-

Allied conspiracy was not strong enough, and the chosen leader incapable of performing his task. At the time of the landings themselves Giraud was ineffective and his presence constituted merely an additional complication for Eisenhower, which he could well have done without. Having committed themselves publicly to Giraud, however, after twenty-four hours' wrangling over his precise status at Gibraltar, the Americans would have looked foolish if they had not found some role for him to play.[5]

Giraud's earlier pretensions (he had at first demanded that he replace Eisenhower as Supreme Allied Commander) soon evaporated when he reached Algiers late on 9 November and found that he had little or no influence to barter for so exalted a position. By that time a great deal had happened and both Murphy and the local American commander, General Ryder, had already opened negotiations with Darlan and Juin. After briefly being placed under house arrest by supporters of the conspiracy, the latter had quickly regained control over the situation. Juin, with or without Darlan's approval, had then instructed his troops to maintain 'elastic but non-aggressive' contact with American troops, pending a clarification of the situation. It is clear, however, that some of his more spirited commanders interpreted this directive pretty liberally, and equally clear that some of the Americans in Algiers, as at Oran, and Casablanca, were more than a little trigger-happy. Since it was evident that if fighting continued for very long it would become more and more difficult to bring it to an end, Juin had secured Darlan's consent to negotiate a cease-fire in Algiers, notwithstanding direct orders from the Pétain government to continue resistance. The cease-fire for Algiers was duly negotiated on the evening of the 8th, less than twenty-four hours after the landings had begun.[6]

This seems in retrospect to have been the decisive moment. The French troops returned to their quarters and the American forces had the opportunity to consolidate their position. Darlan no less than Juin must have known that it would be difficult to reactivate French resistance, particularly as the American guarantees to respect the French position in North Africa were becoming widely known. Juin's motives were fairly clear: after token resistance he wished to reach agreement with the Americans and join them in building up their joint forces for the liberation of France. Darlan's are more obscure. Some authorities hold that he genuinely had not made up his mind at this stage whether to join forces with the Americans or to call on the Axis for help. Certainly he had already suggested that the German air force should attack Allied shipping at Algiers and he at first ordered resistance to the invaders and apparently instructed the Tunisian forces to co-operate with the Germans, who began to fly in troops there on the following day. On the other hand, it seems hardly possible that so shrewd a man as Darlan did not realize that by agreeing to a cease-fire in Algiers he had lost full control of his own situation and that it would be difficult to regain it. Opinions differ, but it is the view of the present writer that from this moment onwards Darlan knew that he had to come to some agreement with the Americans and that he had decided to do so. His later hesitations and equivocations were due to a desire to obtain the best possible terms for France – and for Admiral Darlan. It is consistent with this view that when Ryder had enquired whether it would be possible to negotiate a general cease-fire, Darlan had not rejected the possibility, as his orders from Vichy dictated, but merely said that he must consult Vichy and talk to Eisenhower himself. It was in response to this that Eisenhower decided to send his deputy Clark to negotiate with Darlan.[7]

Clark arrived late on the afternoon of the 9th and Giraud soon afterwards, but it was immediately apparent to Clark that the latter carried no weight with the small group of men whose word counted for something in North Africa. As Eisenhower was afterwards to write to his military superiors, in North Africa at that time the name of Marshal Pétain was still 'something to conjure with'; all the French senior officers were agreed that only Darlan could 'assume the Marshal's mantle' and give a semblance

of legality to a general cease-fire. It was therefore Darlan
to whom Clark directed his attention. After prolonged
and acrimonious discussion on the morning of the 10th,
and by a combination of threats and promises, the American was able to induce Darlan to issue the orders for a
general cease-fire in Algeria and Morocco, assuming full
authority 'in the Marshal's name'. At Casablanca the order
to the French to cease resistance arrived just in time to
prevent the enthusiastic Patton from storming the town.
At Oran the Americans had already forced their way in
and compelled the local commander to surrender. Of the
three main targets of the invasion it was the only one that
had to be taken by assault.[8]

The Vichy government's response was immediate. They
had little choice in the matter, for they were in the position of a man with a pistol to his head, threatened at any
moment with a German occupation of the whole of
France. They had to consider not only their own fortunes
but the conditions of life for all their countrymen, possibly for years ahead. Even so the actions of the Vichy
government were in general in the spirit of Weygand's
advice to 'do the minimum that would satisfy the Germans'. They had refused to declare war against the United
States, contenting themselves with the statement that the
latter had by its actions effectively broken off relations with
them; and they only agreed to the German use of Tunisian air bases and the admittance of German troops into
Tunisia under threat. Even so some of the Vichy government wished to support Darlan's action in ordering a
cease-fire and refuse German requests for co-operation in
Tunisia; but they were overruled by Laval who was des-
perately attempting to stave off a German invasion of unoccupied France in personal negotiations with Hitler. On
the afternoon of the 10th, therefore, Vichy reiterated the
orders to the North African commanders to continue resistance against the Americans. Darlan thereupon attempted to revoke his cease-fire order and declared himself
'a prisoner of the Americans'. Possibly he genuinely felt
that the ground had been cut from under his feet, or

possibly his motive was simply to strengthen his bargaining position. At all events the cease-fire continued to be generally obeyed, and as a result, by the morning of the 11th, Casablanca, Oran and Algiers were already firmly in American hands.[9]

Whatever Darlan's difficulties, they were about to be resolved. On the evening of the 10th Hitler finally decided that there was no more to be gained by maintaining the fiction of the Vichy government's independence, and ordered his troops to march into unoccupied France. The troops began to move in at seven o'clock the following morning, Vichy ordering no resistance to be offered, but protesting in vigorous terms. When the news reached Algiers, Darlan seized the opportunity to announce that the Marshal was no longer a free agent and that he was therefore re-assuming full authority 'in the Marshal's name'. Ignoring an order from Vichy appointing Noguès, the Resident-General in Morocco, as the Vichy representative in North Africa, Darlan summoned the latter to meet him at Algiers; and for the first time Noguès chose to accept Darlan's authority, not Vichy's. For both men the final decision had really been made in favour of collaboration with the Americans and resistance to the Germans. The signature of the Darlan-Clark agreement on the 13th, by which Darlan became head of the civil government and Giraud the head of the armed forces, followed inevitably, and its ratification by Noguès, Juin and Eisenhower was no less inevitable.[10]

The final balance-sheet showed that only five days in all had been consumed in these negotiations, and the prize was all Morocco, Algeria and ultimately West Africa as well, at relatively little cost. But two major prizes had eluded the invaders – the French Fleet and Tunisia. So far as the former was concerned, the delay was probably not decisive. Darlan had finally ordered the French Fleet to sail for North Africa on the afternoon of the 11th, but from the point of view of its commander, de la Borde, the Pétain government was still the legal government of France and Darlan no longer had any authority, even in

North Africa. He refused to sail and when the Germans, after some hesitation, decided to occupy the port, he ordered the Fleet to be scuttled. Three battleships, seven cruisers and one aircraft-carrier went to bottom with many smaller warships. It is indicative of the deep scars left by the British attack on French ships at Mers-el-Kebir two years earlier that the commander of a great fleet should, even after the occupation of his country, have preferred to destroy his ships rather than preserve them to join in the task of liberation. But it may be doubted if the delay in sending the order to sail for North Africa made the slightest difference, since it is clear that de la Borde would not have obeyed such an order from anyone except his superiors at Vichy.[11]

So far as Tunisia is concerned, the verdict may well be otherwise, but here too the reason why the invaders did not gain what both Eisenhower and the British Chiefs regarded as 'the ultimate prize' are complex. Some part of the delay in getting Anderson's forces on the move may have been due to the confusion on shore. Nevertheless, the leading elements of that force set out from Algiers two days after the landings. They were in Bougie, further up the coast, on the 11th and at Bône, close to the Tunisian frontier, on the 12th. The Germans for their part had begun to land troops in Tunisia on the 9th, but by this stage probably had no more than 2,000 men there, certainly less than Anderson was concentrating on the frontier, not to mention the ill-equipped Tunisian 'division' commanded by General Barré. But Anderson's force was at the end of a long supply line from Algiers, with a background of civil disorder and confusion in his rear. His forces were widely dispersed over a fifty-mile front and were being committed piecemeal to the battle-field. It took Anderson and his immediate subordinate Evelegh a week after their arrival on the frontier to sort the troops out into any kind of order, and to concentrate them sufficiently so that Anderson felt justified in ordering them to advance on Tunis. A few days later the winter rains began, reducing the forward air-strips and dirt roads on which he

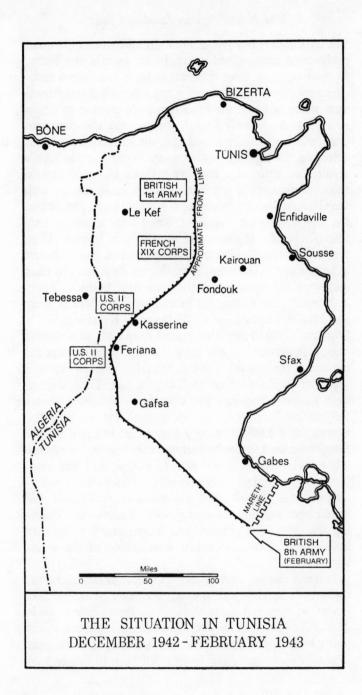

BÔNE

BIZERTA

TUNIS

BRITISH
1st ARMY

•Le Kef

Enfidaville

FRENCH
XIX CORPS

Kairouan

Sousse

Tebessa•

Fondouk

U.S. II
CORPS

Kasserine

U.S. II
CORPS

Feriana

Sfax

•Gafsa

ALGERIA
TUNISIA

APPROXIMATE FRONT LINE

Gabes

MARETH
LINE

BRITISH
8th ARMY
(FEBRUARY)

Miles

0   50   100

THE SITUATION IN TUNISIA
DECEMBER 1942 - FEBRUARY 1943

was dependent to a sea of mud. In addition to his other problems Anderson had to try, in the middle of a battle, to weld units of three different nationalities into a homogeneous force. The wonder is not so much that mistakes were made but that the First Army got as close to Tunis as it did. Anderson's British troops, and the American units which gradually joined him, did in fact display considerable daring and resource, even recklessness. As a result they suffered some severe losses in proportion to their numbers in a number of sharp engagements with the German forces between 24 November and 2 December. On the latter date the First Army was in places only fifteen miles from Tunis and twenty from Bizerta. Then they were checked. Gradually the balance of power shifted in favour of the Germans, operating on short interior lines and supplied by sea and air from Axis bases in Sicily little more than a hundred miles away. In addition, they had the advantage in Field-Marshal Kesselring of a Supreme Commander who was not only more experienced than Eisenhower but less bogged down in political negotiations at the crucial moment. On 2 December Anderson reported to Eisenhower 'If I cannot take Tunis in two days I must withdraw'. The next day Eisenhower regretfully advised him to pause and consolidate, pending the renewal of the offensive on 9 December. But it was clear that Anderson's forces had temporarily 'run out of steam'. They had suffered over 1,000 casualties, and lost more than seventy tanks. As Eisenhower's official diarist put it, 'Overnight it looked as if we would be stalemated and would have to begin the slow process of methodical building up, just as Alexander and Montgomery had to do at Alamein.' This was a just appreciation of the situation.[12]

It was a case of 'so near and yet so far'. If one asks why, the answer must be not so much because Eisenhower and Anderson were not up to their jobs – in the face of great difficulties they did as well as could be expected – but partly because the French commanders in Tunisia, caught in a mêlée of conflicting orders, fell back in the end on inaction, which benefited the Germans; partly because the Americans failed to trust their French allies in Africa sufficiently and give them enough time to organize their coup; but even more because of the original decision not to attempt landings at Bougie, Phillipeville or Bône in the initial assault. The roots of the strategic failure in Tunisia lay in the determination of Marshall and King to put much of the weight of the invasion at Oran and at Casablanca, over 1,000 miles from the Tunisian object-ive.[13]

(iii) THE AXIS DEFEAT IN TUNISIA

The first attempt to gain Tunisia had failed. In the long run there were compensations for the strategic reverse involved. In the course of the six month campaign which followed a large German army was drawn into the Tunisian bridgehead and a substantially German air force was also kept fully employed. Meanwhile the crucial nucleus of battle-hardened Anglo-American divisions was created for future operations and new and as yet untried American commanders gained the experience they needed. Patton, Bradley, Truscott and many others all won their spurs in the Tunisian campaign. Thus the two objectives which Roosevelt had kept firmly in mind throughout the strategic arguments of 1942 – that the Americans should fight and gain experience against the Germans and that the latter should be compelled to commit some resources against them which might otherwise be used on the Russian front – were both better served by this outcome than they would have been by the immediate occupation of Tunisia. On the other hand, the length of the Tunisian campaign finally ruled out the possibility of 'Round-Up' in 1943. Marshall had served the President's purposes by the stand he had adopted in August better than he knew, and better than he had served his own.[14]

Such considerations were of course scant comfort to Eisenhower, who felt that he had failed to secure the big prize. Realistically, however, he settled down in January to build up his forces, sort them out from the confused disorder in which they had been thrown into battle and create separate British, French and American sectors of the Front under national command, pending the arrival of better weather. It was now clear that Tripoli which it was originally thought might be taken from the west by Eisenhower's forces, would in fact fall to the Eighth Army, which had defeated Rommel at Alamein at the end of October, and was now advancing into Tripolitania. It seemed, too, that Rommel would succeed in extricating a good part of the Afrika Corps from Libya and bring it across the frontier to join up with the German Fifth Panzer Army under Von Arnim, who had succeeded the original German commander Nehring. During the last weeks of January Rommel was shepherded warily towards the Tunisian frontier by Montgomery's forces. In the first week of February he crossed the frontier and took up positions in the French-built Mareth Line, facing Montgomery but with his rear towards the American forces in Tunisia.[15]

The political problems in Algiers had now begun to sort themselves out. Darlan's assassination, on Christmas Eve 1942, removed a source of embarrassment. The subsequent installation of Giraud as head of the French civil government, however unsuitable, had at least made possible a coalition between the Gaullists and the North African French, and a common Anglo-American policy in the area – though it was to take some time to bring it about. Unfortunately the political problems in Algiers were reflected at the front. The original intention, that Anderson's First Army headquarters should co-ordinate all ground forces on the Tunisian front had not worked, because the French refused to serve under British command and Fredendall, who commanded the US Second Corps in the southern sector of the front, failed to co-operate sufficiently with either the British or the French. Anderson, lacking real authority, was often blamed, and still is, for mistakes which were not wholly his fault. The British general's weaknesses were probably more of temperament and personality than military capacity, but these were of considerable importance in the situation. Consequently even Eisenhower's final insistence at the end of January that the French as well as the Americans should come firmly under First Army command did not much improve matters. It was not until Alexander took over as commander of all ground forces in Tunisia at the end of February that the situation really improved. The replacement of Fredendall in command of II Corps, first by Patton and then by Bradley, and the partial withdrawal of the French forces temporarily from the line considerably eased Alexander's task, and helped to make the final complete victory in Tunisia possible. The French forces for their part had done well but they were still ill-equipped and in need of relief. In the final stages the French XIX Corps was to play a full part in the battle.[16]

Before the climax was reached, however, the Americans had suffered a sharp reverse in the battle of Kasserine – a rebuff that precipitated Fredendall's relief. Eisenhower had originally intended that II Corps should concentrate in the south and attack towards the port of Sfax in an attempt to separate Rommel's forces from von Arnim's. His tours of inspection, however, had convinced him that many of Fredendall's troops were still ill-disciplined, soft and not fully trained – a judgement which should have led him to replace Fredendall immediately. He did not do so, however, but wisely cancelled the order for the offensive, leaving the main thrust against Rommel and towards Sfax to come from Montgomery's experienced Eighth Army. But Montgomery was still engaged in his methodical way in clearing the port and harbour at Tripoli and concentrating his forces for the attack on the Mareth Line. Taking advantage of the temporary lull in that quarter, von Arnim and Rommel struck out at II Corps, to gain more elbow room and safeguard their communications. Fredendall's force of three divisions had been over-extended and was thinly spread out. Moreover, faulty intelligence prevented Anderson from releasing reinforcements for the threatened sector of the front in good time.

The Americans were driven back from the line Gafsa-Fondouk towards Corps headquarters at Tebessa, with the loss of over a hundred tanks, fifty guns and more than 1,500 casualties. For a moment it seemed that the Germans might achieve a complete breakthrough, capture Tebessa and the American supply base at Le Kef and roll up the front from the south. Eisenhower acted quickly, however, scraping together reinforcements and rushing them to the front. Rommel was finally halted in the Kasserine Pass, and with Montgomery's forces now approaching the Mareth Line he decided it was more politic to withdraw. The Americans had suffered a nasty shock, but in the final analysis the fact that they had eventually held the Germans and seen them withdraw gave them the self-confidence they needed. Patton's vigorous methods when he assumed command for the next month or so completed the progress. As in the Battle of the Bulge two years later, a sharp reverse proved the foundation for future victory.[17]

At the beginning of March General Alexander took office, as Eisenhower's deputy, commanding British, French and American troops in Tunisia. The Allied forces in Tunisia – First and Eighth Armies, the French XIXth Corps, and US II Corps – were now for the first time grouped effectively for operations, under a proper system of command and under commanders all of whom were up to their jobs. Alexander's handling of the Americans was a little unsure at first – he too was new to the job of Allied commander – but with Patton thrusting towards Rommel's rear, Montgomery on 20 March turned and broke through the Mareth position, advancing successively to take Sfax, Sousse and Enfidaville up the coast. The Germans were now penned up in a relatively small bridgehead south and west of Tunis and Bizerta. Rommel, having failed to obtain Hitler's permission to attempt the evacuation of as much of his force as possible – the only sensible course for the Germans at this stage of the campaign – was now withdrawn to Germany and overall command vested in von Arnim. Alexander's 18th Army Group was poised for the *coup de grâce*.[18]

In his plan for the final defeat of the Germans, Alexander decided to use First Army in the main role, rather than Eighth Army, which was facing a difficult position in the mountains at Enfidaville. Moreover the chance of surprise was greater, since it was thought that von Arnim would probably expect the main attack to come from the more famous and more experienced force. In preparation for this offensive Alexander transferred some Eighth Army formations to the First Army sector. In addition, the whole of the US II Corps was moved bodily to the northern sector opposite Bizerta. Originally Alexander had intended to use only two of II Corps' four divisions, but Eisenhower, on Marshall's prompting, insisted that the whole formation should be used and should have a worthwhile objective. It was necessary, he explained to Alexander, that American public opinion should see their troops in a triumphant role after the reverse at Kasserine, or they might otherwise become disillusioned with the European war. Thus for the last time the spectre of 'Pacific First' appeared in the North African scenario. Alexander accepted the arguments. Whether Eisenhower and Marshall were justified in interfering, for nationalistic reasons, with what the former's biographer describes as 'a logical military arrangement which allowed for the most efficient use of resources' is a difficult question to answer. The arguments are very fairly set out by Eisenhower's official diarist, and perhaps the reader should be left to judge for himself.[19]

In the upshot II Corps, now under Bradley's command, performed very well in the last stages of the campaign. Following the opening attack by the British IX Corps on 22 April, II Corps launched a general attack towards Bizerta on the 30th. By 1 May the Germans were in retreat and on the 7th the British entered Tunis and the Americans Bizerta. The German-Italian army fell back into the Cape Bon peninsula where on the 13th they surrendered. Little or no attempt was made to evacuate them by sea – only a few hundred escaped – and the destruction of the German-Italian armies in Africa was complete. About 230,000 prisoners were taken, with about 200 tanks and 1,200 guns – a capitulation on the Stalingrad scale. Almost exactly six months after the landings in Morocco and Algeria the Allies were at last masters of the North African shores.[20]

The Consequences of 'Torch'

Marshall and the US Chiefs of Staff had argued when the decision to launch the North African operation was taken that it would almost certainly rule out a cross-Channel attack in 1943 and must be regarded as a substitute for it. The mounting of 'Torch' would inevitably draw on the best units the two countries had available, including most of the US forces already in Britain. Its overall demands, especially in shipping, would probably delay the planned programme for the transport of further US troops to Britain ('Bolero') by about four months – and it was already obvious that the original hopes for the 'Bolero' build-up (twenty-five US divisions) had been over-optimistic. The realistic facts in the autumn of 1942 suggested to the US army planners that after 'Torch' had been launched the further movement of US troops to Britain would probably mean that no more than four or five US divisions would be available for 'Round-Up' in the spring of 1943. It would not in fact be possible to launch a really powerful cross-Channel attack. In accordance with this view, and reflecting the US Chiefs' judgement the previous month that the Allies were now committed to a defensive 'encircling' strategy in 1943, a strategic appreciation approved by the Combined Chiefs of Staff in August assumed that North Africa would be occupied and then 'intensified operations' would be 'conducted therefrom'.

This was a dangerous line of argument for Marshall to allow to hold the field. On the one hand it opened the way for further commitments in the Mediterranean, an idea Marshall heartily disliked. On the other hand it allowed Admiral King and others who thought like him to argue that since nothing really worthwhile was to be attempted in Europe in 1943, the United States' effort should be concentrated on the Pacific. A 'chink in the door' was indeed made in December 1942 when the US Chiefs of Staff considerably enlarged the concept of 'strategic defensive' operations against Japan to allow for various operations including an offensive in Burma in 1943.[1]

Churchill was at first unwilling to accept that a major cross-Channel attack in 1943 was now ruled out. His combative spirit rebelled against the notion that the North African operation, which would require at most thirteen to fifteen divisions, should effectively rule out an operation for 1943 for which the Allies had been envisaging the employment of *forty-eight* divisions; and he was intensely conscious of what the Soviet reaction would be when they were told again 'No Second Front in Europe this year'. But if this were really the consequence, then it was all the more important that at the end of the North African campaign the Anglo-American force should not be locked up uselessly there, but should be employed in some operation against the Axis that *was* practicable – an invasion of Sardinia, for example, or Sicily. Roosevelt was inclined to share this view. The build-up of US troops in Britain should certainly continue as far as possible and the cross-Channel attack should not be ruled out altogether, but there was also much to be said for exploiting success in the Mediterranean – in Sardinia, Sicily, perhaps even Italy and the Balkans. As usual, Roosevelt had a good deal of sympathy with Churchill's strategic outlook. Both men were attracted by the idea of maintaining some kind of fictitious threat to North-West Europe, thus forcing the Germans to keep troops there, while in fact assaulting the Axis on its vulnerable southern flank and in its least reliable quarter – Italy. It was the policy which Churchill called, in a memorandum of 25 November 1942, assaulting the 'soft underbelly' of the Axis.[2]

Meanwhile Marshall had begun to have second thoughts. For the second time he was caught in the situation where the overriding principle of 'Europe First' was in danger of being whittled away, and yet the only practicable operations in the European theatre looked like being operations which he considered strategically unsound.

Again it was Churchill and the British Chiefs of Staff who were proposing them and again his own Commander-in-Chief seemed to be leaning in that direction.

The pattern exactly repeated itself. Marshall once again concluded that the important thing was to keep the idea of the cross-Channel attack in being, if not for 1943 then for 1944, and to press for the continued build-up of US forces in the UK for this purpose. In the meantime Mediterranean operations might have to be sanctioned, but on the smallest and least ambitious scale that Roosevelt and Churchill would agree to. Perhaps, if all went well in North Africa, it might still be possible to mount some operation across the Channel in 1943. On 14 December Dill wrote to Churchill that Marshall still after all believed 'Round-up' was possible, provided the United States continued to devote its main efforts to building up its forces in Britain rather than sending them to North Africa for the expansion of Mediterranean operations. As Dill put it, 'Marshall prefers even a modified 'Round-Up' [ie smaller than was at first envisaged] to such operations as the invasion of Sicily or Sardinia'.[3]

In January of 1943, therefore, just as had been the case six months earlier, Marshall found himself setting out for a conference with the British, this time at Casablanca, knowing that he would have to play a lone hand. He could expect little help from King, who did not share his strategic outlook, and he could not rely on the President. Indeed he had been forced to admit to Roosevelt that his own War Department planners were divided amongst themselves and with those of the Navy; he could not argue that there was a united view in favour of a cross-Channel attack in 1943.[4]

Surprisingly, in view of the importance of the issues, the US Chiefs took with them to this conference only a minimum of planning staff and other advisers. In golfing parlance, as one observer put it, 'they left most of their clubs behind'. King's chief naval adviser even had to ask Mountbatten for the loan of some of his Combined Operations Planners, with the paradoxical result that the pre-

sentations of the US Chief of Naval Operations were influenced by a British viewpoint. Perhaps Marshall knew
that he was going to lose. By the time the participants assembled at Casablanca, it was already apparent that the
main assumption on which Marshall and indeed Churchill
had based their view that 'Round-up' in 1943 might still
be possible had not been fulfilled. Clearly Tunis was not
going to be taken or North Africa cleared by an early
date. A campaign extending into the spring or early summer was now inevitable. This really settled the matter. It
might just have been possible to close everything up in
the Mediterranean at the end of 1942 and bring the bulk
of the troops, landing craft etc. back to England in time
for a cross-Channel attack some time in 1943. In April or
May it would really be impossible to do so.[5]

The British case therefore prevailed, as it was more or
less bound to do. Marshall found that even his own man
on the spot, Eisenhower, was of the opinion that the Allies
could not keep their best troops idle for the best part of
1943: and, even if they could be got back to Britain in
time for a cross-Channel attack, at most that attack would
be launched by twenty-one divisions, not the forty-eight
which the American planners themselves had originally
considered necessary for success. Marshall could only
argue that Allied strategy should not be dictated by the
mere desirability of 'maintaining momentum', and pose
the pertinent question 'Where would an attack on, say,
Sicily, actually lead to?' To which Brooke's logical but
discomfiting answer was 'To the knocking-out of Italy
from the war' – and perhaps to an Italian campaign or
possibly a Balkan one. This of course was precisely what
Marshall feared. Nonetheless, he could not hold out
against the logic of the situation. As usual Dill and Portal
helped to find a formula which would enable Marshall to
accept the situation gracefully. Sicily, then, was to be the
next objective, but the 'Bolero' build-up of American
troops in Britain was to continue as fast as shipping became available, so as to allow at least the *possibility* of
a cross-Channel attack in the autumn of 1943 with the

united forces available, if circumstances seemed propitious. As a further concession to Marshall's views, the final agreed programme did not mention an invasion of the Italian mainland. Yet by the time the question of future strategy again came up, in the summer of 1943, it had become all too clear that an invasion of Italy (the logical next step after Sicily) could and should be mounted in the autumn, while a cross-Channel attack could not. Rightly did the British Secretary to the Conference record 'our ideas have prevailed almost throughout'. The official US historians basically accept this view of the conference.[6]

In a nutshell, therefore, the strategic consequence of the decision to invade North Africa in 1942 was that which Marshall had always feared: namely that the decisive attack across the Channel was postponed, not till 1943 but till 1944, and the Allies spent the year 1943 in operations in the Mediterranean, in Africa, Sicily and Italy. The question must be asked again, as it was asked then, and often since, was this on the whole for the best, as Churchill and the British Chiefs certainly thought? Or was it for the worst, as Marshall thought? One American historian at least has written a persuasive book arguing the latter very strongly. But Professor Higgins's case, which Professor Ambrose and Colonel L. J. Myer and other US writers also seem to accept, is that the cross-Channel strategy really depended on all Allied efforts in Europe being devoted to the build-up and training of American forces in Britain in 1942, as a prelude to an attack across the Channel in overwhelming strength in 1943. Eisenhower himself certainly accepted in later life, as Marshall never did, that a cross-Channel assault *in 1942* with limited forces and inadequate landing craft would almost certainly have been a disaster; and even if successful in achieving a lodgement would have delayed the landing of the main assault, without drawing any German troops from the Russian front.[7]

The argument therefore revolves around two questions: firstly whether, given the most favourable circumstances, a cross-Channel attack *in 1943* would have been successful.

It is not certain that it would have been. Lord Mount-batten, who was accepted by the Americans no less than by the British as the foremost authority on amphibious operations, holds the view now, as he did then, that the chances of real success in 1943 were dubious. Certainly German coastal defences were weaker in 1943 than in 1944, but so was Allied air-power and the Allied ground forces available. The US forces would have been less well-equipped and presumably inexperienced. There would not have been the number and variety of specialized landing-craft available in 1943, and in particular the means and 'know-how' to overcome beach-obstacles. 'Torch' was at the time the most ambitious, largest-scale amphibious operation ever attempted. 'Round-Up' would have been on a similar scale. But 'Torch' went in against relatively weak and uncertain opposition which soon ceased, while 'Round-Up' would have faced vigorous and determined opposition by German troops whose morale was much higher in 1943 than it was in 1944 after a full year of defeat.

It is at least open to question therefore whether a cross-Channel attack would have been successful in 1943, even had it been politically possible to concentrate all efforts on the 'build-up' for it during the previous year. But was it in fact possible? This is the second question, and here one can bring in Marshall himself on this side of the argument. In after years that great man conceded that in fact Roosevelt and Churchill were right on this point. American and British public opinion, no less than the pressure to assist Russia, meant that American troops could not spend the whole of the crucial year 1942 simply training for the great operation of 1943. This meant that the real alternatives were not 'a cross-Channel assault in 1943' or 'North Africa in 1942'. The alternatives were a cross-Channel attack *in 1942* or North Africa in 1942; and there can be very little doubt that in preferring 'Torch' to 'Sledgehammer' Churchill and Roosevelt made the right decision.[8]

Finally one must ask the question 'What were the long

term political effects of the decision for "Torch"?' So far
as Anglo-American relations were concerned, the long-
drawn out and heated arguments did not poison these
relations as they might well have done. On the contrary,
out of these protracted discussions there emerged, so far
as the major participants were concerned, a genuine mutual respect and understanding which formed a strong
foundation for a war alliance which was to be in many
respects closer and more effective than any in history. The
'special relationship' which was to be an important factor
in both American and British foreign policy for the next
twenty years was forged in this period. Much of this result was owed to the two principals, to the special talents
of men like Dill, Hopkins, Portal, Harriman and Mountbatten, and, at the operational end, to the particular
genius for inter-allied co-operation of the top-level commanders, particularly Eisenhower, Alexander, Cunningham and Tedder. They established the precedents for
inter-allied co-operation and the machinery that made it
work for the rest of the war. The final contribution was
made by Marshall, who had the magnanimity to see –
more than once – his cherished ideas go down in defeat
without allowing it to create any lasting bitterness.

The effects of the decision on two other allies, the
Russians and the French, were less happy. Soviet bitterness over the – as they saw it – callous decision to leave
the Russian people to bear the brunt of the German on-
slaught for two years (indeed, as it turned out, for three)
was not confined to Stalin. Anglo-Soviet relations at the
end of 1942 fell to their lowest level during the Alliance
and there was much recrimination, much of it private
but some of it semi-public, over the lack of a Second
Front and the simultaneous suspension of convoys to
Russia. The original communiqué after the Molotov visit
apparently promising a 'Second Front in 1942' had been
much played up in Moscow. The public 'let-down' and
sense of disappointment was all the greater. It revived
in full force all the suspicions which Soviet leaders had
long cherished, that the real objective of British foreign

policy had always been to embroil Russia and Germany and that Churchill was now quite content to see them bleed each other white. Roosevelt and the Americans, it was felt, were not so much to blame, but at the very least they were Churchill's dupes.

Things improved somewhat after the success of 'Torch', however, and the Russian victories at Stalingrad. But Soviet suspicions of Western good faith lingered on. Just how important the episode was in the long term is more debatable. Whatever decision had been made, the Soviet Union would still have been led after the war by men like Stalin and Molotov, pathologically suspicious of the West and imprisoned in a cage of dogma which made them constantly on the look out for evidence of Western bad faith and duplicity, and of course often provoking the very behaviour which they expected. It may be doubted whether the 'Second Front' controversy made any major contribution to the post-war breakdown of the Alliance or the 'cold war' which developed in the late 'forties', though the extent to which Soviet ruling circles in general and the Soviet public shared the general sense of disappointment may have contributed to the ease with which anti-Western policies were accepted and supported in the Soviet Union.[9]

So far as France was concerned, the principal factor which has to be measured is the effect of the unfortunate Darlan episode and its sequel on the attitude of de Gaulle and those who supported him, coming as it did immediately after his total exclusion from the operation. Robert Murphy has been severely criticized here, and he deserves some of the criticism, as do Hull and Roosevelt himself. They should not have allowed themselves to be influenced so much by resentment over the Saint Pierre episode, outrageous though de Gaulle's behaviour had been. Murphy for his part certainly underestimated Gaullist support in North Africa, and overestimated that which Giraud could command. On the other hand he was not wrong in thinking that those whose word immediately counted – the North African hierarchy – regarded de

Gaulle as a traitor and that the presence of Free French forces initially would certainly exacerbate the situation.

Roosevelt and Hull were mistaken in their insistence on debarring de Gaulle from all information about the operation, particularly since its likelihood became so widely known that de Gaulle found out anyway. But they were right to exclude his forces from participation in the landings.[10]

The effects and the rights and wrongs of the Darlan 'expedient', as it soon became known, will always be debated; and the fact that Roosevelt and Churchill both backed away from it subsequently in the face of public outcry should not be allowed to obscure the fact that they had both come close to sanctioning it in advance. As Roosevelt put it to Churchill, quoting an old Balkan proverb, 'It is permitted to walk with the devil, until you have crossed the bridge.' From Moscow Stalin, an expert in such matters, concurred. One was justified perhaps in dealing with men like Darlan when so much was at stake. To Eisenhower and Clark certainly the agreement was a straightforward matter of saving American lives: and they could point to the fact that US casualties were only one tenth of what had been expected. British and French casualties were also correspondingly reduced. Some historians think that it was American promises rather than Darlan's authority which influenced the situation: but promises have to be made to someone, and that someone needed to be able to secure the co-operation of the Vichy authorities. If it had not been Darlan it would have had to be someone else – perhaps Noguès. Eisenhower was probably right in thinking that no one else available could have produced the desired results. If he could not deliver Tunisia and the French Fleet, Darlan could and did deliver Morocco, Algeria and West Africa. The mistake was not so much in making the arrangements with Darlan, but firstly in agreeing to terms which allowed him to prolong the obnoxious Vichy regime in full, and imprison pro-Allied officers; and secondly in continuing the arrangement with the ineffable Giraud, even after his lack of influence and political skill had become apparent. Yet even there it could be argued that an assassination in such circumstances was bound to create a situation in which someone had to be pushed quickly into the breach; and Giraud was the least compromised of the available candidates.

The American overall view on French affairs was not unreasonable in the circumstances, namely that neither they nor the British should impose a government on France, but leave it to the free choice of a liberated people after the war. But it was unrealistic to think that one could meddle in French politics without supporting one side or another and so to some extent pre-judging the issue. There was no 'conspiracy' here, no deliberate desire to impose an American sphere of influence on the French Empire. It was a case of mistaken judgement, mistaken both in thinking that de Gaulle and his movement could be long excluded from so important a French sphere, and also that once there he could be kept in a subordinate role and prevented from taking his rightful place at the head of Free France. It is not surprising that a French leader in these circumstances should have felt resentment: but it was unfortunate that de Gaulle's temperament should have been so deeply suspicious that the episode became magnified in his mind to the proportions of conspiracy against de Gaulle – and therefore against France. Among the less fortunate consequences of 'Torch' was the fact that the maladroit American handling of de Gaulle before, during and after the operation stored up grievances in his mind which were to affect Franco-American and Franco-British relations for as long as de Gaulle had any influence on them. And that, as things turned out, was to be a very long time.

Finally one must consider the possibilities inherent in the thesis that the decision in favour of the North African rather than the cross-Channel strategy did in effect delay Allied victory in the West for at least a year. If that were so then certainly Britain, exhausted by a further year's effort, emerged weaker, and the Soviet Union stronger

from the conflict than need have been the case. This thesis
has already been considered in its main details, and it has
been argued that an attack across the Channel in 1942
would have been a disaster and that it was not in fact
possible simply to wait and build up for such an attack
in 1943. History is certainly not merely a matter of a
deterministic series of events, but this particular decision
was as near as it is possible to get to an 'inevitable' decision. Moreover, of course, a cross-Channel attack in
1943 would not necessarily have been successful, nor, if
successful, necessarily decisive in ending the war in 1944.

More fundamentally, however, one can take comfort
from the thought that the destinies of nations are not
often decided by such factors as the difference between
five and six years of war. The roots of Britain's post-war
decline (and also that of France) reach back into the pre-
war era and before. The process itself was largely conditioned by the pace of political, economic and technological change. Certainly the Second World War acceler-
ated the process. But this was due to the stark fact of
British participation in a long and costly struggle, rather
than to the way the war was fought or the strategic decisions taken in the summer of 1942.

APPENDIX

Strategic Full Circle

(A) WASHINGTON WAR CONFERENCE (ARCADIA): AMERICAN
AND BRITISH STRATEGY. (ABC – 4/CS.I.) (WWI – FINAL)
(MEMORANDUM BY THE UNITED STATES AND BRITISH
CHIEFS OF STAFF.) JANUARY 1942.

III Steps to be taken in 1942 to put into effect the General
Policy:

13. Closing and tightening the ring around Germany......
......The main object will be to strengthen this ring and
close the gaps in it, by sustaining the Russian front, by
arming and supporting Turkey, by increasing our strength
in the Middle East, and by gaining possession of the
whole North African coast......

......16. It does not seem likely that in 1942 any large-
scale land offensive against Germany, except on the
Russian front, will be possible......

......17. In 1943 the way may be clear for a return to the
Continent, across the Mediterranean, from Turkey into
the Balkans, or by landings in Western Europe.

(B) OPERATIONS IN WESTERN EUROPE – THE MARSHALL MEM-
ORANDUM (TAB A, ABCI) (MEMORANDUM BY GENERAL
MARSHALL FOR THE LONDON CONFERENCE) APRIL 1942.

Western Europe is favoured as the theatre in which to stage
the first major offensive by the United States and Great
Britain . . . Our proposal provides for an attack by a combat
force of 48 divisions as soon as the necessary means can be
accumulated in England – estimated at 1 April, 1943 . . .
included: preparations for an 'emergency offensive' by the
fall of 1942 . . . This limited operation would be justified
only in case:
(1) The situation on the Russian front becomes desperate,
ie the success of German arms threatens the immediate collapse of Russian resistance.

(2) The German situation in Western Europe becomes critically weaker......
......US troops that can be made available in England by 15 September, (1942)......
......2½ Infantry Divisions and 1 Armoured Division.
or
1½ Infantry Divisions and 2 Armoured Divisions.

(C) OPERATIONS IN 1942-3 (CCS 94)
(MEMORANDUM BY THE COMBINED CHIEFS OF STAFF)
JULY, 1942.

It having been decided that 'Sledgehammer' is not to be undertaken, we propose the following plans for 1942-3:
......That if......by 15th September......'Round-Up' appears impracticable of successful execution (in 1943), the decision should be taken to launch a combined operation against the North and North West Coast of Africa at the earliest possible date before December 1942.

FOOTNOTES

PROLOGUE

n.1 cf. J. M. Burns, *Roosevelt The Soldier of Freedom* (Harcourt Brace, New York, 1970) pp.11, 26.

n.2 See G. Warner, *Iraq and Syria 1941* (Davis Poynter, London, 1974) for the most recent account of these campaigns.

n.3 Burns, op. cit., p.102, 112. R. S. Sherwood, *The White House Papers of Harry Hopkins*. (London, Eyre and Spottiswood, 1948) Vol. I, pp.303-5, 344. W. S. Churchill, *The Second World War*, Vol. III, (London, Cassell, 1950), p.350.

n.4 Sir A. Bryant, *The Alanbrooke War Diaries*, Vol. I, (London, Collins, Fontana PB 1965) pp.327, 437-8, 440-1.

n.5 As late as May 1942 the British Chief of Imperial General Staff estimated that there would be at very most ten trained U.K. divisions available for a cross-Channel attack. At that time the landing craft available were only sufficient to land 4,000 men in the first assault. Later in the year there would be sufficient landing-craft to land one division initially (about 15,000 men): by 1943 a two-division front would be possible. (Bryant, I, 298-9, 312). (Confirmed by Earl Mountbatten to the author). Allied shipping losses in 1941 amounted to about four million tons. In the first half of the year they averaged between four hundred thousand and five hundred thousand *a month* (Churchill, III, p.687). cf. J. Leasor, *War At The Top* (London, M. Joseph, 1957) pp.191-2.

n.6 Churchill, III, pp.479, 489. T. H. Higgins, *Winston Churchill And The Second Front* (Toronto, Oxford, 1958) p.78.

n.7 Bryant, I, p.298.

n.8 M. Matloff and E. M. Snell, *Strategic Planning for Coalition Warfare*. (Washington, U.S. War Department, 1953) p.55, citing Item 10, Exec. 4, 31.7.41. F. C. Pogue, *Ordeal and Hope*, (London, MacGibbon and Kee, 1968) p.144. Churchill, III, pp.481-5, 489. J. R. M. Butler, *Grand Strategy*, Vol. III, Part II (London, H.M.S.O., 1964) pp.725-30.

n.9 Churchill, III, pp.479-90. The quotation is on p.490.

n.10 Churchill, III, p.339. As Churchill rightly points out, the latter comment applied also to the Americans initially, i.e. that they had little idea of the difficulties of amphibious warfare.

n.11 H. Feis, *Churchill, Roosevelt, Stalin*. (Princeton, N. J. Princeton University Press 1957 PB) p.11, for Soviet demands on the U.S.A. Churchill, III, pp.342-6, for the Churchill-Stalin correspondence.

n.12 Feis, p.13.

n.13 Feis, pp.16-17.

n.14 For the Churchill-Maisky interview, see Churchill III, pp. 405-9 and Maisky's own account in I. Maisky, *Memoirs of a*

Footnotes

Soviet Ambassador. (London, Hutchinson, 1976) pp.190-1.
See also Feis, pp.14-17 and The Earl of Avon, *The Reckoning.*
(London Cassell, 1965) pp.275-6. Avon (Antony Eden) was
present at the Churchill-Maisky meeting in his capacity as
Foreign Secretary. Lord Beaverbrook was Minister of Supply,
Harriman Roosevelt's personal representative in London.
Hopkins would have been the logical American representative
on the supply mission to Russia, but was too ill to return
to Moscow. (Sherwood, p.360).

n.15 Sir L. Woodward, *British Foreign Policy in the Second World
War.* (London, H.M.S.O., 1962) p.153. (single volume edition).

n.16 Feis, pp.23-25; Cordell Hull, *Memoirs,* Vol. II, (London
Hodder and Stoughton, 1948) p.1166; Churchill, III, pp.
559-60; Eden, pp.291-7, and 299-300, gives his account of the
talks with Stalin on these matters, and military questions,
during which he raised the question of Soviet participation
in the war against Japan, thus neatly reversing the 'Second
Front' issue. See also Churchill III, pp.557-8.

n.17 Churchill, III, p.560. On Soviet territorial demands, see
F.O. memo W.P. (42) 69.

n.18 Churchill, III, p.539.

n.19 Matloff and Snell, pp.42-8, citing J.B. 325, series 642-5. See
also Pogue, pp.123-4.

n.20 Burns, p.87.

n.21 Butler, *Grand Strategy,* Vol. II, pp.342-4; Matloff and Snell
pp.22-24. For 'Plan Dog' see Matloff and Snell, pp.25-28
and Pogue, p.126 for Marshall's attitude to it. The quotation
is Pogue, p.127.

n.22 Matloff and Snell, loc. cit. citing WPD 4175-15; Churchill
III, p.489; R. M. Leighton and R. W. Coakley, *Global Logistics and Strategy, 1940-43* (Washington, U.S. War Department, 1955) pp.43-56. Roosevelt inserted the qualification
'navally' into the statement that 'U.S. operations' should facili-
tate the exertion of its principal military effort in the Atlantic
or the Mediterranean' – the qualification applying only to the
Mediterranean (Matloff and Snell, p.30, citing JB 325, Series
674).

n.23 Burns pp.86-7. Matloff and Snell pp.28-30, citing WPD 4175-
18.

n.24 Higgins, pp.46, 66. Matloff and Snell, pp.34-48, citing JB
325, series 642-5 et al. Pogue pp.127-8. Burns, loc. cit. For
Anglo-American Staff talks, see British series B.U.S., 1-40
(CAB 99/5).

n.25 Matloff and Snell, p.46.

n.26 General Francisco Franco had been dictator of Spain since
the Nationalist victory in the Civil War of the mid-thirties.
His general attitude to the war is discussed in Ch. IV.
Marshal Phillipe Pétain became head of the authoritarian
Vichy French regime in June 1940 after the defeat of France.
The Vichy French position is discussed in Ch. I.

n.27 Sir I. Kirkpatrick. *The Inner Circle*. (London, Macmillan, 1959) p.195.

n.28 Churchill III, pp.123-5; Burns, 127. Matloff and Snell, p.50, citing JB 325, series 694.

n.29 Churchill III, p.479.

n.30 Pogue, pp.125-6. F. Williams, *A Prime Minister Remembers* (London, Heinemann, 1961) p.51.

n.31 Pogue, p.160. The planners' figure was eight million, which included two million for the Army Air Corps (Matloff and Snell, pp.59-60, citing WPD 4494-21, et al).

n.32 Burns, p.87.

n.33 Burns, p.91. H. L. Stimson and McG. Bundy, *On Active Service In Peace And War*. (New York, Harper Bros., 1947). Other 'militant' members of Roosevelt's Cabinet were Navy Secretary Knox, and Interior Secretary Ickes. Hopkins shared their general viewpoint on the war, but unlike them was, in this period, still concerned to reflect his chief's viewpoint rather than influence it. [Cf WM 41/86, Aug. 25, 41]

n.34 At the beginning of the year Marshall had stressed that the U.S. was in no way committed to take military action 'unless we are attacked'. In July he felt still that any break with Japan should be delayed till the last possible moment 'because of our state of unpreparedness'. In November, however, he informed newspapermen that 'the United States and Japan were on the brink of war'. Pogue, pp.128, 183, 202, citing Marshall, interview 15 Jan., 1957, Pearl Harbour Hearings (Naval Court of Inquiry) pt. 32, p.560. See also Pogue pp. 121-2, for Marshall's general attitude to the war.

n.35 Eden's comment that this was a 'gratuitous act' which 'sealed the fate' of Germany and Italy is fully justified. Had they held their hand U.S. strategy must of necessity have been 'Pacific First'. (Eden, p.315).

n.36 Sherwood, pp.427, quoting the Report of the Commission of Inquiry into Pearl Harbour; see also Churchill, III, p.535; Eden, p.306.

n.37 Eden, pp.308-9; Sherwood, pp.432-3. According to British sources Hopkins was much more forthcoming on his second visit in July, predicting incorrectly (and contrary to the President's orders if the story is true) that 'the U.S.A. could be in the war in six weeks'. Sir J. Kennedy *The Business of War* (London, Hutchinson, 1957) p.411, cf. Sherwood, I, p.312 for Roosevelt's instructions.

n.38 Eden, p.311. See Hull, II, p.1059. The latter (Chs 78-80) contains a full account of the negotiations with Japan.

n.39 Stimson, pp.86-7; Sherwood, p.428; Pogue, pp.209-10, citing WPD 4544-16. Hull, II, p.1090; Eden, p.306; and Hull, II, p.1087; Sherwood, I, p.432.

Footnotes

CHAPTER 1

n.1 Burns, p.286.

n.2 Viscount Templewood, *Ambassador on Special Mission* (London, Collins, 1946) pp.34-43, 49-53, 67-71, 93-5. G. Warner, *Pierre Laval And The Eclipse of France*, (London, Eyre and Spottiswood, 1968) pp.235, 252-3. See also D. Detwiler, *Hitler, Franco and Gibraltar* (Wiesbaden, F. Steiner Verlag, 1962). Hitler's directive for Operation 'Barbarossa' (The invasion of Russia) was signed on December 18th 1940.

n.3 Hull, II, pp.955-6 and Churchill, III, p.209. Equally worrying to the British and the Americans was the possibility that Vichy might voluntarily cede the use of bases in North and West Africa to the Germans as was mooted in the abortive Darlan-Abetz agreement of May 28th 1941. Hull, II, pp.962-4, Pogue, pp.54-5 and S. Conn and B. Fairchild, *The Framework of Hemisphere Defence* (Washington, US Dept. of the Army, 1960) Ch. XI, W. L. Langer, *Our Vichy Gamble*, (New York, A. Knopf, 1947) p.143. This book contains the best sustained defence of the US Vichy policy from the State Department's viewpoint. For Roosevelt's and the Navy Secretary's 'responsiveness' see Churchill, III, p.489 and F. L. Loewenheim et. al. *Roosevelt and Churchill*, (London, Barrie and Jenkins, 1975) p.162. See also Prologue, n.30.

n.4 See Pogue, (loc cit) for the theoretical danger to Latin America. Knox's dire prognostication is recorded in Langer, loc. cit. For American plans and attitudes to West Africa which Hull's statement to Halifax reflected, see Matloff and Snell, pp.103-4 citing JB 325, series 729.

n.5 Sir Alan Brooke's reflection on the advantages of opening the Mediterranean is recorded in Bryant, I, p.298. See also Churchill, III, pp.577-8. A general British statement of the advantages of gaining N. Africa is reproduced by H. C. Butcher, *Three Years with Eisenhower* (London, Heinemann, 1946) p.32. cf. British COS memorandum (Arcadia Conference) Dec 22, 1941 (WW1).

n.6 As Churchill discovered in his Adana conversations with the Turkish government in January 1943, the Turks would have required massive re-equipment and would have been a drain on Allied resources rather than an accession to them. Bryant, I, p.469.

n.7 For some British views of US troops' combat-readiness see Bryant, I, pp.343-4, and Lord Ismay, *Memoirs* (London, Heinemann, 1960) p.257. Ismay was Churchill's personal representative on the British Chiefs of Staff.

n.8 The rights and wrongs of the British decision to attack the French ships at Oran will always be a matter of dispute. Many of the British naval commanders on the spot had their doubts about its wisdom and necessity, including the Commander-in-Chief, Admiral Cunningham. cf. Viscount Cunningham of Hyndhope, *A Sailor's Odyssey*, (London, Hutchinson, 1951) pp.244-5. Cunningham was able to immobilize the French squadron at Alexandria without bloodshed, though the repercussions of Oran made his task more difficult. That the latter caused very bitter and lasting French resentment against Britain is unquestionable nor that it very much strengthened the hands of the 'collaborationists' at Vichy. cf. *Warner, Laval*, p.196.

n.9 In *Troubled Neighbours*, ed. N. Waites (London, Weidenfeld and Nicolson, 1971) Ch. 9.

n.10 C. de Gaulle, *War Memoirs*, Vol. I, (London, Weidenfeld and Nicolson, 1953) pp.188-191. Lord Chandos, *Memoirs*, (London, Bodley Head, 1962) pp.246-50. The latter subsequently described de Gaulle as 'white with rage' over his treatment by Britain in the Syrian affair. (1st Lord Chandos to the author, 27th April, 1971).

n.11 Even the more patient and friendly Eden once remarked to de Gaulle, 'Do you know that you have caused us more difficulties than all our other European allies put together?' 'I don't doubt it', replied de Gaulle, 'France is a great power' (de Gaulle, *War Memoirs*, Vol. II, (London, Weidenfeld, 1959) p.106.

n.12 The most celebrated statement of his attachment to the American alliance by Churchill to de Gaulle occurred in their acrimonious discussions in June 1944, when Churchill said, 'Each time I have to choose between you and Roosevelt, I shall always choose Roosevelt' (de Gaulle, II, p.227). Churchill gives a different account of this interchange (V, 556) but de Gaulle's version is supported by Eden (p.453). The US attitude to de Gaulle, particularly the State Department's, is summarized by Hull in his Memoirs (II, pp.961-2). Roosevelt's was not very different and became more hostile as time went by. (Cf. Loewenheim, pp.344-5). See also D. S. White, *Seeds of Discord* (Syracuse, University Press, 1964) for the early history of American relations with de Gaulle.

n.13 Churchill, Vol. III, (pp.577-8); Hull, II, pp.1129-37; Sherwood, I, pp.456-66. The latter (p.465) describes how Roosevelt's feelings gradually became more exacerbated. The amount of space devoted to this relatively unimportant matter in these two books is itself some justification for the view expressed in the last sentence of this paragraph. De Gaulle's lack of ability (and possibly desire) to win the friendship of the Americans is exemplified by Pogue's account of his first meeting with Marshall (pp.413-14). Cf. Sherwood II, pp.682-90.

n.14 Burns, p.286.

n.15 Cf. Langer, op. cit., and Admiral W. Leahy *I Was There* (New York, Whittlesley House, 1950) for the Vichy policy, also Hull, II, Chs. 69, 75, 82, 84, R. Murphy, *Diplomat Among Warriors* (London, Collins, 1964) p.109 and Ch. 6. Leahy was Ambassador to Vichy till the autumn of 1942.

n.16 Warner, *Laval*, pp.23-4, 95, 139-40, 191-2, and passim.

n.17 Churchill, III, 113-6. See also Woodward s.v. pp.103-4. Darlan's son has provided an apologia for his father in A.

Footnotes

Darlan, *L'Amiral Darlan Parle* (Paris, Amiot-Dumont, 1952) but 'time-server and opportunist' are words not ill-deserved in relation to this man. Hull, II, pp.962-4. See also Warner, Laval, p.278 and the German documents cited by him, D.G.F.P. Series D, Vol. XII, Nos. 491, 559.

n.18 Churchill, III, p.209. De Gaulle I, pp.88, 188, 235, 244-5. Later he was to say bitterly that 'the Anglo-American powers never consented to deal with us as genuine allies'. (*Memoirs*, II, p.262).

n.19 For US views of de Gaulle see references cited n.12. 'It is well known that he (Roosevelt) didn't trust de Gaulle. He believed we should not impose de Gaulle on the French people, but that the French should be allowed to select their own postwar leadership' (Averell Harriman to the author). Cf. de Gaulle, pp.15, 46-8.

CHAPTER II

n.1 The party included Field Marshal Sir John Dill, the retiring Chief of Imperial General Staff; Sir Dudley Pound, First Sea Lord; Sir Charles Portal, Chief of Air Staff; Lord Beaverbrook, Minister of Aircraft Production; and Leslie Hollis and Ian Jacob of the War Cabinet/Chiefs of Staff Secretariat. For the outlook as it seemed to the newly appointed CIGS, Alan Brooke, see Bryant I, 235-7, 241-2. cf. Kennedy, pp.185-189.

n.2 Other British leaders realistically accepted that the United States must ultimately take the lead. cf. Eden, p.316. For the advantages enjoyed by the British, through experience and better organization see Pogue, p.262, Ambrose, p.23, Bryant, I, p.240. American war-planning machinery existed only in embryo, and the US Joint Chiefs of Staff as an entity was created by Roosevelt ad hoc to meet the need for an equivalent to the British body.

n.3 Churchill, IV, pp.185-90, Sherwood, II, pp.516-7. For Churchill's attitude to Roosevelt see Churchill III, pp.588, 608. Sherwood, I, 470. Roosevelt's general attitude to Churchill is well summed up in Loewenheim pp.3-13. A slightly different complexion is put on this in E. Roosevelt, *As He Saw It.* (New York, Duell, Sloan and Pearce, 1946) pp.25, 35-6 and passim, but Elliot Roosevelt's knowledge of the relationship was only fragmentary. See also Lord Moran, *Churchill, The Struggle For Survival* (London, Sphere Bks., PB, 1968) pp. 47-8 and Burns passim. Mrs Roosevelt's judgement is in E. Roosevelt, *This I Remember*, (New York, Harper, 1949) p.255.

n.4 On Hopkins, Churchill, III, pp.21-2. Sherwood, I, pp.3-13, 202-3 and passim. Pogue, pp.24-6.

n.5 Bryant, I, 449-50, Ismay, pp.253-4, Cunningham, pp.465-6. Pogue pp.84-6. Both Arnold and King have given their accounts of the war in H. H. Arnold, *Global Mission* (New York, Harper, 1949) and E. J. King and W. M. Whitehill, *Fleet Admiral King* (New York, Norton, 1952). cf. Leasor, pp.186-7.

n.6 Roosevelt's growing trust in and reliance on Marshall is universally testified to. It is best exemplified by the remark the President made to Marshall when he decided that the latter could not be spared from Washington to command the invasion of Western Europe 'I feel I could not sleep at night with you out of the country'. (Sherwood II, p.793).

n.7 That Brooke was generally acknowledged as the fittest person for his position is worth saying, since it is by no means true of all his immediate predecessors, See P. J. Grigg, *Prejudice and Judgement*, (London, Cape, 1948) pp.419-20. Field Marshall Montgomery, *Memoirs* (London Collins, 1958, pp. 59, 534) Ismay, p.318. For various aspects of the Brooke-Churchill relationship see Bryant, I, pp.19, 21-3 and passim, J. Leasor, op. cit. As Brooke himself said, he had to 'weather many storms' (Bryant, I, 245), cf. Kennedy, pp.178-9.

n.8 On Marshall, Dill and Brooke, see Churchill III, p.609, Pogue, pp.272, 284, Sherwood, I, p.482, Bryant, I, p.233. Sherwood II, p.528, Bryant, I, pp.295, 299. Later Marshall and Brooke developed a greater degree of liking and respect for each other (Pogue, pp.308-10. Kennedy. p.284).

n.9 ABDA = American, British, Dutch, Australian. The command included the East Indies, Malaya, New Guinea and Burma. Brooke thought the separation of Burma from the India Command absurd and dangerous. (Bryant, I, p.242). Cf. CR 18, Dec 26, 41 (Arcadia records) also CR 25, 27, 30.

n.10 Churchill is eloquent in his memoirs on the dangers of 'Pacific First' at this juncture (III, pp.567-8). For the Darlan feelers and prospects for 'Super-Gymnast' see III, pp.561, 575-6. See also Sherwood, I, p.473.

n.11 See Matloff and Snell, pp.104-5, citing WPD 4510, 4511-12, 4511-26. A typically cautious comment by Marshall is recorded by Pogue, p.288. See also Memo of Decisions at the White House, Dec 21, 1941, WDCSA 381 (SS). At this meeting Stimson and Marshall had secured the President's approval for the War Department memorandum which 'played down the value of American action in the Mediterranean' (Burns, p.180).

n.12 Churchill, III, p.545.

n.13 Bryant, I, pp.234-5, 242, Ismay, pp.242 ff. Churchill's forecast of 'Severe punishment' was to the Commons on December 11th 1941 (III, p.552).

n.14 Bryant pp.240-2, Pogue, p.244, citing WPD 4639-3, Sherwood I, pp. 443-4.

n.15 The comment on Marshall's preoccupation at 'Arcadia' with organization is from S. E. Ambrose, *The Supreme Commander* (London, Cassel, 1971) p.25. On the UN Declaration see Hull, II, 1114-16 and Sherwood I, pp.450-5. cf. Burns p.178. Churchill's preoccupation with strategy is amply evidenced by his elaborate memoranda for the Conference prepared en route (III, pp.575-85).

n.16 Ambrose pp.25-6, citing EP 22 and 23; Pogue, pp.276-80, citing ABC 337, Arcadia Development File, Sec. II; Churchill III, pp.598-600. Brooke agreed with Marshall in favouring unity of command (cf. Kennedy, pp.206-7).

n.17 Churchill, III, p.597. See also Sherwood, I, pp.469-71, Churchill, III, p.607, and p.608. Pogue pp.41-5, and pp. 277-8. Bryant, I, p.241. The quotation is from Pogue, p.275. 'Arcadia' records CR 17, Dec. 25, 41; CR 21, Dec. 27, 41; cf. CR 22, 25, 27; WM 42/8, Jan. 17, 42. For 'Supreme Commander' directive, WW1, Final 'Arcadia' records).

n.18 Churchill, III, p.599. Burns, p.183. Sherwood, I, p.481. The quotations are from Sherwood p.482 and Ismay p.245.

n.19 On the American lack of experience in joint interservice command and planning and the improvised nature of their early arrangements see Pogue, pp.262, 270; and Dill's part, p.284. The figures for CCS meetings are given, among others, by Ismay p.244. Brooke's mature judgement on the CCS is in Bryant, I, p.262 and Churchill's in III, pp.608-9.

n.20 Sherwood, I, p.449 (WDCSA 381.SS). British Records CR 17 (Arcadia).

n.21 Churchill III, pp.620-4.

n.22 Bryant, I, p.244.

n.23 The crucial part of the argument for North African operations in this memorandum is contained in Churchill, III, pp. 575-7. This memorandum illustrates very well the way in which the British approached the problem from a Mediterranean angle – *North* Africa is described as 'urgent' whereas 'the mastering of Dakar and the West African establishments' is viewed as a more leisurely process. The American tentative plans for an operation had seen the occupation of Dakar as first priority (Matloff and Snell, p.103 citing WDCSA 381.SS and 'Black' and 'Barrister' Development File, G-3 Registered Documents). See also Matloff and Snell p.105 for Roosevelt's desire to get 'American troops fighting across the Atlantic' citing WPD 4402-136 and his interest in the Prime Minister's proposal'. See also p.101, citing JB 355, Series 707, 11/9/41 and WPD 4494-13, for the US planners' opposite view that 'the main effort' should be 'in Western Europe', while Africa and the Middle East should be classed as 'subsidiary theatres'. See also Sherwood, I, p.473, Higgins p.88, and Churchill III, pp.574, 588-9 for Roosevelt's favourable attitude.

n.24 This admission is contained in the same document (WPD 4494-13) referred to above in n.23. This document is quoted in full in Sherwood, I, pp.413-423. The case for attacking an enemy operating on interior lines somewhere on his furthest periphery (Churchill's case) is put in paragraph 17 as well as Churchill could have put it himself.

n.25 Burns, p.180. Churchill, III, p.589. Roosevelt's change of attitude on the 23rd is referred to by Burns and Pogue, p.268 citing WPD 4402-136 and WDCSA 334. See Arnold, p.303, Matloff and Snell pp.104-8, D. D. Eisenhower, *Crusade in Europe* (London, Heinemann, 1948) pp.77-8. Mr Averell Harriman, among others, does not think Roosevelt at this time contemplated an occupation of N. Africa *without an invitation* (Averell Harriman to the author) but confirms that Roosevelt wanted early 'military action'. cf. British 'Arcadia' records CR 43, Jan. 4, 42 (Annex XXI), also CR 15, Dec. 24, 41. The British Chiefs of Staff themselves accepted this qualification (ie the necessity of French consent to the landings) at this time. COS 42/5/o, Jan. 31, 42. For date of 'Super-Gymnast', WW 17, Jan. 20, 42.

n.26 Burns' comment is in his biography, op. cit., p.181. The opposite view is in Higgins, p.94. The official historians' conclusion is 'The American planners could scarcely doubt that once the Japanese offensive was contained, if not before, the North African operation would again become the first question of American-British strategy' (Matloff and Snell, p.119). Churchill's belief in the *ultimate* necessity of winning the war on land in Europe is however testified to by others, including Earl Mountbatten. The latter recalls that the essence of his appointment to Combined Operations was 'to prepare for the invasion of Europe'. (Earl Mountbatten to the author). Churchill's remarks are quoted from III, pp.583 and 585. For US commitment to WW1 see also 'Arcadia' records CR 21, Dec. 27, and CR 57, Jan. 10, 42; also WW 14, Jan. 13, 42; WW 17, Jan. 20, 42.

n.27 See also Churchill III, p.590, 606. See also Matloff and Snell, pp. 108-111 citing WDCSA 334 and 381 and WPD 4402-136, ABC 337 for 'Magnet' plans. On the effect of Pacific reinforcements on Atlantic movements see pp.114-117, citing especially Minutes of Conference at White House, 12 Jan. 42. Super-Gymnast Development File G.3. Registered Documents. See also Churchill III, p.624, Bryant p.288. The conflicting of Churchill's and Marshall's strategy is in ABC-4/CS-1, 31 Dec. 41, cited in G. A. Harrison, *Cross-Channel Attack* (Washington, US Army Dept. 1951) p.9. Churchill's subsequent reflections are in III, p.585-6. See also Sherwood, pp.472-9. See also Grigg pp.369-70, for the views of Spaatz and Wedemeyer. The relevant British document is WW1 (Final). (See Appendix.)

n.28 Matloff and Snell, pp.117-8 citing Super-Gymnast File (see n. 27).

n.29 Roosevelt's comment is cited by Sherwood, I, p.479.

CHAPTER III

n.1 See Ch. II, n.26.
n.2 'Of 132,000 US troops embarked in the first three months of

1942 only about 20,000 sailed for Iceland and N. Ireland. During the same period over 90,000 left for stations along the "line" Hawaii-Australia.' (Matloff and Snell, p.147, citing OPD (WPD) Weekly Status Maps AG 061). Churchill's acceptance of 'several months' delay for 'Gymnast' is in IV, p. 168, and Roosevelt's agreement p.173.

n.3 Stimson and Marshall thought Roosevelt no less than Churchill dangerously prone to 'dispersionist' ideas. cf. Pogue, p.306, citing an interview with Marshall 5th October 1956. cf. also Stimson, p.416-7.

n.4 Churchill, IV, pp.289-90.

n.5 Stimson, p.214; Eden, p.317; cf. also Pogue, pp.323, 326; Ambrose, p.16, citing EP 73; Matloff and Snell, p.177; Ambrose, pp.30-33 (EP 160); On shipping losses, Churchill IV, pp.109-15, 176. Ironically, Eisenhower's memorandum was drafted less than a fortnight after the tentative Combined Chiefs' plan for 'Super-Gymnast' had been approved (on February 19th). Fredendall was to command. (K. R. Greenfield, *Command Decisions* (Washington, Army Department, 1960) p.176.

n.6 'Eisenhower's plan was bold and imaginative and – for 1942 at least – impossible' (Ambrose, p.31) cf. Matloff and Snell, pp.178-9, citing JCS 23, App. II, (14 March '42). In fact by April Marshall could only promise 3½ US divisions for a cross-Channel operation in 1942 (see Appendix).

n.7 Churchill's opposition to concentrating on 'Bolero' *only* in 1942 was early made apparent to the Americans (III, p.581). For the early 'use' of 'Sledgehammer' as code-name for a *limited* cross Channel attack see COS 42/7/0 13, Mch, 42. cf. Kennedy, pp.210, 222.

n.8 Churchill, IV, pp.167-175; Sherwood pp.515, 523-5; Pogue, p.365. The quotation is from Pogue p.259. See also Matloff and Snell, pp.179-180.

n.9 General Douglas MacArthur, Supreme Allied Commander, South-West Pacific. He made every attempt to change US strategic priorities in favour of his theatre. The British plan envisaged landing troops in the vicinity of Le Havre *in the early summer of 1943* 'under conditions of severe deterioration of military power' and with the enemy 'weakened in strength and morale' (Matloff and Snell, p.179-80, citing Br War Cabinet – Jt Plng Study, 9 Dec. 41 and CPS 26/D in ABC 381 Bolero 16.3.42). The 'Combined Planners' responsible to the Combined Chiefs of Staff had also concluded from their study in March that 'it was not possible to put on the Continent the ground forces necessary for invasion'. This was no doubt one reason why Hopkins urged that the OPD plan should not be referred to the CCS but be taken directly to London. (Matloff and Snell loc. cit.,) cf. Matloff and Snell, pp.183-5.

n.10 Estimates of what number of troops could be transported to the UK in 1942 varied at this time. The US Services of Supply estimate was about three divisions by mid-September

(Leighton and Coakley, p.20). This was about the least optimistic – and the most accurate. Roosevelt to Churchill on the Hopkins mission, Lowenheim, p.202, and Churchill, IV, p.281.

n.11 Churchill IV, p.293; Sherwood, II, p.531.

n.12 On the political motive see Pogue, pp.265, 315. The argument for Churchill's 'prescience' is fairly discussed by Sherwood (II, p.594). The quotation is from Churchill, IV, p.615.

n.13 Moran, p.50; Eisenhower, pp.213-4; Bryant, I, pp.298-9. Earl Mountbatten shared Brooke's views to the full. Brooke 'could see no hope whatever of a successful invasion in 1942' (Bryant, I, p.311). 'I was sure it wouldn't work and I kept on saying so' (Earl Mountbatten to the author).

n.14 That Marshall in effect reversed the tentative order of strategic priorities agreed at 'Arcadia' is clear, and since Churchill and Roosevelt had only agreed that Gymnast should be 'shelved' or 'postponed', not abandoned, it could be said that in this instance Marshall was advocating going back on a previous agreement with an ally. It is partly this which leads the official American historians, using unusually critical language, to describe the manner in which Marshall's proposals were drawn up and presented as 'irregular' and to go on to say 'The course of action urged by the War Department was at variance with the long-standing plans and expectations of the British Chiefs of Staff' (Matloff and Snell, p.190). That Marshall knew well enough how little there was to be said for 'Sledgehammer' as a military operation is virtually conceded by his biographer (Pogue pp.316-7, 345) and that he showed a certain lack of candour in advocating it, when it was 'Round-Up' he really cared about. Cf. Greenfield, p.183. 'Sledgehammer' was envisaged by the Americans as occurring only in the event of what Earl Mountbatten describes as 'two opposite and extremely unlikely assumptions' (Earl Mountbatten to the author) – namely the imminence of a Russian collapse or a situation in which the Germans were gravely weakened. The latter condition was the only one really accepted by the British Chiefs of Staff, and that was of course very unlikely. cf. COS 42/25/0, Ap 14, 42; 42/45/0, May 27, 42; 42/51/0, June 8th, 42; WM 42/73, June 11, 42. DO (42) 10, April 14, 42.

n.15 For British Chiefs' views on 'Sledgehammer' at this time and reaction to US proposals see COS 42/9/0, March 17th, 42; 42/12/0, March 21, 42; 42/15/0, March 28, 42. For the subsequent fortunes of 'Sledgehammer' see COS 42/36/0, May 5th, 42; 42/38/0, May 8, 42; 42/45/0 May 27, 42; 42/46/0, May 27, 42; 42/48/0, June 1st, 42; 42/52/0, June 15th, 42; War Cabinet minutes WM/42/73, July 11, 42; WM 42/87, July 7th, 42; and others for this period.

n.16 Sherwood, II, pp.528. Hopkins is the sole authority, but he is usually reliable, and Churchill's tone as he describes it accords with the former's later attitude – an attitude which

Churchill himself concedes was not wholly candid. For the meetings with Marshall see Bryant, I, pp.296-300; Sherwood, pp.539-542; Pogue pp.308-320; Churchill, IV, pp.282-6 and the official British records, COS 42/21/0, Ap 8, 42; 42/23/0, Ap 9, 42; 42/24/0, Ap 10, 42; 42/25/0, Ap 14, 42; and War Cabinet minutes WM 42/54, Ap. 29, 42 (NB Churchill's remark 'We are not committed to carry out such an operation this year'.) For Marshall's admission, DO (42)10, April 14, 42.

n.17 Pogue, p.318, citing Exec 1, Item 5d. Sherwood, II, p.542. Churchill's expansive remark is in his Memoirs, quoting the official record of the Defence Committee Meeting on the 14th April. (DO (42)10, April 14, 42).

n.18 For the question of Churchill's candour, see Burns pp.231-2, Stimson p.216. Mr Averell Harriman's view was expressed in a letter to the author, in which he adds that when he saw Churchill at this time the latter 'considered there was very little chance of "Sledgehammer" being a possibility'. (Averell Harriman to the author). cf. Ismay pp.249-50, Pogue p.520, Bryant, I, p.296, Churchill IV, pp.283, 286, 289-90. See also Loewenheim, p.206. Maisky refers to Churchill's behaviour as a 'hypocritical manoeuvre' (p.281). The reader must judge for himself.

n.19 Sherwood, II, pp.531, 535. Earl Mountbatten recalls that during this visit Marshall (like Hopkins) constantly stressed the necessity of an agreement on European operations to stave off the pressure for 'Pacific First'. (Earl Mountbatten to the author). cf. Bryant, I, p.299. See also Churchill loc cit. For Churchill's earlier advocacy of a cross-Channel attack, see Leasor, pp.166, 181. For Hopkins' reminder to Churchill of the pressure for 'Pacific First', see also DO (42), April 14, 42.

n.20 Pogue, p.318, citing Exec 1, Item 5c. For Marshall's qualifications on 'Sledgehammer' see COS 42/25/0, Ap. 14th, 42. Pogue, p.319. See Churchill, IV, pp.395, 581-90.

n.21 For the Molotov visit see Churchill, IV Ch. XIX, especially pp.293, 297-300. See also Eden, pp.323-330. Churchill's remark to the Chiefs of Staff about the Second Front is in COS 42/46/0, May 27, 42. For Soviet accounts see Maisky, Part IV, Chs. 2, 3, 4, especially pp.281-285. See also Trukhanovsky, *British Foreign Policy in the Second World War*, (Moscow, Progress, 1970), Chapters Three, Four. Woodward, Vol. II, pp.244-262. See also Sherwood II, p.559. Also WM 42/68, May 26, 42.

n.22 Sherwood II, Ch. XXV, especially pp.513-33, 566-8, 570-3, 579, 582; cf. Loewenheim, p.217. For Marshall's caution see also Pogue pp.326-7 (confirmed by Hopkins, Sherwood, II, p.573). That Roosevelt and Marshall believed that 'Bolero-Sledgehammer' held the field at this period is amply borne out by their defence of its claims against other calls on US resources, especially the Pacific, recorded in Matloff and Snell, (ABC 381 and JC3 48 and WDCSA 31 (SS) 6 May 1942). In the latter paper Roosevelt states emphatically that it was 'essential that active operations be conducted in 1942', with the 'principal objective' of helping the Soviet Union, but adds the interesting qualification '*if* we decide that the only large-scale operation is to be in the European area, the element of speed becomes the first essential'. This qualification suggests that Roosevelt was well-informed of British doubts about 'Sledgehammer' and that what Stimson called his 'secret baby' (North Africa) may still have been in his mind. Churchill's repeated assertions that he and Roosevelt thought alike on these matters were probably not far off the mark. cf. Greenfield, p.181.

n.23   For British 'consternation' which is glossed over by Churchill, see Eden, p.330; cf. COS 42/51, June 8, 42 and Churchill IV, pp.303-4. For the second Molotov visit, Eden p.330; Bryant; I, p.327; Churchill, p.305. The text of the aide-memoire (Annexe, WM 42/73 June 11, 42) is in Churchill, IV, p.305 and has been freely cited elsewhere. Maisky's statement that it was 'thrust into Molotov's hand' at the last minute hardly alters its language or its significance. cf. War Cabinet conclusions WM 42/73, loc. cit. Churchill, IV, p.310. His note laying down the two (impossible) conditions for the operation is on p.311. cf. COS 42/51/0, June 8th, 42. For Stalin's later interpretation of the communiqué, WM. 42/95, July 23, 42.

n.24   On obligations to Russia, Churchill, IV, p.242 and passim; Bryant, I, p.314-5. The heavy losses suffered in Convoy PQ 17 and the Russian reaction was particularly resented (Churchill, IV, pp.234-42).

n.25   See Maisky, loc. cit. For the impression made by Mountbatten, see Sherwood, II, p.581. For an American view of the 'pledge' aspect of Roosevelt's assurances to Molotov see Pogue, p.527; Matloff and Snell (pp.232-3). Others, including Mr Averell Harriman, hold the view that 'Roosevelt did not commit himself to a Second Front in 1942' (Averell Harriman to the author). cf. War Cabinet Minutes WM 42/85, July 3rd, 42.

n.26   That Roosevelt had it in mind particularly to encourage the Russian people is the view of Mr Averell Harriman among others (Averell Harriman to the author).

n.27   For the incorrect American view that Mountbatten reflected (according to Hopkins) the Chiefs of Staff viewpoint (and by implication not necessarily his own) see n. 13. In fact Mountbatten told Roosevelt that 'Sledgehammer' was 'not on' (Earl Mountbatten to the author). (See Minute, 24th mtg. CCS 10 June 1942 and Minute 27th mtg. CCS 19 June 1942). See also Sherwood, II, pp.587-88. Cf. J. Terraine, *The Life and Times of Lord Mountbatten* (London, Arrow Books, Hutchinson, 1968) p.127. cf. meetings of Chiefs of Staff cited n. 15, esp. COS 42/48/0 of June 1st.

n.28   Bryant I, p.330. As Churchill puts it, that he decided to leave the country at a critical stage in the Desert Battle was indica-

Footnotes

tive of the urgency of an Anglo-American meeting (IV, pp. 336-7). The latter's comment to Brooke about the necessity of 'some good talks as regards a Western Front' (ie 'Sledgehammer') is quoted in Bryant, I, p.332.

n.29 For Marshall, Eisenhower and Mountbatten see Terraine, p.124-5; Pogue p.312; Eisenhower, pp.75-76. Mountbatten had joined the Chiefs of Staff, as a full member, in March, 1942 in his capacity as Chief of Combined Operations.

n.30 For the reference to 'the difficulties of 1942' see Churchill, loc. cit. Mountbatten's remark is in Terraine, p.126.

n.31 That Roosevelt deliberately chose to meet Mountbatten alone with Hopkins, but without the Chiefs of Staff (and the embarrassment it caused him vis-a-vis the latter) was confirmed by Earl Mountbatten to the author. See also A. C. Wedemeyer, (*Wedemeyer Reports*) (New York, H. Holt, 1958) pp. 136-9 and FRUS Europe, 1942, III, pp.582-3. The substance of what I have said here is based on the letter from Earl Mountbatten to the President, recorded in Sherwood II, pp.587-8, supplemented by a personal interview with Earl Mountbatten on July 21st, 1975. The estimate of six or eight divisions is Churchill's (IV p.342) cf. COS 42/46/0, May 27th 42, WM/42/73, June 11th, 42. Not only the number of the landing craft available but their capacity was a crucial factor. Until Mountbatten took over Combined Operations the previous year, planning had mainly been in relation to relatively small-scale raids and the size of landing craft reflected this. Their capacity was about 30 men, and since no more than 30 craft could be easily handled at night in close company this meant only about a battalion could be put on shore in one place. To land even as much as a division simultaneously – which was the size of force which available landing craft made it possible to lift by the time of the Dieppe raid in August – meant a highly complex operation. The building of the larger landing craft (LCTL), first suggested by Captain Hughes-Hallett and sketched out by Mountbatten to Marshall in April, revolutionized the situation – but these were slow in building. (Earl Mountbatten to the author). cf. COS 42/59, June 25th, 42. Cf Churchill IV pp. 298, 430; Matloff and Snell, p.180, 186, 192-4 and elsewhere. Cf also Pogue, p.330, citing interview with Marshall, 5 Oct, 56. Eisenhower, who visited England at this time, concluded it might be possible to land only ten-twelve divisions *even by 1943*, cf. Higgins, p.122.

n.32 Stimson, p.216; Pogue 328.

n.33 Cf. Pogue p.327-8; Higgins p.117; Terraine p.126.

n.34 At this time Marshall thought Suez might fall in two weeks; and Roosevelt is supposed to have remarked to Wendell Wilkie, setting out on a round-the-world trip that he might find both Cairo and Moscow in enemy hands (A. Werth, *Russia At War* (London, Pan, 1964), p.444). Cf. Stimson, p.220; Higgins p.133 ff.

n.35 Churchill, IV p.398; Bryant I, pp.336-7. Cf. Pogue, p.329; Matloff and Snell pp.237-9, citing Min. 27th & 28th Mtgs. CCS, 19/20 June 1942, and Exec. 1, Item 4. Cf also W. F. Craven and J. L. Cate *Army Air Forces in World War II* (Chicago UP 1948), Vol. I, p.571.cf. Pogue p.333; Churchill, IV, p.344; Craven and Cate, II, p.46; Matloff and Snell pp. 239-244; Stimson pp.423-4; Sherwood pp.592-7. Cf. COS 42/61, June 30, 42 and 42/66, July 8, 42; WM 42/82, June 27, 42, and WM 42/87 July 7th, 42. For the attractions of 'Bolero' to both British and Americans, Kennedy, p.224.

n.36 Churchill IV, loc. cit. p.112; ISO Playfair, *The Mediterranean And The Middle East* (London, HMSO, 1960) Vol. III, p.274; Churchill IV, p.344; Eisenhower, p.61.

n.37 For the demise of 'Sledgehammer', see following documents and Churchill IV, pp.391-2, for his dismissal of the operation and his case to Roosevelt. COS 42/61, June 30, 42; 42/62, July 1, 42; 42/63, July 2, 42; 42/65, July 6, 42; 42/74, July 17, 42; 42/75, July 15, 42; WM 42/87, July 7, 42 and WM 42/88, July 8th, 42; cf. Kennedy, pp.253-4, 257-8. Portal was the only real advocate of the operation among the Chiefs of Staff (COS 42/45/0, May 27, 42.) cf. also WP 42/78, July 2, 42 and message, War Cabinet to British Joint Staff Mission, JSM 420, July 8, 42.

n.38 Pogue, p.340, citing Stimson's Diary for 10 July 42.

n.39 Matloff and Snell pp.267-276, citing OPD 381, gen 73, (FDR to Marshall, 14 July 42); WDCSA Bolero (SS); Tab 10, Item 1, Exec. 5.; WDCSA 381. See also Stimson, p.425; Sherwood, II, p.597, 601-6; Pogue, p.340-1. Sherwood, presumably reflecting Hopkins, thought this threat was not entirely bluff. Marshall, however, stated in an interview in 1956 that it *was* bluff as far as he was concerned – but not for King. Cf. Stimson Diary 12 July, 1942; Sherwood, II, pp.604-6. Roosevelt ordered them to press for 'Sledgehammer' and if they could not secure agreement on this, 'to determine another place for US troops to fight in 1942' – either the Middle East or North Africa. Matloff and Snell, pp.276-8 (WDCSA 381, 1(SS) cf. COS 42/71, July 10, 42. (Dill to British C/S).

n.40 Higgins, p.153.

n.41 Eisenhower, p.79 and Butcher, pp.15, 21, 23.

n.42 Bryant pp.352-7; Pogue pp.343-8; Sherwood, pp.608-12; Bryant p.353. See also Butcher, pp.9, 18, 19-26; Ambrose, p.71 (EP 379). See also Butler, *Grand Strategy III*, pp.633-8 and War Cabinet WM 42/94, July 22, 42. Brooke's estimate at this meeting was that 'Sledgehammer' would mean pitting six or seven allied divisions against 25 to 40 German divisions available in Western Europe. Cf. also WM 95/96, July 23, 24, 42. Marshall was advised at this time that only *two* US divisions would be readily available. M. W. Clark, *Calculated Risk* (London, Panther, 1956), p.36.

n.43 Matloff and Snell p.278 (WDCSA 381, 1 SS); Butcher, p.24; Ambrose, p.74 (EP 389); Eisenhower, pp.81-2; Sherwood, II,

p.611-12; Matloff and Snell pp.282-3 (WDCSA 381, 1 SS);
and pp.279-81 (CCS 94 in ABC 381); WM 42/95, July 24,
42. The objective of 'Torch' was defined as 'to gain control
of the whole coast of Africa up to Tunis'. The British and
US planners were instructed to begin planning immediately
(COS 42/76, July 27, 42; WM 42/96, July 24, 42.) See also
Records of London Conference CL and CCS 32-33, July
24/25, 42.

n.44 Stimson, p.221.

CHAPTER IV

n.1 Different versions of the numbers involved are given in
various sources, some of the confusion arising from the failure
to distinguish assault forces from 'follow-up' troops. But in
fact the numbers allocated to the operation varied somewhat
during this period. See G. F. Howe, *North West Africa*
(Washington, Dept. of the Army, 1957) pp.42-53, 63-4; Playfair, *Mediterranean and Middle East, IV*, p.126; M. Howard,
Grand Strategy IV, (London, HMSO, 1972) p. 137, for some
conflicting figures. The figures given in the text here are approximately those agreed by Churchill and Roosevelt at the
beginning of September. Ultimately it was envisaged that a
force of something like twelve or thirteen British and US
divisions would be engaged in North Africa (Howard, loc. cit,
Howe loc. cit). Clark, who was in charge of planning the
operation gives a figure of 110,000 for the 'initial' landings.
In the upshot seven British carriers were made available inside the Mediterranean and five US carriers for the Casablanca
landings, after Churchill and Roosevelt had ordered other
theatres to be 'stripped to the bone'.

n.2 Burns, p.285. The US War Department's view was that the
operation had less than a fifty per cent chance of success
(Butcher p.46).

n.3 Pogue, p.349.

n.4 For Marshall's reservations, Matloff and Snell, pp.280-1;
Butler, *Grand Strategy* III, pp.633-6. The relevant official
paper is CCS 94 in ABC 381. Marshall argued that the decisions meant the Western Allies had accepted 'a defensive encircling line of action for the Continental European Theatre'
in 1943. (This was the American version of Churchill's
'Closing The Ring'). The War Cabinet wished to remove
some of these qualifications, on the ground that they blurred
the decision; but Brooke persuaded them not to, on the
ground that the Americans had gone a long way to meet them
(Bryant, I, p.357; WM 42/96, July 24, 42.) For Churchill's
hopes for 'Round-Up' in 1943 *and* 'Torch' in 1942 see Churchill IV, p.581 ff. and Marshall's comment, Pogue, p.347.
Brooke certainly also doubted if 'Round-Up' in 1943 was
either possible or desirable (Bryant, loc. cit.) and Mount-

batten also had already formed that conclusion (Terraine, p.127). For Roosevelt's view Sherwood pp.653-4. Eisenhower was instructed to produce an 'outline plan' immediately after the July decision. cf. COS 42/83, August 7, 42. WM 42/127 Sept. 2, 42.

n.5 Leasor, pp.192-3, (confirmed by Earl Mountbatten to the author).

n.6 Sherwood, pp.611-12, 615; Pogue p.348-9; Matloff and Snell, pp.283-4, citing Notes of a White House meeting of July 30th where Roosevelt reaffirmed his decision (TAB 14, Item 1, Exec 5); Pogue, p.401, (citing WDCSA 381). For Dill's suggestion, Churchill, IV, p.407. See also Stimson, Diary 10th August, 1942 (Pogue 349).

n.7 Churchill, IV, Chs. XXVI–XXIX; Bryant, I, Ch. 9; Butler, *Grand Strategy III*, Ch. XXVIII; Ismay, p.264.

n.8 Churchill IV, pp.527-8; Field Marshall Montgomery, *Memoirs* (London, Collins, 1958) p.117; N. Nicolson, *Alex.* (London, Weidenfeld and Nicolson, 1973) pp.161-2. As Nicolson remarks, it was indicative of Churchill's unusual patience that he allowed Alexander a free hand in fixing the date for the offensive. (cf. Churchill IV, p.467).

n.9 Maisky pp.302-3 and Trukhanovsky, Ch. Four. See also Werth pp.437-447. Churchill's desire to honour his commitments to Stalin is reflected in his message to Roosevelt, IV, p.476.

n.10 Churchill, IV, p.474.

n.11 For Eisenhower's and Clark's appointment and the British reaction, Bryant, I, 357, 435; Pogue, pp. 337-9, 348, (citing letter Eisenhower to Ward 15th April 51, OCMH files); Churchill to Roosevelt July 31st (T 1066/2); COS 42/82, 6 Aug. 42; Loewenheim, pp.232-3; Churchill IV, p.422, 484; Ambrose, pp.6, 81-2; Clark, pp.24, 41; Eisenhower, pp.11, 80. The original intention was that Eisenhower should deputize for another American (the British expected Marshall to assume command eventually) and that he should have a British deputy. The former idea was dropped because Marshall did not want it, the latter in order to give the appearance of an 'all-American' invasion. Later in Tunisia Alexander took on the role of deputy to Eisenhower and ground forces commander originally allotted to him. It is clear that Marshall and King intended Eisenhower to have the command from the beginning. cf. COS 42/84, Aug. 7, 42; WM 42/101, Aug. 15, 42.

n.12 Cunningham, pp.470, 479-80; Butcher pp.102, 104-5; Playfair, *Mediterranean and Middle East*, IV, p.113-4; and Howe, pp.36-7. Cf. COS 42/146, Oct. 13, 42. Eisenhower, p.93, (cf. Ambrose, p.188); Clark, pp.42-3; Cunningham, p.477; Nicolson, pp.176-7). For Eisenhower's formal directive (COS W/244), see below, n. 18.

n.13 For the difficulties with the US navy, see Cunningham loc. cit. and Butcher, p.42. Eisenhower apparently expressed a touching faith in King's goodwill, which is hardly borne out by the facts. (cf. Ambrose, p.81, Eisenhower, p.100. COS 42/146, Oct. 13, 42). Cunningham's valuable role was often praised by Eisenhower, who had the highest opinion of him (Eisenhower, pp.99-100, cf. Butcher p.108). But Cunningham himself, though willing to serve under Eisenhower's command, apparently felt differently about accepting Alexander in the same light, when the latter was Eisenhower's deputy and Eisenhower had to be away (private information). For Portal's role see Pogue, p.271. A characteristic intervention by him at the Casablanca conference is recorded in its proper place. For Hewitt's 'indoctrination' at Combined Operation HQ see Leasor, p.193. (Confirmed by Earl Mountbatten to the author). On Air Command, COS 42/79, Aug. 2, 42; COS 42/83, Aug. 7, 42.

n.15 The difference in view was not entirely one of nationality. The British Joint Planners, however, produced a plan on August 15th emphasizing the importance of 'forestalling the Germans in Tunisia' and therefore seizing ports as far east as possible, and certainly including Algiers among the first objectives; (JP (42) 721), which Eisenhower approved. Brooke however continued to have doubts, and in particular agreed in this instance with Marshall that the Casablanca landings should not take place later than those inside the Mediterranean (COS (42) 101 of 27th Aug.). Bryant surprisingly does not really bring this point out, though he quotes Brooke's description of the final compromise – ie landings at Casablanca, Oran and Algiers but not further east ¬ as 'a much wiser plan' (Bryant, I, p.406, cf. also p.357). Pogue pp.402-3. Pogue also ignores the differences among the British Chiefs of Staff as well as blurring the important point that *simultaneous* landings east of Algiers were dropped. Cf. COS 42/100, Aug. 26, 42; & COS 42/102, 27th Aug. 42 for Brooke's views.

n.16 Churchill, IV, pp.474, 479; Ambrose p.87 (citing EP 403). The War Cabinet had accepted the necessity for the operation to have an 'all-Americans' veneer (WM 42/95, July 24, 42). See also JIC 42/316 (COS 42/98). British estimate of Spanish danger, COS 42/86, Aug. 11, 42 – and of Vichy resistance WM 42/114, Aug. 20, 42. Loewenheim p.244, cf. Pogue, p.411, cf. JIC 42/386, (Annexe to COS 42/140, Oct. 7, 42).

n.17 Churchill felt that Hitler's decision to put nearly 100,000 men into Tunisia was 'a grave strategic error', even though it delayed the end of the Tunisian campaign and made 'Round-Up' in 1943 impossible (IV, p.591).

n.18 See Pogue p.403; Ambrose p.87 (citing CCS 38th Mtg. 28th Aug., EP 403, 430, 448 and ABC 1, Sec. 1). Howard, pp.121-136; Howe pp.27-29. Eisenhower's judgement of 23rd August that the forces allocated were insufficient to achieve the objectives given him was based to a considerable extent on the in-

itial unwillingness of the two navies to furnish his needs. See
eg his memo to the Chiefs of Staff (COS (42) 97 (o) of
23,8.42.) cf. Butcher pp. 48, 50, 58-9 and p.51 (Entry for
August 15th). Cf. Bryant, pp.403-6; Ismay, p.262. COS
42/86, Aug. 11, 42; COS 42/88, Aug. 12, 42. For directive to
Eisenhower, COS 42/90, Aug. 14, 42 (Annexe). For Marshall's
concern about Spain, COS 42/96, Aug. 21, 42; COS 42/98,
Aug. 24, 42; COS 42/100, Aug. 26, 42 and JSM 365, COS
42/101, Aug. 26, 42, and especially COS 42/102, Aug. 27, 42
and Annexe I; cf. Clark, pp.47-8, 51-2. Also US docs. ABC
381 (7-25-42) of Aug 9, 42 and Aug 22, 42.

n.19 Ambrose, p.94 (citing Eisenhower to Marshall, EP 453).
Churchill, IV, pp.475-87, p.486 (n) and Ambrose, p.95. Cf.
Sherwood, II, pp.625-7, and Loewenheim pp.243-250. COS
42/103, Aug. 27, 42; COS 42/105, Aug. 29, 42; COS 42/106,
Aug. 31, 42. Cf. Kennedy, p.261.

n.20 These appear to be the approximate figures employed in the
actual assaults, though different authorities vary somewhat.
See n.1. A further 20,000 British troops were to enter Algeria
within a week of the landings (Howe, p.43).

n.21 Churchill, IV, pp.453-5, 487; Butcher, p.82; COS 42/81,
4th Aug. 42; COS 42/84, 10 Aug. 42; COS 42/85, 11th
Aug. 42; WM 42/107, 17 Aug. 42; WM 42/127, 2 Sept.
42.

n.22 Ambrose, p.96; cf. Churchill IV, pp.477, 484; Loewenheim,
p.244. The Germans had about 10,000 men in Tunisia by
November 22nd and about 18,000 by the end of the month.
(Howe, p.258, citing German 5th Panzer Army, Taetigke-
itsbericht, 15th November – 31st December) cf. Playfair,
Mediterranean and Middle East IV, p.172. Bryant gives a
figure of 50,000 Axis troops by December 22nd (op. cit., p.
441). cf. CCS 57, Jan 15, 42.

n.23 For a full discussion of the Spanish issue, see an excellent
summary in Howard, *Grand Strategy IV*, Ch. IX. Cf. Churchill IV, pp.482, and 474. Cf. JIC 42/386 (Annexe to COS
42/140, Oct. 7, 42).

n.24 For the Franco-Hitler meeting, Warner, p.235; Templewood
pp.94-5, pp.310-12.

n.25 Howard, p.161; Templewood, pp.62-63 and ibid pp.50-3,
73 for Beigbeder, pp.56-58 for Suner.

n.26 Churchill, IV, p.488. For plans in the event of Spanish intervention (Operation 'Backbone'), Howard, pp. 163-6; Hoare's
visit, Templewood p.161-4; Howard, pp.159, 162-3; Bryant
p.407 and Eden p.346. Hoare strongly advised a UK – US
assurance to Franco about Spanish territory. Churchill's
unsent letter to Hopkins is in his IV, p.485. See also Hull,
II, p.1191. COS 42/95, Aug. 24, 42 (Annexe II,); COS
42/99, Aug. 25, 42; COS 42/148, Oct. 15, 42; COS 42/149,
Oct. 16, 42. Cf. Clark, p.55 for Hoare's views.

n.27 For fuller accounts of US Vichy Policy see Langer, Warner,
Hull op. cit., and *Foreign Relations of the United States*

(FRUS) II, 1942, Europe (Washington, Dept of State, 1962), Admiral W. D. Leahy *I Was There* op. cit., passim.

n.28 Churchill IV, pp.434, 542-3; Loewenheim pp.249, 251; Eden p.346. The coldness of Roosevelt's reference to de Gaulle in the middle of a series of cordial exchanges is note-worthy, and perhaps prompted partly by Churchill's criticism the day before of Roosevelt's proposed message to Pétain (Sherwood, pp.643-4). In this message Roosevelt cites Leahy, who had spent most of the previous two years at Vichy, as his authority. Murphy's view also carried weight (see Murphy, pp.133-4). De Gaulle's mordant comment on Murphy that 'he was familiar with the smart world and inclined to believe that France consisted of the people he dined with in town' (de Gaulle, II, p.15) is a little unfair, but Murphy's views were inevitably influenced too by his Vichy contacts. Cf. Langer, pp.217-8; Sherwood I, p.474. WM 42/114, Aug. 20, 42. For Free French foreknowledge of the operation, COS 42/93, Aug. 18. 42; COS 42/148, Oct. 15, 42; and COS 42/149, Oct. 16, 42.

n.29 For the relative weight of US and German pressure in a key instance see Warner, pp.287-9. The quotation from Ambrose is on p.107. For the Bergeret incident, Warner, p.319 (citing Pétain trial proceedings p.261). The incident is illustrative of the extent to which Allied plans percolated through to Vichy; which has a bearing on the question whether Darlan's arrival in North Africa was entirely accidental.

n.30 Darlan p.157, 165; P. Tompkins, *The Murder of Admiral Darlan*, (London, Weidenfeld and Nicolson, 1965) p.64. Tompkins uses a variety of French sources, in the case Admiral J. Docteur, *La Grande Enigme de la Guerre: Darlan*. (Paris, Couronne, 1949) which are suspect, because of their obvious desire for self-justification. However since the contact named, Lemaigre-Dubreuill, was known to be in contact with members of the Vichy government (Murphy, p.149) it does not seem unlikely that he informed Darlan. For Darlan's approaches to the US see FRUS (1942) II, p.237, 248-9, 283-4, 392-3 etc. and Murphy, pp.151-2 (latter also for attitude of London and Washington, cf. also Butcher, pp.121-2; Ambrose, pp.105-6, citing EP 558). Warner (p.319-20) thinks Darlan's presence in Algiers fortuitous, and regards Darlan, pp.183-7, as conclusive on this point. One has to ask, however, how reliable the latter is. The present writer's view is that Darlan would have found some other reason to return to Africa if his son's illness had not provided one. Cf. Langer, pp.325-6; Pogue, p.415 (citing OPD Exec. 5, Item 8).

n.31 For the negotiations with Giraud and Mast, Murphy pp. 148-158; FRUS, 1942, Europe, pp.331-3, 394-7, 405-10, 423-6; H. Giraud, *Un Seul But, Victoire*, C. Mast, *Histoire d'Une Rebellion*, (Paris, Plon, 1969), Chs. VI-XI; Butcher pp.93-5, 121-3, 128-38; Ambrose, pp.99-100, 105-10; Clark, pp.58, 66-90. The 'cloak and dagger' meeting in Algeria is amusingly described by Clark and Murphy: it is not clear why it was necessary to hazard the safety of the deputy C-in-C when a staff officer would have done just as well. FRUS II, pp.412-7.

n.32 Ambrose, p.106-10; Butcher, 121-2; Burns, p.291; Mast, pp.102-3; Langer pp.321-5; Eden, p.345.

n.33 de Gaulle, (on Giraud) II, pp.15-18. For a cutting opinion by Eisenhower of Giraud at a later date see CCS 57, Jan. 15, 42.

n.34 On Juin, Murphy, pp.149, 163. As Murphy says, Churchill's recollection is at fault in thinking Juin was 'the leading hope' (Churchill, IV, 548), but it may be that a mistake was made in not admitting Juin to the plot. It is unlikely the latter's pledge to the Germans (on his release from imprisonment) not to fight against them, would have weighed with him; and in any case the same applied to Mast. Murphy's indirect contacts with Juin and the latter's own statements had in fact convinced the American it was unsafe to go too far with Juin, who *did* attach importance to his obligations to Vichy. While Juin for his part had learnt a good deal from these interchanges, though like Darlan he was taken by surprise by the actual date of the landings. cf. A. Kammerer, *Du Debarquement Africain Au Meutre De Darlan* (Paris, Flammarion, 1949) pp.149-153; Mast, pp.145-6; Howe, pp.78, 84-5; A. L. Funk, *De Gaulle, The Crucial Years, 1943-44* (Norton, University of Oklahoma, 1959) pp.34-5. The conspirators were not told the actual date of the landings till the last minute, and things might certainly have gone better if they had been given more notice (Murphy pp.154, 160; FRUS 1942, II, pp.406, 423-4;) cf. Mast. pp.136, 149, for a slightly contradictory account on this point.

n.35 Cf. Calvocoressi and Wint, pp.370-4. An interesting footnote is provided by Murphy, pp.157-8. Patton's forces were landed at Port Lyautey rather than the more suitable Rabat, in order not to antagonize the Sultan of Morocco whose residence was Rabat.

CHAPTER V

n.1 The landings and the campaign are described in detail by the official US and British historians, Playfair, *Mediterranean and Middle East IV* (op. cit.,) and Howe, *Northwest Africa* (op. cit.,). Shorter but quite well-researched accounts are in V. Jones, *Operation Torch* (London, Pan, 1972) and K. Macksey *Crucible of Power* (London, Hutchinson, 1969). Eisenhower (op. cit.,), Clark (op. cit.,) and Alexander (*Memoirs*, London, Cassell, 1962) have all given their accounts. Of the commanders in the assaults, only Patton had experience (in the First World War) of handling a large formation in battle.

Footnotes

n.2 A. Hillgruber (ed.) *Kriegestagebuch Des Oberkommandos Der Wehrmacht*, Vol. II, Part II (Frankfurt, 1963) p.901 and G. Warlimont, *Im Hauptquartier Der Deutschen Wehrmacht* (Frankfurt 1962), p.918. cf. Playfair, pp.134-6, 159-60; Churchill, IV, p.545; Cunningham, p.483; Howe, p.174, (citing SKL/1 Abt., Kriegestagebuch, Pt.A, 1-30).

n.3 On Michelier, (and Noguès) see Kammerer, pp.330-332, 339-44 ff; Howe, pp.93-5; Murphy, pp.144-5; Warner, *Laval*, p.332.

n.4 On decision not to attack ports directly, Howe, pp.40-2, 46-8, 50-2. General plan of attack, Howe, Ch. III; Playfair, Ch. V. On the landings themselves, Howe, Chs. V-XIII; Playfair, Ch. VI. On casualties, Butcher, p.173; French casualties were approximately 3,000 (de Gaulle, II, p.39). Churchill, IV, p.548.

n.5 Churchill, IV p.473; On Giraud's ineffectiveness, etc. Eisenhower, pp.110-4, 121; Murphy, pp.173-5; Kammerer, Ch. XIV-XV; Giraud's own account, Butcher, pp.145-6, 165.

n.6 For the Darlan-Juin-Murphy-Clark negotiations, see Murphy, loc. cit; Howe, pp.249-52, 262-70; Clark, pp.102-16; Darlan, Ch. VIII. cf. Kammerer, Chs. IX-XV (p.293 for Pétain's response to Roosevelt's letter and message to Darlan). Cf. Ambrose pp.118-124.

n.7 On Darlan's equivocations, Ambrose, loc. cit; Warner, *Laval* pp.328-332; Howe, loc. cit; Darlan's tendency to equate French interests with his own and identify France with himself was not after all unique. In this respect if in no other, he resembled de Gaulle.

n.8 For Eisenhower's assessment of the situation, Ambrose, pp. 128-9 (citing, Eisenhower to CCS, EP 622); also Eisenhower, pp.121-3. His statement that 'French sentiment here does not remotely agree with prior calculations' reflects on Murphy's judgement and those of his assistants. Cf. Kammerer, p.397. For the end at Casablanca, Howe, pp.171-4; at Oran, Howe, pp.220-5.

n.9 Weygand's remark to Laval, Warner, p.325, citing H. Nogueres, *Le Suicide De La Flotte*, (Paris, Laffont, 1963) p.483; Vichy response to German pressures, Warner, p.334-5, citing inter alia Nogueres pp.444-5 and G. Auphan, *Histoire De Mes 'Trahisons'* in *Les Grimaces de L'Histoire*, (Paris, Les Iles d'Or, 1951) pp.297, 281. Cf. Kammerer, p.408, for the order to continue resistance; Darlan, p.204; Clark p.113.

n.10 For Vichy reaction to German occupation, Warner, *Laval* pp.336-8; Kammerer, p.433. Darlan and Noguès reaction, Darlan, pp.206-8; Kammerer, pp.458, 471-5; Clark, pp.111-117; Murphy, pp.175-6; Eisenhower, pp.118-21.

n.11 For rallying of French West Africa, Howe, pp.270-2; Murphy, p.179; Kammerer, Ch. XXV; Darlan, pp.209-13; the French Fleet, Warner, pp.340-1, 355-7; Kammerer, pp. 442-5, 446-8, 470, 540-2; Darlan, pp.214-16; Cunningham, pp.506-7; Playfair, pp.163-4.

n.12 For early stages of Tunisian Campaign, Howe, Chs. XV-XVIII (p.291, for date of advance into Tunisia) Playfair, Ch. VII (pp.186, 188 for onset of bad weather etc., p.169 for Anderson's approach to the campaign and his difficulties) Anderson's decision to halt, Playfair, pp.181-2; cf. Ambrose p.142 (citing EP 685); Butcher pp.181, 188; Eisenhower, pp.124-37.

n.13 On French actions in Tunisia, Warner, pp.341-6; Kammerer, pp.321-6, 357-65, etc; Howe, pp.245-60, 287; Playfair, pp. 162-3, 170-1, 174. Barré felt he could not risk his ill-equipped troops against the Germans but preferred to withdraw gradually towards the Algerian frontier, where, after initial hesitations, he threw in his lot with the Allies, Estéva, the Resident-General in Tunisia, decided to collaborate with the Germans. Cf. Eisenhower, p.155.

n.14 Patton commanded Western Task Force attacking Casablanca, and subsequently US II Corps in Tunisia, March to April, 1943; Bradley succeeded Patton in command of II Corps in the final stages of the campaign; Truscott had commanded the attack on Port Lyautey under Patton and later, as Deputy Chief of Staff AFHQ, commanded Eisenhower's advanced command post. On Marshall's influence on the outcome, Pogue, p.424.

n.15 Eisenhower's disappointment, Ambrose p.147; his reorganization of command and difficulties in organizing American and French troops in a unified command, Howe pp.350-1. On expectations re. capture of Tripoli from West cf. Nicolson, p.165; Eisenhower, pp.140-1.

n.16 Space does not permit an account of the tortuous circumstances surrounding the assassination of Darlan, as a result of a conspiracy in which Gaullists and Royalists were both implicated (there is no real evidence that either de Gaulle himself or British intelligence services were privy to the plot, as has sometimes been suggested). See Tompkins, passim, and Kammerer, Ch. XXVI. For Giraud's succession and US, British and Gaullist reactions see Howe, pp.355-9; Ambrose, pp.146-148; Clark, pp.123-5. Murphy pp. 181-2, FRUS 1942, II, pp.493-6, de Gaulle, pp.69-77. Opinions vary on Anderson's capacities (see n. 12, Ch IV). There are few defenders of Fredendall, yet he had performed well in the initial landings. He seems to have been suffering from battle fatigue (Ambrose, pp.173-5). Alexander was appointed at the Casablanca Conference, but did not take over immediately. For French troops in Tunisia, Butcher, pp.212-223.

n.17 For Kesselring, see Howe, Ch. XXIII; Playfair, Ch. XII; Eisenhower's judgement of US troops and Fredendall, Ambrose, pp.152-4, 166-9; Eisenhower, pp.156-7, 163.

n.18 For Alexander's initial impact and occasional 'unsureness', Howe, pp.475-6; Nicolson, pp.173-5, 176-7, 180-4; L. Farago, *Patton: Ordeal And Triumph* (London, Mayflower, 1969) pp. 137-9 and ff.; Ambrose, pp.177, 180.

Footnotes

n.19 Final stages of the campaign and Allied re-grouping, Playfair Ch. XVII; Howe, Part Seven; for II Corps' role, Ambrose,
pp.183-4; Butcher, p.244; Nicolson, pp.187-8.

n.20 Doubt has sometimes been thrown on the figure of Axis
troops which surrendered (cf. Macksey, p.300) and the British
official historians admit that an exact figure is difficult to give
(Playfair, IV, p.460). However the figure of nearly a quarter
of a million seems fairly accurate (cf. Howe, p.666) and is
accepted by both Eisenhower (p.174) and Alexander (p.39).

EPILOGUE

n.1 For effect of 'Torch' on 'Bolero' and 'Round-Up', Matloff
and Snell, pp.317-8, 322-27, 354-5; British Chiefs' view, COS
42/97, Aug. 22, 42. For August CCS strategic appreciation,
CCS 97/3, CCS 36th Mtg. 14 Aug. 1942; for US Chiefs of
Staff enlargement of 'strategic defensive' in Pacific, G. Harrison, *Cross-Channel Attack* (Washington, US Dept. of the
Army, 1951) p.36, citing JCS 167/1 (JCS 46th meeting).
At about this time a message from the US War Department
to London strongly suggested that the Americans were cutting
down on preparations for 'Round-Up'. Roosevelt assured
Churchill this was only a temporary measure, occasioned by
the needs of 'Torch', the Pacific, and the Russian front.

n.2 For Churchill's reaction, Churchill, IV, pp.581, 584-5;
Loewenheim, p.255 (in this letter Churchill expresses his hope
that Tunisia could be occupied by the end of November);
Matloff and Snell, loc. cit. (citing ABC 381, 4-B, EP 513);
Roosevelt's view, Harrison, p.35; Howard, p.254; 'Soft under-
belly' Churchill, IV, p.586; cf. WM 42/127, Sept. 2, 42.
For development of British ideas of strategy see JPS 849
(Annexe to COS 42/139, Oct. 6, 42;) also COS 42/144,
Oct. 10, 42. cf. Leasor p.221. Brooke certainly thought talk
of 'Round-Up' in 1943 had now become unreal (Bryant, p.
531).

n.3 Marshall's change of mind, Churchill, IV p.590; Matloff and
Snell, pp.363-4 (citing Minutes of White House Meeting 10,
Dec. 42., Tab. 42, Item 2, Exec. 5).

n.4 US planners' uncertainty, Matloff and Snell, p.324; Harrison,
p.38 (citing OPD files, Item 1, Exec 10); cf. Bryant, I,
p.453, quoting Brooke's diary.

n.5 On US lack of staff at Casablanca, Bryant, I, p.447 and
footnote. On the use of British naval planners, Earl Mountbatten to the author. The latter's view is that it would have
been impossible to 'close down the Mediterranean' and concentrate on 'Round-Up' in 1943, unless the decision to do so
had been made at the beginning of the campaign.

n.6 Brooke's opinion of the way the British view prevailed,
Bryant I, pp.451-2. Cf. Ambrose pp.158-9 (and for Eisenhower's views); 'Round-Up' prospects, Bryant, I, p.454;

Marshall at Casablanca, Harrison, p.40; Brooke on Italy, Bryant, I, p.455; and Portal, p.453; Final agreement, pp.461-2; cf. Harrison, pp.42-5; CCS Mtgs. 55-69; cf. Howard, Chs. XIII-XIV. CCS 155/1 (19/1/42) is the relevant document. Cf. Kennedy pp.283-4 cf. CCS 170/2, and CCS memoranda 153-172, passim.

n.7 Higgins' book (op. cit.,) contains the fullest argument for the view that the adoption of British strategy 1942-3 was 'for the worse'. See also Greenfield, pp.196-8. For Eisenhower on 'Sledgehammer', 'Torch' and 'Round-Up', Eisenhower p.79; Cf. Ambrose, pp.75-6. Marshall's view, Pogue, pp.342, and his interviews of 28th September, 5th October and 13th November, 1956 with Marshall.

n.8 Earl Mountbatten's views, cited in this paragraph, were expressed in an interview with the author. Marshall's subsequent admission on impossibility of inaction in 1942 is from his interview of 13 Nov. 1956, cited Pogue, p.330. Tank landing craft were not available till 1943. The formidable rocket-firing craft not till later.

n.9 On Soviet views, Werth, pp.443, 355; Maisky, Chs. 3, 4. Maisky asserts that Churchill lied in saying that he did not think 'Torch' ruled out 'Round-Up'. The most charitable construction one can put on this slur is that Maisky has not bothered to read the evidence.

n.10 Cf. Ch. IV, n. 28.

BIBLIOGRAPHY

Alexander of Tunis, Earl: *Memoirs*, London, Cassell, 1962.

Ambrose, S. E. *The Supreme Commander*, London, Cassell, 1971.

Arnold, H. H.: *Global Mission*, New York, Harper, 1949.

Avon, Earl of: *The Reckoning*, London, Cassell, 1965.

Bradley, O. M.: *A Soldier's Story*, New York, Holt, 1951.

Bryant, Sir A. (ed.): *The Alanbrooke War Diaries*, (Two Volumes), London, Collins, 1957.

Burns, J. M.: *Roosevelt, The Soldier of Freedom*, New York, H. Brace, 1970.

Butler, J. R. M. (ed.): *Grand Strategy III*, London, H.M. S.O. 1964.

Butcher, H.: *My Three Years with Eisenhower*, London, Heinemann, 1946.

Calvocoressi, P. and Wint, G.: *Total War*, London, Penguin Press, 1972.

Chandler, A. D., Jnr (ed.): *The Papers of Dwight David Eisenhower* (5 vols), Baltimore, John Hopkins, 1970.

Churchill, W. S.: *The Second World War*, (six volumes), London, Cassell, 1948-54.

Clark, M. W.: *Calculated Risk*, London, Harrap, 1951, also Panther PB, 1956.

Darlan, A.: *L'Amiral Darlan Parle*, Paris, Amiot-Dumont, 1952.

De Gaulle, C.: *War Memoirs* (three volumes and documents), London, Weidenfeld and Nicolson, 1955-60.

Eisenhower, D. D.: *Crusade in Europe*, London, Heinemann, 1948.

Farago, L.: *Patton, Ordeal and Triumph*, London, Barker, 1966, and Mayflower PB, 1969.

Feis, H.: *Churchill, Roosevelt, Stalin*, Princeton, University Press, 1957.

Foreign Relations of the United States, 1942 (seven volumes), Washington, Department of State, 1962.

Giraud, H.: *Un Seul But, La Victoire*, Paris, Julliard, 1959.

Higgins, T. H.: *Winston Churchill and the Second Front*, Toronto, Oxford, 1958.

Howe, G. F.: *North West Africa*, Washington, Department of the Army, 1957.

Howard, M.: *Grand Strategy, IV*, London, H.M.S.O., 1972.

——: *The Mediterranean Strategy in World War II*, London, Weidenfeld and Nicolson, 1968.

Hull, C.: *Memoirs* (two volumes), London, Hodder and Stoughton, 1948.

Ismay, Lord: *Memoirs*, London, Heinemann, 1960.

Kammerer, A.: *Du Debarquement Africain au Meutre de Darlan*, Paris, Flammarion, 1949.

Kennedy, Sir J.: *The Business of War*, London, Hutchinson, 1957.

King, E. J. and Whitehill, W. M.: *Fleet Admiral King*, New York, Norton, 1952.

Langer, W. L.: *Our Vichy Gamble*, New York, Knopf, 1947.

Leahy, W. D.: *I Was There*, New York, Whittlesey House, 1950.

Leasor, J.: *War at the Top*, London, M. Joseph, 1959.

Leighton, R. M. and Coakley, R. W.: *Global Logistics and Strategy, 1940-3*, Washington, US Department of the Army, 1955.

Loewenheim, F. L. *et al.*: *Roosevelt and Churchill*, London, Barrie and Jenkins, 1975.

Maisky, I.: *Memoirs of a Soviet Ambassador*, London, Hutchinson, 1967.

Matloff, M. and Snell, E. M.: *Strategic Planning for Coalition Warfare*, Washington, D.C., Department of the Army, 1953.

Mast, C.: *Alger, 8 November 1942*, Paris, Plon, 1969.

Moran, Lord: *Winston Churchill, the Struggle for Survival*, London, Constable, 1966

Murphy, R.: *Diplomat among Warriors*, London, Collins, 1964.

Nicolson, N.: *Alex*, London, Weidenfeld and Nicolson, 1973.

Playfair, I. S. O.: *The Mediterranean and the Middle East, III*, London, H.M.S.O., 1960.

Playfair, I. S. O.: and Moloney, C.: *The Mediterranean and the Middle East, IV* (London, H.M.S.O., 1966)
Pogue, F. C.: *Ordeal and Hope*, London, McGibbon and Kee, 1968.

Sherwood, R. S. (ed), *The White House Papers of Harry L. Hopkins*, (two volumes), London, Eyre and Spottiswood, 1948.
Soviet Commission on Foreign Diplomatic Documents, *Correspondence Between Churchill, Roosevelt, Stalin*, Moscow.
Stimson, H. L. and Bundy, McG.: *On Active Service in Peace and War*, New York, Harper, 1947.

Templewood, Viscount: *Ambassador on Special Mission*, London, Collins, 1946.
Terraine, J.: *The Life and Times of Lord Mountbatten*, London, Hutchinson, 1968, and PB, Arrow, 1969.
Tompkins, P.: *The Murder of Admiral Darlan*, London, Weidenfeld, 1965.
Trukhanovsky, L.: *British Foreign Policy in the Second World War*, Moscow, Progress, 1969.
Truscott, L.: *Command Missions*, New York, Dutton, 1954.

Waites, N. (ed): *Troubled Neighbours*, London, Weidenfeld and Nicolson, 1971.
Warner, G.: *Pierre Laval and the Eclipse of France*, London, Eyre and Spottiswood, 1968.
Werth, A.: *Russia at War*, London, Barrie and Rockliffe, 1964, also Pan, PB, 1965.
White, D. S.: *Seeds of Discord*, Syracuse, University Press, 1964.
Woodward, Sir L.: *British Foreign Policy in the Second World War*, (five vols) London, H.M.S.O., 1970 – 75, and Single-volume edition.

NOTE: This book was finished before the author was able to obtain a copy of a new book by Professor A. L. Funk – *The Politics of Torch*, Kansas UP, 1974.

DOCUMENTARY SOURCES

BRITISH DOCUMENTS
The following documents are available in the Public Record Office, London:

(1) War Cabinet Minutes and Memoranda (WM and WP Series, filed under CAB 65, 66, 68)
(2) Defence Committee Minutes and Memoranda (D.O. Series, filed under CAB 69)
(3) Chiefs of Staff Committee Minutes and Memoranda (C.O.S. Series, filed under CAB 79)
(4) Records of Washington War Conference (Arcadia) (C.R. and W.W. Series), 2nd Washington Conference and London Conference (filed under CAB 99)
(5) Combined Chiefs of Staff Committee Minutes and Memoranda (C.C.S. Series, filed under CAB 88)
(6) Records of Casablanca Conference (filed under CAB 99, also CAB 80.)
(7) Prime Minister's Papers. (Filed PREM III-IV).

AMERICAN DOCUMENTS

The main diplomatic documents are available in published form, viz:

Foreign Relations of the United States (7 volumes)
   1942 (Washington, Department of State, 1962)

The following collections of documents are cited by F. C. Pogue (*Ordeal and Hope*), S. E. Ambrose (*The Supreme Commander*) and the official US Historians; and are referred to in the footnotes:

(1) War Department Chief of Staff Army (WDCSA)
(2) War Plans Division (WPD), after March 1942 Operations Division (OPD), especially high policy file of the Executive Office, OPD (Exec.), and Strategic Policy Group (ABC)
(3) U.S. Joint Chiefs of Staff Minutes and Memoranda (J.C.S.)
(4) Joint Board memoranda (J.B.)
(5) The Papers of Dwight David Eisenhower (EP)

These documents are in Washington, mainly in the Departmental Records Branch, Adjutant General's Office (DRP AGO), or in the office of the Chief of Military History (OCMH).

INDEX

ABC 1, 31–3
ABDA Command, 61, 69
Abetz, Otto, 52, 193
ACROBAT, 13, 22–3
Adana talks, 183
Afrika Corps, 17, 162
Alexander, General Sir Harold, 121–2, 129, 160, 163–5, 173, 196–7
Alexandria, 184
Algeria, 121, 129, 132, 140, 143, 150, 153, 156, 157, 166, 198, 200
Algiers, 34, 76, 126, 128–9, 131, 133, 145, 150, 152–5, 157–8, 162, 175, 197
Ambrose, Professor Stephen, 171
Anderson, General Sir Kenneth, 125–7, 132, 158, 160, 162–3, 202
ARCADIA, *see* Washington Conference
Argentia talks, 21, 25, 33, 56, 75, 77
Arctic supply route, 18, 26, 192
Arnold, General Henry, 59, 75, 87
Arzew, 152
'Atlantic First', 61–3, 66, 71–4, 80, 84, 87–8, 95, 113–4, 168
Attlee, Clement, 34
Auchinleck, General Sir Claude, 22–3, 64, 79, 91, 105, 121
Australia, 69, 82, 88, 189
Azores, 33

BACKBONE, 198
Balkans, 77–8, 89–90, 168, 170, 178
Baltic States, 17, 24, 26, 99
BARBAROSSA, 33, 183
Barré, General Georges, 158, 202
Battle of Britain, 17, 136
Battle of the Atlantic, 24, 60
Battle of the Bulge, 164
Beaverbrook, Lord, 25, 68, 76, 80, 93, 181, 185

Beigbeder, Colonel Juan, 137
Belgium, 77
Benghazi, 22–3
Bergeret, General Jean, 143, 199
Béthouart, Maj-General Émile, 144, 147, 150
Bizerta, 43, 160, 164–5
Black Sea, 24
BOLERO, 13, 72, 77–8, 86, 91–4, 97, 100, 107–11, 114, 167, 170, 189, 191, 194, 203
Bône, 129, 131, 158, 161
Bougie, 158, 161
Boulogne, 88
Borguiba, Habib, 147
Bradley, Maj-General Omar, 161, 163, 165, 202
Brazil, 42–3
Brooke, General Sir Alan, 59, 60, 65, 70, 90, 93, 95, 104–110, 121, 127, 137, 170, 183, 185–7, 190, 193–5, 197, 203
Bulgaria, 17
Burma, 64, 69, 73, 82, 168, 186
'Burma Road', 36
Burns, W. B. 76, 94

Cairo, 109, 121, 193
Calais, 88, 102
Cape Bon, 165
Cape Matifou, 152
Casablanca, 43, 76, 125, 127–37, 144, 150–57, 161, 195, 197
Casablanca Conference, 169–171, 203–4
Caucasus, 109, 122
Chandos, Lord, 184
Chaney, Maj-General James, 32
Chatel, General Yves, 146
Cherbourg, 102, 115
Chiang-Kai-Shek, General, 36–8
Chiefs of Staff Committee (British), 99, 101–2, 115–6, 190–2, 197, *see also* Brooke, Pound, Portal, Mountbatten
China, 36–38, 66
Churchill, Winston, 15, 24, 26, 32–4, 39, 46, 52, 54–5, 59, 63–

Hewitt, Admiral Kent, 125, 127,
197
Hoare, Sir Samuel, 137–8, 198
Hoare-Laval Plan, 51
Holland, 37, 67, 69, 73, 77
Hollis, Brigadier Leslie, 185
Hong Kong, 64
Hopkins, Harry, 24–5, 39, 57–8,
61, 68, 70, 80, 87–90, 93–5,
98, 101, 103–4, 114–116–7,
120, 138, 173, 181–2, 185,
189–94, 198
Hughes-Hallett, Captain John,
193
Hull, Cordell, 24, 27, 39, 49,
139–40, 174–5, 182–4
Hungary, 17
Hyde Park (Roosevelt's home),
107–112

Iceland, 22, 30, 35, 78, 189
Ickes, Harold, 182
India, 16, 43, 57, 64, 82, 88,
109, 186
Indo-China, 37–8
Indomitable, 65
Indonesia, *see* East Indies
Iran, 17–18
Iraq, 16
Ismay, Lord, 70, 94, 131, 183
Italy, 21, 35, 37, 43–44, 51, 63,
77, 79, 83, 89, 117, 130, 135,
142, 147, 168, 170–1, 204

Jacob, Maj-General Sir Ian, 185
Japan, 23, 28, 36–9, 61–5, 72–3,
103, 109, 168, 182, 188
Joint Army-Navy Board (US),
28, 72
Joint Chiefs of Staff (US), 101,
106–7, 109–10, 113–6, 132,
153, 167–9, 185, 193; *see* also,
Marshall, King, Arnold
Jordana, General Francisco, 139
Juin, General Alphonse, 141,
146–7, 150, 152–7, 200–1
JUPITER, 97

Kasserine, 45, 163–5
Kesselring, Field-Marshal
Albert, 160
Kharkov, 17, 102

Kiev, 24
King, Admiral Ernest, 59, 68,
73, 84, 87–8, 95, 108, 114,
120, 123, 126, 128, 132, 161,
167, 169–70, 194, 197
Knox, Colonel Frank, 21, 30, 43,
68, 87, 182–3

Laval, Pierre, 51, 143, 156
Leahy, Admiral William, 79,
139–40, 143, 184, 199
Lebanon, 16, 48
Le Havre, 88, 189
Le Kef, 164
Lemaigre-Dubreuill, Jacques,
199
Lend – Lease Act, 35, 66
Leningrad, 17, 24
Les Andelouses, 152
Libya, 16, 18, 20–2, 42–5, 62,
64, 121, 136
Lloyd George, Earl, 20
Low Countries, 18, 83

MacArthur, General Douglas,
88, 95, 189
McNarney, Lt-General Joseph,
94, 97
Madagascar, 140
MAGNET, 22, 72, 76, 78, 82–
3, 87
Maisky, Ivan, 25, 181, 191–2,
204
Malaya, 23, 37–8, 64–5, 69, 73,
82, 186
Malta, 18, 20, 43, 133, 149
Mareth Line, 162–4
Marshall, General George, 44–5,
58–9, 66, 70–76, 78, 80, 103–
4, 106–12, 121–3, 161, 167–8,
172–3, 183, 184, 187–9, 191,
193, 202; views on strategy
before Pearl Harbour, 28–34;
accepts inevitably of war with
Axis, 35–6, 182; opposed to
North African operation, 44,
81, 186; relations with Brooke,
60, 186; friendship with Dill,
60–1; urges 'Unity of Command', 61, 67–9; favours
Cross-Channel attack, 63, 77;
obtains reversal of North

Index

African Strategy, 83–9, 190; at London Conference (March 1942), 90–8; and Molotov mission, 100–1; threatens reversal of 'Germany First', 113, 194; accepts abandonment of SLEDGEHAMMER, 115; insists on qualifying TORCH decision, 119, 195; regards TORCH as ruling out ROUND-UP, 120, 195; and Eisenhower's appointment, 124–5, 196; opposes US concentration inside Mediterranean, 128–32, 198; distrusts Darlan, 145; insists on adequate role for US troops, 165; continues to favour Cross-Channel Attack, 169–71, 203; accepts Sicilian, but not Italian campaign, 170; postwar views on Cross-Channel versus Mediterranean strategy, 171, 204

Marshall Memorandum, 86, 96, 178

Mast, Maj-General Charles, 144, 147, 150, 199–200

Maurois, André, 49

Mersa, 152

Mers-el-Kebir, 21, 158, 183, 184

Michelier, Admiral François, 150

Midway Island, 65

Molotov, Vacheslav, 98–107, 173–4, 191–2

Monnet, Jean, 49

Monroe Doctrine, 43

Montgomery, General Sir Bernard, 59, 121–2, 160, 162–4

Moran, Lord, 90

Morgenthau, Henry, 35–6, 83

Morocco, 34, 126, 136, 138, 147–8, 150, 153, 156–7, 166, 175

Moscow, 17, 24, 193

Moscow Conference (August 1942), 121, 132

Mountbatten, Vice-Admiral Lord Louis, 101, 104–8, 110, 120, 127, 169, 172–3, 180, 188, 190–7, 203–4

Murphy, Robert, 51, 79, 140–8,

152, 154, 174, 199–201

Mussolini, Benito, 136

Myer, Colonel L. J., 171

Napoleonic Wars, 20

National Committee, see Free France

Nehring, General Walther, 162

New Guinea, 186

New Zealand, 82

Ninth Corps (British), 165

Nineteenth Corps (French), 163–4

Noguès, General Auguste, 41, 53, 146–7, 157, 175

Norway, 24, 76, 83, 97, 99, 101–2, 116

Northern Ireland, 22, 189

North-West Africa, see French North Africa, Dakar

Oceania, French, 48

O'Connor, Maj-General Sir Richard, 22–3

Odessa, 24

Operations Division (US War Department), 87, 89, 169, 187, 189, see also War Plans Division

Oran, 43, 47, 52, 126–133, 144, 150, 152–7, 161, 197, 201

OSS, 144

'Pacific First', 88, 91, 114, 165, 167–8, 182, 186, 189, 191; see also King

Paris Protocols, 52

Pas de Calais, 102

Patton, Maj-General George, 125–6, 131, 152, 161, 163–4, 200, 202

Pearl Harbour, 23, 27, 30, 44, 62–5, 82, 109, 139

Pétain, Marshal Phillipe, 33, 41, 44, 46, 50–2, 79, 134, 139, 141–3, 150, 153–5, 157, 181, 199

Phillipeville, 129, 161

Phillipines, 23, 38, 64–5, 69, 73, 82

Poland, 24, 26, 39

Port Lyautey, 152, 200, 202